D0285480

Health Information Management

In almost all Western countries, concerted efforts are made to stimulate the use of information technology (IT) in health care. Yet the number of success stories are few and the frustrations many. *Health Information Management* is a new textbook that introduces readers to the challenges, the lessons learned and the new insights of health information management at the start of the twenty-first century.

With a strong international orientation and a critical eye on many traditional information management views the book illustrates key developments by drawing on examples from different countries. This comparative approach provides readers with a comprehensive and well-balanced perspective to this core management topic in the health care field. It highlights how seemingly 'technical' management decisions affect both clinicians and patients, and how the unpredictable nature of technology development in complex organizations may be handled.

Featuring case studies and an overall practitioner's perspective, this is an accessible textbook that combines theoretical backgrounds and starting points with practice-oriented guidelines and advice on the best methods for bringing these ideas to the challenges of everyday health care management. Topics covered include:

- Patient care information systems
- Integrating quality improvement
- Information strategy
- Implementing information systems

An original and refreshing textbook on this core health care topic, this is essential reading for students of health care management and health care practitioners alike.

Marc Berg is Professor of Social-Medical Sciences at the Institute of Health Policy and Management, Erasmus University Medical Centre, Rotterdam.

ROUTLEDGE HEALTH MANAGEMENT SERIES

*Edited by Marc Berg, Robbert Huijsman, David Hunter,
John Øvretveit*

Routledge Health Management is one of the first series of its kind, filling the need for a comprehensive and balanced series of textbooks on core management topics specifically oriented towards the health care field. In almost all Western countries, health care is seen to be in a state of radical reorientation. Each title in this series will focus on a core topic within health care management, and will concentrate explicitly on the knowledge and insights required to meet the challenges of being a health care manager. With a strong international orientation, each book draws heavily on case examples and vignettes to illustrate the theories at play. A genuinely groundbreaking new series in a much-needed area, this series has been put together by an international collection of expert editors and teachers.

Health Information Management
Integrating information technology in health care work
Marc Berg with others

Health Information Management

Integrating information technology in health care work

Marc Berg

with Cé Bergen, Enrico Coiera,
Heather Heathfield, Bert Huisman,
Marleen de Mul, Arjen Stoop and
Brit Ross Winthereik

Routledge
Taylor & Francis Group

LONDON AND NEW YORK

First published 2004
by Routledge
11 New Fetter Lane, London EC4P 4EE

Simultaneously published in the USA and Canada
by Routledge
29 West 35th Street, New York, NY 10001

Routledge is an imprint of the Taylor & Francis Group

Typeset in Perpetua and Bell Gothic by
Florence Production Ltd, Stoodleigh, Devon
Printed and bound in Great Britain by
The Cromwell Press, Trowbridge, Wiltshire

British Library Cataloguing in Publication Data
A catalogue record for this book is available from the British Library

Library of Congress Cataloging in Publication Data
Health information management/[edited by] Marc Berg.
    p. cm. – (Routledge health management series)
        1. Medical records – Management.   2. Information storage
    and retrieval systems – Hospital.   I. Berg, Marc.   II. Series.

RA976.H387 2004
362.1'068'4–dc21   2003012421

ISBN 0–415–31518–2 (hbk)
ISBN 0–415–31519–0 (pbk)

Contents

CONTENTS

Illustrations

FIGURES

TABLES

Contributors

Marc Berg is a physician and health scientist. He is currently professor of Social-Medical Sciences at the Institute of Health Policy and Management, Erasmus University Medical Centre, Rotterdam, The Netherlands. His areas of interest include health information management and quality management. He has published many articles and books, including *Rationalizing Medical Work. Decision Support Techniques and Medical Practices*, 1997, Cambridge: MIT Press, and, with Stefan Timmermans, *The Gold Standard: An Exploration of Evidence-Based Medicine and Standardization in Health Care*, 2003, Philadelphia: Temple University Press.

Cé Bergen is a physician, with a Masters in Business Administration and a Masters in Health Informatics. He worked as a senior-consultant for PriceWaterhouse Coopers for many years, and gained much experience doing interim management, developing and implementing information strategies and leading large scale information system replacements. Some years ago, he started his own consulting agency (Bergen Consulting).

Enrico Coiera is a physician with a PhD in computer science. He is Foundation Chair in Medical Informatics within the Faculty of Medicine at the University of New South Wales, Australia. He is also Co-director of the Centre for Health Informatics, and an Adjunct Professor in Computer Science at the University of New South Wales. He is the author of many publications, including the widely used *Guide to Medical Informatics, the Internet and Telemedicine*, Oxford University Press, 1997 (currently in its 2003 2nd Edition as *Guide to Health Informatics*).

Heather Heathfield is a computer scientist. She is currently managing director of IT Perspectives Ltd, a company that provides an extensive range of research and health informatics consultancy services to its (predominantly UK) clients.

She is also well known for her academic research in decision support systems, electronic patient records and evaluation of IT in health care.

Bert Huisman holds a Masters in Business Administration/Business Informatics from the Rotterdam School of Management. He has 20 years' experience in health care IT, primarily with international health care software companies. Today, he works part-time as a researcher in the Research group on Information Technology in Health care practice and Management (RITHM) at the Institute of Health Policy and Management, Erasmus University Medical Centre, Rotterdam, The Netherlands. He is currently working on a PhD on IT implementation strategies in health care. He is a partner in Van Gelderen & Associates, a consulting firm dedicated to health care.

Marleen de Mul is a health scientist. She is currently working as a researcher in the Research group on Information Technology in Health care practice and Management (RITHM) at the Institute of Health Policy and Management, Erasmus University Medical Centre, Rotterdam, The Netherlands. Her areas of interest include evaluation of electronic patient records and IT supported quality systems in health care.

Arjen Stoop is a nurse and health scientist. He is currently working as a researcher in the Research group on Information Technology in Health care practice and Management (RITHM) at the Institute of Health Policy and Management, Erasmus University Medical Centre, Rotterdam, The Netherlands. He is writing a PhD on the topic of evaluation of IT in health care.

Brit Ross Winthereik holds a BA in ethnography and social anthropology and a MA in science and technology studies. She is currently located in the Rotterdam Research group on Information Technology in Health care practice and Management (RITHM) at the Institute of Health Policy and Management, Erasmus University Medical Centre. Her PhD project focuses on the consequences of the use of an electronic patient record for work in general practice. Areas of key interest are: classification, the construction of accuracy, accountability and autonomy and cross-national comparison.

Series preface

In almost all Western countries, health care is in a state of radical transformation. How can we meet the needs and demands of increasingly empowered 'consumers', contain costs, incorporate 'evidence based' modes of working, and re-motivate health care professionals — and all at the same time? The health care systems in Western countries are usually compared and contrasted along their axes of difference: nationalized versus fully market-driven; tax-based versus insurance-based financing; 'gatekeeping' general practitioners versus self-referral to hospital care. Yet, with the exception perhaps of the USA, these health care systems are struggling in strikingly similar ways to achieve the optimal balance between market incentives and government controls; and between professional self-regulation and explicit accountability to patients and payers. It has become clear that simple solutions will not work: neither 'the market' nor 'state control' offers the complete answer to the challenges that face us. Equally, neither 'professional self-regulation' nor 'paying for performance' offers the simple recipe that will heal our health care system's woes.

New models of health policy and health management are needed throughout the Western world, including a shift from a downstream preoccupation with health care services to an upstream focus on the health of communities and its improvement, tackling the widening 'health gap' between social groups; novel conceptions of organizing integrated care and chronic disease management; new approaches to performance management; innovative and realistic information management; effective human resource management; new models for managing clinical work; and so forth. These new models and approaches need to be theoretically sound, empirically based, and speak to professionals and patients and the problems facing them.

There is a great and urgent need for leadership in health and health care, and the many managers and professionals who end up in health management roles currently lack a well-defined series of textbooks to equip them with the requisite knowledge and insights derived from experience and research. We do not need more management hype, or yet another management fad or fashion that is unthinkingly applied to health care. These days more than ever, however, we do need to learn from each other's experiences and mistakes, and we need to be able to communicate and build upon 'best practices' developed elsewhere.

The *Routledge Series on Health Management* aims to meet these needs by providing health care managers with the theoretical knowledge, practical insights and concrete examples they require in today's rapidly changing health care environment, including experiences from adjacent fields (e.g. business, service industry, and so forth) where relevant. The series has a strong international orientation, comparing related developments and drawing on examples from different countries. The series is aimed at Masters students, other postgraduate students and also at experienced managers providing them with an up-to-date overview of the latest developments in their particular field(s) of interest. The books in the series contain a balanced mix of theoretical backgrounds and starting points on the one hand, and practice-oriented advice and guidance on the other in order to show how these theoretical concepts might be applied to concrete management challenges. Finally, each book pays explicit attention to the 'practitioner perspective': each book contains direct accounts or case studies, often written by practitioners, of the relevance (or otherwise) to them of the issues presented.

Prof. Dr. Marc Berg, MD, PhD
Prof. Dr. Robbert Huijsman, MBA, PhD
Prof. Dr. David J. Hunter, MA, PhD, HonFPHM, FRCP(Edin.)
Prof. Dr. John Øvretveit, PhD

Acknowledgements

I would like to thank all those who contributed to this book: the named co-authors, who worked hard to prepare this volume, and Els Goorman, Paul Harterink and Saskia Plass, with whom I cooperated some years ago and who contributed to some of the earlier work from which parts of this book derived. Further I would like to thank Francesca Poynter and Rachel Crookes, for starting up this project and for their never ending enthusiasm and faith in this undertaking. Finally, thanks to all the other members of the Rotterdam Research Group on Information Technology in Health care practice and Management (RITHM), and to Vasilie Getrouw and Marlies Hellendoorn for their support in organizing and handling the work that was part and parcel of preparing this book.

Chapters 2 to 4 from this book have emerged from the Dutch report *De Nacht Schreef Rood: Informatisering van Zorgpraktijken* (Berg, M., E. Goorman, P. Harterink, and S. Plass, 1998, Den Haag: Rathenau Instituut). Parts of the following articles were drawn upon in Chapter 2 to 5: Accumulating and Coordinating: Occasions for Information Technologies in Medical Work, Berg, M. 1999, *Computer Supported Cooperative Work* 8: 373–401; Search for Synergy: Interrelating Medical Work and Patient Care Information Systems, Berg, M., 2003, *Methods of Information in Medicine*, in press; The Contextual Nature of Medical Information, Berg, M., and E. Goorman, 1999, *International Journal of Medical Informatics* 56: 51–60; Embodying the Patient: Records and Bodies in Early 20th Century US Medical Practice, Berg, M., and P. Harterink, 2003, *Body and Society*, in press. Chapter 6 is based upon material presented in a trio of papers, which set out a broad framework for understanding how humans interact with each other, through the use of technology: When Conversation is Better than Computation, Coiera, E. 2000, *Journal of the American Medical Informatics Association* 7: 277–86; Mediated Agent Interaction, E. Coiera, 2001, in S. Qualglini, P. Barahona and S. Adreassen (Eds.), *AIME 2001 – Proceedings of the 8th Conference on Artificial Intelligence in Medicine Europe*, Springer Lecture Notes in Artificial Intelligence no. 2101, and Mediated

Interaction Design, Coiera, E. in press, *International Journal of Medical Informatics*. Chapter 9, finally, is based upon Implementing Information Systems in Health Care Organizations: Myths and Challenges, Berg, M. 2001, *International Journal of Medical Informatics* 64: 143–56.

Chapter 1

Introduction

In all Western countries, concerted efforts are undertaken to enhance the use of Information Technology (IT) in health care. National, regional and institutional projects abound to bring the shared Electronic Patient Record (EPR) into being, and to support the care process with order communication and decision support techniques. IT, it is hoped, can help reduce medical errors and increase the quality of health care delivery through optimizing communication. Likewise, extensive use of Internet technologies and electronic patient records could enhance the position of the patient (provide him/her with relevant medical information and access to their own records). Simultaneously, it could provide governments, payers and patient organizations with comparable information on the performance of individual professionals and organizations.

Yet there are only a few real success stories in health care IT, and the frustrations are many. It has become clear that the design and introduction of IT in the health care sector is a complex endeavour, encompassing the simultaneous management of technological innovation and organizational change. This book will introduce the reader to the challenges, lessons learned and new insights of Health Information Management at the beginning of the twenty-first century. It focuses on some of the theoretical reasons *why* introducing health care IT appears to be 'a more complex task than putting a man on the moon' (Collen, 1995: 353). Simultaneously, it attempts to provide the reader with concrete insights and lessons on how to handle these complex issues more successfully.

FOR WHOM IS THIS BOOK?

The book focuses on the development and implementation of health care IT, on making a health care IT strategy and on evaluating health care IT as part and parcel of these undertakings. Importantly, this is not a technical volume, but a text focused on the *organizational processes and management of design, implementation and evaluation of such systems.* Health Information Management, in our view, is the job of handling the information requirements of a health care organization. In the past century, 'health information management' was often a term reserved for those making and archiving the paper medical records of an institution. A book on 'health information management' would have been a rather specialized endeavour, focusing on how to make forms, how to archive records, the legal responsibilities of record keepers, and so forth. Not the reading material physicians or general managers would dive into.

At the beginning of the twenty-first century, however, the field of 'health information management' has fundamentally changed. Only 20 years ago, 'the information systems department' was usually a small organizational unit, part of the Finance Department, whose organizational 'niche' position reflected the limited strategic importance of information systems, and their small impact on the organization. Nowadays, however, 'information management' has become of much more strategic importance to the organization, with 'information managers' at work within many different departments, and a 'Chief Information Officer' (however labelled) who reports directly to or is often even part of the Board of Directors.

This migration 'upwards' and diffusion through the organizational chart is no mere fashion or management hype. Health care organizations are information-intensive industries, with at least three different types of 'information' that are of core importance to a professional organization such as a hospital or GP practice:

1 *information about individual patients* (gathered in the 'patient record');
2 *aggregate information about the processes and outcomes of the organization* ('management' information, which can also be for the professionals themselves to help them monitor and improve their current performance);
3 *information about diagnostic and therapeutic decisions and procedures* (the professional and organizational 'knowledge' required to handle patients optimally, often embedded in guidelines or protocols).

The Patient Care Information System (PCIS; see below) is where all these different forms of information are required and/or are generated. It is the core node in the information network of a health care organization, and, as such, of core importance to health information management.

Currently, then, health information management deals first and foremost with the challenge of *integrating health information systems in health care work in such a way that the quality of that work is improved.* This sounds obvious, but, as this book will show, it is not. Health information management is about the complex task of handling technical innovation *simultaneously with* organizational transformation. Yielding strategic benefits from PCIS, it will become clear, requires vision and basic information management knowledge for every manager or professional whose responsibilities include the (re-)organization of health care work or the generation or utilization of management information from that work. This, indeed, includes many people – but in current information-intensive organizations such as health care institutions, IT *does* affect many people.

This book, then, is of importance to both the (future) health information manager, and to those professionals and general managers whose responsibilities touch upon the deployment of IT in the organization – whether at the strategic or the implementation level.

A READER'S GUIDE

This book focuses on what we call 'Patient Care Information Systems' (PCIS): all those systems that are used primarily by health care professionals and patients, and that are primarily oriented at the support of their tasks (such as electronic patient records, order communication systems, patient cards, patient information systems). Systems that bridge the primary care process and secondary work processes in health care organizations, such as management information systems and registration systems for scientific research are included. Systems that primarily focus on financial administration, human resource management and so forth are not addressed here.

This is not an ordinary handbook. Significant parts of this book are not written in the form of 'how to' manuals, but are aimed at providing an *understanding* of the tasks of information management; of the organizational processes and management of design, implementation and evaluation of PCISs. Subsequently, these and other chapters also give concrete guidelines for (information) managers and professionals to handle these tasks.

We argue, maybe a bit counter-intuitively, that those readers whose responsibilities are not *primarily* oriented towards information management concentrate first and foremost on the more conceptual chapters. A core insight of this book is that many PCIS projects run to the ground because of wrong expectations of what these technologies can do (at the level of the workfloor and for the organization), and how their implementation should be managed. The book touches upon the familiar high hopes and dreams surrounding information technology, and the frustrations of professionals when these high hopes cannot be realized instantly ('my nephew can do this in one evening!'). Since the conceptual chapters are full with concrete examples and are directly oriented towards the real-life issues that managers and professionals face in their daily, information-intensive work, these chapters (concentrated in Part I of this book) are not 'difficult' or 'dry'.

Part I, then, 'Understanding health care work and the role of IT' attempts to underscore the strategic importance of IT, the nature of IT and its development, and the nature of health care work. It will push the reader to understand the phenomenal challenges of creating true synergy between health care work practices and PCIS systems. Simultaneously, it will set high stakes for the ambitions that can and will have to be pursued in twenty-first century health care.

Chapter 2 focuses on the nature of information technology innovation. Through a historical account of the paper-based patient-centred record, and the subsequent quest for its electronic sequel, the entanglement of information technology, information management and its social and organizational context is emphasized.

Subsequently, Chapters 3 and 4 deal with the nature of health care work and of health care information, and with the way PCIS systems can transform this work. This transformation, we will argue, can easily be a negative development: systems abound that truly 'interfere' with work rather than support it. Only through a thorough understanding of the nature of health care work and information can systems be developed and implemented that can help this work become more patient-oriented, more effective, more efficient, and more professional-oriented.

This last sentence, we will argue in Chapter 5, is no mere slogan. Western health care is in dire need for means to cross the 'Quality Chasm', as it has been labelled by recent, widely embraced reports from the US Institute of Medicine (Committee on Quality of Health Care in America, 2001). Information technology, we will argue in Chapter 5, is a *sine qua non* in the effort to transform health care work so that it can hope to meet the challenges facing it. Crucially, however, IT will not be able to fulfil this role in the form of yet the next IT 'hype'. It is not more *intelligent technology* that we need: it is *intelligent use* of already existing technologies. As will become abundantly clear in this chapter and others, properly developing and implementing IT in health care practices is primarily about *organizational development*. Technology is crucial – but secondary.

In Chapter 6, this latter theme is picked up again in a discussion about the proper position of Information Technology in the *interaction space* for humans in complex organizations such as hospitals. This chapter challenges us to see even the *design* of systems as a shift from a focus on the technology to the people that are using it. Only in that way, the chapter argues, can information systems become truly useful.

In Part II, 'Information strategy, implementation and evaluation', we will build upon these insights and discuss some of the information management tasks. Here, we will dive deeper into the topics of IT strategy development, PCIS implementation and PCIS evaluation. More than in Part I, the emphasis is directed towards providing practical guidelines for the health information manager.

Chapter 7 discusses the challenges of information strategy development. It discusses the very nature of strategy and strategy formation, and it focuses on the *alignment* between the information strategy and the organizational strategy. The complexity of both information technology and health care organizations, the chapter argues, makes the attempt to align their mutual *development* a sheer impossible – yet crucial! – challenge.

Chapter 8, subsequently, sets out to give the reader some concrete instruments with which he/she can manage this process. It discusses the goals of the information strategy, gives guidelines to how it should be drafted, and, more importantly, what it should contain. These instruments do not solve the complexity, nor do they constitute a simple roadmap towards success. Yet they are the tools that health information managers – and health care organizations – can draw upon to maintain on course. They are a means to ensure that the strategy development process is seen as the vital process that it is, and to ensure that it remains focused on the tough questions that any ambitious IT strategy will certainly bring along.

Chapter 9 then turns towards the issue of the *implementation* of a PCIS. Arguing for the strong intertwinement of IT and work practice, it restates the point that PCIS implementation is a form of *organizational development*, and argues how this has consequences for the management of any PCIS implementation project. As Chapter 7, this chapter demonstrates the complexity of such projects, and argues for a knife-edge balance between intense, bottom-up user-participation and strong visionary management, and between controlling the development process and letting go of control.

Chapter 10, then, mirroring Chapter 8, brings the tools that make it feasible to run projects without the 'control' criticized in Chapter 9, and to have projects be both user-driven and management-led. Again, this is no magical recipe, but a set of decision points and steps that, when well handled, sets some of the conditions in place for a 'successful' IT implementation.

Chapter 11, finally, discusses the need for PCIS evaluation. Starting with a sketch of the PCIS evaluation field, it focuses on the so-called *formative* evaluations that should be part and parcel of any PCIS development. A formative evaluation, this chapter argues, is a necessary building block of successful IT development and use: only in this way can the mutual learning potential between 'work practice' and 'PCIS' be fully drawn upon. Although often omitted because of its seemingly supplementary costs, proper formative evaluation ultimately always pays itself back – and often saves the organization for expensive mistakes. The chapter outlines the different domains that a formative evaluation can focus on, and discusses the real-life steps of setting up and performing such an evaluation.

This book has a strong international orientation, comparing related developments and drawing on examples from different countries. It is an ideal handbook for Masters students, other postgraduate trainees, interested professionals and general managers, and will equally provide experienced information managers with an up to date overview of the latest developments in their area. The book will draw heavily on case descriptions and examples (in Case Study Boxes) to illustrate and enrich the main text, but also to enhance their usability for teaching purposes. Every chapter starts with a list of 'key points' and 'key terms' of the chapter, and ends with 'discussion questions' and suggestions for 'further reading'.

A NOTE ON PATIENT CARE INFORMATION SYSTEMS AND TERMINOLOGY

Different authors, different countries, different vendors all use different terminologies for their health care IT products. The medical informatics literature is replete with discussions about whether an Electronic Medical Record should not rather be called an Electronic *Patient* Record (emphasizing the central role of the patient) or, rather, an Electronic *Health* Record (emphasizing the fact that there is much more than just 'medical' or 'disease related' information in a record). For others, a Medical Record is something essentially different from a Health Record – the former being limited to physician's notes and physician-oriented information; the latter being the all-encompassing record on the 'whole patient'.

This book does not want to take a stake in such definition quarrels. Yet it is important to realize that they exist, and that what is precisely meant at any given time by a label such as 'medical record' is not self-evident. Often, terminology oversells the underlying product: at best, the intelligence of 'intelligent systems' lies in their design and their use; at worst, 'intelligent systems' are an affront to any intelligent person working with it. Similarly, a 'data warehouse' and 'data mining' allude to highly lucrative activities and the 'golden nuggets' of information that the organization has at its fingertips. 'Databases' and 'doing searches' sound much less interesting, although that is basically what lies beneath the rhetoric.

We will use the term 'Information Technology' (IT) throughout this book, although some prefer the term 'Information and Communication Technology' (ICT). We intend no definition quarrel here either, although we do not focus on telecom applications, for example.

As said, we will here use the term 'Patient Care Information Systems' (PCIS) to address those systems that are used primarily by health care professionals and patients, and that are primarily oriented to the support of their tasks. Among others, the following systems that we will encounter in this book belong to this category (for more technical details, please consult a leading Medical Informatics handbook such as (Coiera, 2003; van Bemmel, 1997)).

Table 1.1 *Some examples of patient care information systems*

Electronic Patient Record (EPR)	The EPR is primarily a database containing patients' information. Through its *retrieval* functions it should allow the health professional easy access to stored patient information. Through its *input* functions, it should allow adequate and easy storage of patient information. In this book, the terms 'patient record' and 'medical record' are used interchangeably.
Patient Information System (PIS)	A Patient Information System is a system that is primarily oriented towards a patient, allowing electronic access to his/her record and/or to (individualized) patient education material. It could also contain modes of electronic communication with health care professionals and/or decision support modules.
Physician Order Entry (POE)	Order Entry systems allow professionals to order tests, additional investigations, drugs and other 'services' electronically. Results are also reported back electronically, and often, intermediate steps can be monitored. POE systems explicitly attempt at having the *doctor* perform these tasks, which should, amongst others, reduce errors due to illegible handwriting and miscommunication. Since the orders that are given and the results that are received should also be part and parcel of the EPR, a POE is often designed so as to be able to fulfil the role of an EPR.
Decision-Support Technique (DST)	A decision support technique attempts to improve decisions taken by health care professionals through providing the professional with salient advice, reminders or alarms at the proper time. Also, systems that actively guide professionals through separate steps in a decision or action process are sometimes called DSTs. DSTs can be built into EPRs and POEs. The latter combination especially affords the production of protocollized order sets, automatically generated advice and reminders when an order is given (or is forgotten), and so forth.
Medication System	A medication system is like a POE system focused especially on handling and monitoring a patient's medication. (Indeed, POE systems usually encompass medication systems.) It allows professionals to overview and prescribe medication, and it may monitor and check omissions, dosing mistakes, interactions and so forth. Further, it may be integrated with an automated dispensing system and/or electronic drug administration support. An example of such an addition could be robot-produced, patient-specific, pre-wrapped medication strips and a bar scanner with handheld device through which administering the drugs may become a safeguarded procedure as well.

Table 1.1 *(cont.)*

Hospital Information System (HIS)	Most hospitals still have an HIS: an integrated application supporting a broad range of functions in a hospital. Constructed around a common patient database, laboratory systems, radiology systems, and discharge letter production and storage can all be built in. In addition, the operation of the pharmacy, the kitchen, and the EPR may all be built in as well. Because of their integrated nature, such systems were once highly efficient, but are now seen as outdated. Currently, 'hospital information systems' would ideally exist of a wide array of applications, from different vendors, specialized in only *one* of these functions. In this way, 'best of breed' systems (the best EPR, the best PIS, the best Data Warehousing system, etc.) could be linked together because they all adhere to so-called 'open' standards defining their interfaces.
General Practitioner Information System (GPIS)	Although the term resembles the HIS, the GPIS is usually a stand-alone application, made for an individual GP (or a small group practice). It is basically an EPR with added administration and medication functions, and functions facilitating risk-group management (such as the execution of a preventive influenza vaccination campaign, the monitoring and handling of diabetes patients, and so forth). Many different versions exist (see Chapter 2).
Data Warehouse	A data warehouse is a database that draws information seen as relevant for management information (or research, or teaching purposes and so forth) out of the root databases of the (modules of the) PCIS. In this way, even large queries of the database do not affect overall PCIS performance. More importantly, most HISs are poorly equipped for generating *any* management information, so that a 'data warehouse' is often the only technically feasible way to get to this information with some ease.

REFERENCES

Collen, M. E. (1995) *A History of Medical Informatics in the United States, 1950 to 1990.* American Medical Informatics Association.

Coiera, E. (2003) *Guide to Health Informatics.* London: Arnold.

Committee on Quality of Health Care in America (2001) *Crossing the Quality Chasm: A New Health System for the 21st Century.* Washington: National Academy Press.

van Bemmel, J. and M. Musen (1997) *Handbook of Medical Informatics.* Berlin: Springer Verlag.

Part I

Starting points

Understanding health care work and the role of IT

Chapter 2

Waiting for Godot

Episodes from the history of patient records

Marc Berg and Brit Ross Winthereik

The electronic medical record has been pursued as an ideal by so many, for so long, that some suggest that it has become the Holy Grail of Medical Informatics.

(Kay and Purves 1996)

KEY POINTS OF THIS CHAPTER

- The patient record has been at the centre of health care innovation for at least a century.
- Since its early conception, the history of the patient record is intertwined with the standardization of health care work.
- The development (the construction and implementation) of new record systems (and information technologies in general) implies a transformation of the practice in which it functions. Similarly, during this development process, the technology is transformed as well.
- The still prevailing standard view of technology tends to reduce the complicated and socially relevant concerns involved in the development of (health care) ICT to mere 'technical' problems.
- Bringing the interrelations between technological, organizational and political aspects into the light is a precondition for the development of health care ICT applications that may actually work.
- Although the need for patient care information systems has only grown more acute, the actual track record of ICT in health care is in stark contrast with the golden futures that are often promised.

KEY TERMS

- The (integrated) patient-oriented record
- The electronic patient record
- Standardization
- Health care practice
- Politics of technology

INTRODUCTION

The recent attention for the patient record is all but new. Throughout the twentieth century, it has been a major concern for those engaged in the innovation of medical work. The American Hospital Standardization Movement, for instance, substantially contributed to the introduction of patient-oriented records in the early part of this century, Lawrence Weed's problem-oriented record was introduced in the late 1960s, and for the last five decades the electronic patient record (EPR) has carried along the promise of more effective and efficient care. In the next section one of these developments, the introduction of a patient-oriented record during the early years of the twentieth century in the United States, will be addressed in detail. We will also look at the response to this development in Europe, where the American example was generally well received, with the exception of its strong emphasis on 'standardization'.

The aim of this historical excursion is twofold. First, it is meant to put the current state of affairs in historical perspective. Some consider the introduction of the EPR as the 'next major change' in medical reporting (Ornstein *et al.* 1992), but our historical approach in this chapter will reveal that already at the beginning of the twentieth century standardization was viewed as inevitable for a rational medical practice. Also, the ideal of an integrated patient record – one record with all information on a patient – will appear to be at least a century old. Our perspective is equally meant to illustrate the particular complexity of the issue: after one hundred years the call for standardization is still loudly heard, while a truly integrated patient record still seems a remote prospect.

Second, our historical excursion will generate a better understanding of the current state of affairs. Finding ourselves at the beginning of a new century, it is as if we are looking into a mirror when we see that around 1900 similar issues and concerns were debated in the health care field. What exactly does it mean to radically change practices of medical reporting, to introduce new systems for keeping records in health care, or to aspire to raise the quality and effectiveness of medical work in this way? In most literature on health care IT, technological development is considered a neutral process: one that may either be facilitated or impeded by social factors. In recent studies of technology this view of technology development is called the 'standard view'. Because in this standard view the development of technology is understood as an autonomous, technical process, little attention tends to be paid to the social and political implications of technologies for the practices in which they function.

The history of patient records, however, demonstrates that the construction and implementation of new record systems should be seen as the building of a network, a process in which both medical practice and the record system are significantly changed. Technology development does not follow an autonomous, straight line without intersections. The large number of people and factors involved and the fact that there are always several driving forces and interests at work turn it into a non-linear and unpredictable process. The history of patient records also amply illustrates that the development of technology is no neutral affair. Because technologies reconfigure health care practices, they are deeply involved in intra- and inter-organizational and professional politics. Changes in the way patient records are kept have affected, for instance, the distribution of tasks between professions, the autonomy of physicians, and the authority of the executive boards of hospitals.

In the section 'Terra incognita' (pp. 24–36) we sketch the international developments involving EPRs, zooming in at some European examples of health care information technology development. Our concern is not with providing a full overview of the current state of affairs regarding the role of information technology in the health care sector. Rather, this section is devoted to a brief introduction of the key players in the developments discussed in this book and to a preliminary exploration of the value of the historical lessons for these more recent events.

Capitalizing on the idea that technology development is inextricably bound up with transformations in health care practices, another conclusion is advanced. In the still prevailing standard view of technology, the complicated and socially relevant concerns involved in the development of EPRs are reduced to mere 'technical' problems. Standardization, for instance, is generally conceptualized as a technical problem to be solved by technical commissions. We will argue that with such a problem-definition important political and organizational aspects disappear from sight. Not only is this undesirable from a social perspective, it also leads to unworkable 'solutions'.

The empirical material of this chapter is predominantly focused on the medical record and the medical profession. We opted for this limitation in focus because the developments around record keeping originated here, were very influential, and are well documented.

THE RISE OF THE PATIENT-ORIENTED RECORD

The transition from the nineteenth to the twentieth century was the period in which the hospital became the focal point of health care in the United States. In the years around 1900, it changed from a shelter for the poor into an institution that was organized on a scientific basis. Here, medical professionals, relying on all kinds of technological novelties, offered high quality care. Whereas in the Netherlands and the UK the family doctor as 'trusted adviser' played a central role in health care (which he continues to have to this day), in America the hospital became 'the heart and mind' of the health care system (Mansholt 1931).

Moreover, it was in this period that the medical profession managed to secure its central, autonomous position in society. The reform of medical training in the United States – under the aegis of the American Medical Association (AMA) – led to a reduction of the number of medical schools and the number of licensed physicians. The ensuing concentration of medical training and the establishment of common performance standards caused a consolidation of the professional authority of the AMA.

The American College of Surgeons was equally engaged in the effort to create a tight, homogeneous professional group. It also embraced a centralized approach and established official nationwide standards to be met by surgeons throughout the country. These 'Fellows of the College' had to possess the proper expertise and were not allowed 'to split their fees with doctors who referred patients to them' (Stevens 1989). To this end, an in-depth study of the skills and practices of surgeons was set up around 1915. Surgeons were asked to send in case histories of patients they had operated upon, so that the College could evaluate their work. It turned out, however, that neither the surgeons nor the hospitals were able to submit the appropriate records needed for such a study. Many hospitals simply failed to have general procedures for medical reporting. Only the better hospitals had wards where doctors kept track of the progression of the patients on the ward in a logbook. In such a 'ward record', physicians would enter basic information on their patients, each entry simply following the previous one. Not much information was recorded: a poor patient admitted to one of the leading US East coast hospitals in 1900 with a broken leg might have spent some six weeks there, and have one or two entries in the ward record. Data on individual patients were difficult to trace: information on a single patient was scattered throughout the log, and only if a good index was available could this information be aggregated. In addition to these ward records, physicians kept track of their patient's case history by jotting down catchwords on a note-pad or in a notebook, or simply from memory.

Furthermore, the circumstances under which surgeons had to operate appeared to be so varied that a proper comparison of the case histories was virtually impossible. Some hospitals had operating theatres that were new, sterile and equipped with electric lighting, while operating theatres in other hospitals hardly differed from the average wardroom. In some hospitals one would find specifically trained nursing staff for providing assistance during operations and regular autopsies, while in other hospitals such facilities were nonexistent.

Because of these widely divergent circumstances, the College decided that the quality of surgeons' performance could only be guaranteed if the hospitals where they worked satisfied specific minimum requirements. Laboratory facilities, x-ray facilities, and clean and well-lighted operating theatres with a specially trained nursing staff had to be available. In addition, systematic patient-oriented records, as opposed to ward records, had to be kept for all patients:

> Accurate, accessible, and complete written records must be kept for all patients and should include patient identification, complaints, personal and family history, history of present illness, physical examination, record of special examination such as consultations, clinical laboratory and x-ray results, provisional or working diagnosis, proposed medical or surgical therapy, gross and microscopic findings, progress notes, final diagnosis, condition on discharge, follow up and in case of death autopsy findings.
>
> (Atwater 1989)

Adequate, patient-oriented record keeping was one of the priorities of the Hospital Standardization Movement, co-initiated by the College. Its concern for standardization did not appear out of the blue. It was inspired by the scientifically motivated methods of management that had become popular in American industry and business. This approach favoured a 'scientific' organization of the production process, whereby complex tasks were divided into standardized and clearly delineated subtasks in order to raise the efficiency and controllability of the process as a whole. An accurate, centralized administration was seen as an essential requirement:

> The basis of this standardized service is to know what the hospital is doing, and to record its work in such a way as to enable an appraisement to be made of it. . . . Records, therefore, are a prime essential in any program of hospital standardization. . . . Case records are the visible evidence of what the hospital is accomplishing. . . . Not to maintain case records properly is like running a factory without a record of the product.
>
> (Huffman 1972)

Thus the need to keep records was not only triggered by the need for standards of accreditation. An explicit function of records in industrial contexts involved the monitoring of the activities of employees by the management. Even when the employees were physicians, the management could benefit from having control mechanisms at its disposal, as is illustrated by the following words of a hospital board member:

> The advantage of having a complete hospital record . . ., not a long one, but a complete one, was illustrated to me . . . [The superintendent] had asked the clerk to take the records of four men occupying similar positions on the staff, the man in dispute being one of them, and bring him these men's records of operations for three months, the character of the operation, the result, and the number of days the patient remained in the hospital, so that when this man came to him and said he was being persecuted, he had definite facts to show that his death rate was high, and that the average length of stay of his patients in the hospital was longer than any other man's.
>
> (Bottomley 1918)

Besides allowing for control by the hospital management, it was emphasized that adequate records were essential for the development of medical science. After all, systematic data could be used for evaluating medical interventions and acquiring a better insight in the pattern of specific diseases:

> In a way it marks the beginning of real clinical science, for each operation or each attempt at any other form of curative treatment in any hospital is an experiment. It seems curious that these experiments should not be recorded in most hospitals. Often the facts thus obtained would be of the greatest scientific value.
>
> (Anonymous 1914)

Finally, the keeping of medical records also became relevant in a juridical context as potential evidence in court cases. This function may seem natural to us, but in the early years of the twentieth century this use of medical records was all but taken for granted:

> [S]o called 'bed-side notes' were not admissible in evidence. They were introduced during the examination of a hospital nurse, who was in the hospital at the time the plaintiff was a patient there. She describes the paper as a 'temperature chart, known in the hospital as bedside notes,' and said such notes were taken in each case where a patient was brought to the hospital. The court is not aware of any rule of evidence which makes such a paper, offered under such circumstances, admissible.
>
> (Anonymous 1904)

At first, patient records were too idiosyncratic and insufficiently formalized to serve as legal evidence. When, for instance, it was not clear who had written what and at what date or time, or when the exact status of individual notes failed to be clear, records could hardly fulfil a legal function. Only after practices of record keeping became standardized, patient records began to be accepted as relevant documents in court cases. The institutionalization of writing and reporting procedures opened up the possibility to consider the medical record as an objective account of events, irrespective of the individuals who actually wrote down the notes or data (Smith 1990). The patient record became established as the official document in which everything about a patient's medical treatment could be found:

> Subpoena of the record enables any court to obtain a true statement concerning the patient's care and treatment in connection with insurance claims, employees' liability claims, suit for damages and malpractice.
>
> (Munger 1928)

Obviously, it did not take long for this juridical function to become itself an important incentive for a more complete, standardized recording of data on patients.

Standardized recording of patient data may have been useful in many contexts, but its realization proved no easy task. The Hospital Standardization Movement had to convince hospitals, physicians, and patients of its significance, and an infrastructure for the creation and storage of records had to be developed.

For one, physicians generally saw little use for keeping exhaustive records. In their day-to-day performance, just a few catchwords, jotted down in a log or a notebook, would do in most cases. On the whole, American physicians worked very much on their own. They were associated to hospitals as private physicians, responsible for following their 'own' patients on their therapeutic trajectory during their stay in hospital. These patients tended to see few other physicians and so a physician's memory could suffice. Poor patients could not afford to have their own physician. Their notes – if any – ended up in the ward record, the brevity of which matched the brevity of attention such patients could be expected to receive.

Although the methods of reporting data on patients would do in the eyes of most physicians, the advocates of the Hospital Standardization Movement deemed it absolutely unacceptable. Frequently, they claimed, physicians kept notes and records in an 'exceedingly laconic' manner (Davis 1920):

> The various diagnostic procedures are often neither dated nor signed. . . .
> The bedside notes seldom give a complete picture of the case. There is likewise hardly ever a note as to the condition of the patient at discharge.
>
> (Lewinski-Corwin 1922)

In principle, the records on private patients were patient-oriented, but most physicians kept them to themselves. A more 'public' storage of this confidential information was considered a violation or even betrayal of the unique relationship of trust between doctor and patient. In terms of their administrative value and continuity, these private records could never fulfil the functions as envisioned by the Hospital Standardization Movement. Thus, they equally failed to meet the standards of accreditation as formulated by the College of Surgeons:

> The private patient records are worse than the ward records. In some of the hospitals, no records of the private patients are required for the central file, thus making the relationship of the patient to the hospital purely that of a hotel.
>
> (Lewinski-Corwin 1922)

In a study of the problems of medical record keeping, the lack of motivation among physicians was mentioned as the main obstacle:

> In response to the question of what difficulties were met with, not one hospital mentioned any trouble in getting the clerical part of the work done. The difficulties all seemed to be in getting proper reports of the histories, physical examination, operations, etc. . . . . All this, of course, with the exception of the shortage of house officers, points to a lack of interest and cooperation on the part of the doctors.
>
> (Stevens 1919)

In order to be able to guarantee proficient record keeping, hospitals began to hire new, clerical staff:

> Of course the first thing that suggests itself is to have a competent stenographer who will take down dictations at the time of the visit and after the operations. This stenographer could also take care of the clerical part of the work and the details of the follow-up system.
>
> (Stevens 1919)

In addition to stenographers, the professions of 'record clerk' and 'record librarian' were created. They were in charge of setting up and keeping up to date the central record systems. Generally, they had the right to call on medical staff who failed to complete forms and records properly:

> The record clerk peruses the chart from the first sheet to the last, making notations on the small pad (which is addressed to the intern) of any deficiencies noted on the chart . . . if there are any deficiencies on the chart, the red signal is replaced by a green signal. . . . When the intern has corrected the deficiencies on his record and has returned the slip to the

record office the green signal is then removed from the card. This leaves a clear margin and indicates that the charts in a given area have been checked and are satisfactory in every detail.

(Gilman 1932)

In some cases, clerks took their monitoring task to considerable lengths:

The record room clerk shall post each day on a bulletin board at the entrance of the hospital the number of incompetent histories opposite the name of the member of the staff responsible for their completion.

(Auchincloss 1926)

Such reorganization was no longer just a matter of more staff. The primary location of records was replaced from the ward or the physician's office to the 'record room'. In addition to new technologies, such as dictating machines and pneumatic dispatch for transporting records, many architectural adjustments proved to be necessary as well. These were not always easy to realize:

In older institutions, however, built before the days of hospital standardization or of emphasis upon hospital record-keeping, the installation of a record department has in many cases been a difficult problem. . . . The ideal record room is near enough to the operating room, laboratories, and staff room to make it convenient to access, yet sufficiently secluded to be a suitable place for quiet work, on the part of both the record room staff and the attending doctors, interns, and technicians who may come there to complete unfinished charts, for information, or for research.

(Genevieve Morse 1934)

The new hospitals were designed as centralized high-rise buildings, in part because this type of building reduces the transportation times of the steadily increasing number of forms, records, materials, and patients that were moved up and down between the various offices and wards:

The distance covered in vertical transportation is shorter than that in horizontal transportation — even though in the former case one remains dependent on the proper functioning of elevators and the staff who service them.

(Mansholt 1931)

Another consequence of the vast increase in paperwork was the need to standardize medical terminology. Outpatient clinics and wards were to use the same 'nomenclature of disease and nomenclature of operations' (Genevieve Morse 1934), if at least the notes of one individual are to be comprehensible to another. The use of standardized terminology made it possible, for instance, to compare groups of patients with each other on the basis of the records:

> The cards in the diagnosis catalogue are arranged according to Dr. Post's 'Nomenclature of Diseases and Conditions,' in which entries are grouped primarily under the different systems and secondarily under anatomical parts, in alphabetical order. Thus the cards referring to all the diseases of an anatomical part can be found at a glance.
>
> (Anonymous 1912)

In most cases, the categorization of records and the selection of a particular nomenclature became the responsibility of the new 'medical record professional' (Stokes *et al.* 1933).

It will be clear by now that the implementation of a patient-oriented record required a rigorous transformation of the health care practice in which this record was going to function. In the hospitals, new professional groups were invented and introduced, the routines of physicians and nurses underwent changes, terminologies had to be standardized, and buildings were remodelled. The realization of a new record system was a costly and time-consuming affair which caused substantial financial difficulties for many smaller American hospitals.

European medical professions responded with ambivalence to these American developments. The significance of keeping complete records was underscored, and the facilities created for American physicians were looked at with envy, a Dutch doctor reported:

> While in our country, as far as I know, the doctor is expected to bring his own fountain pen and have a considerable passion for writing, the American doctor has more attractive means at his disposal. Every hospital of some importance has a separate department for managing the case histories, the 'Record Department'. Young ladies, who not only have typing skills but who also know short-hand, are busy in there all day. They help out with every clerical matter.
>
> (Schoute 1925)

However, already the architectural prerequisites for adequate, centrally organized recording of patient data posed a problem to European hospitals:

> One will definitely find many [among the large hospitals in the Netherlands] that are built on the premise of the still prevailing system in Europe, namely the one marked by isolated pavilions, including separate

buildings for the clerical and financial departments. The newer style of building aims to integrate everything as much as possible in one or several buildings, which, consequently, have to have many stories.

(Mansholt 1931)

Official regulations and restrictions stood in the way of such 'rational and efficient' building in the Netherlands. The minimal size of the garden of Dutch hospitals, for instance, was officially linked to the number of beds. As someone commented on this aspect:

In these hospitals the garden was in danger of being sacrificed as well: of the common requirement with us to have 100 square meters of garden for each hospital bed, normally little is left over there. . . . The Americans in general seem to have little feeling for blooming flower beds and shrubs.

(Mansholt 1931)

More important, however, was that the Dutch physicians vehemently opposed the immediate consequences of the 'American system' for the medical profession. The central role of American hospitals as 'custodian' of integrated patient information was unthinkable in the Dutch context. In the Netherlands as in the UK, the hospital was 'no more than one link in the chain of public health care' and, as such, this institution could not take over the overall responsibility for patient information from physicians (Mansholt 1931). When terms such as 'rationalization' and 'standardization' were used in a Dutch medical context, it was to discuss the economic administration of hospitals, or the logistics of its day-to-day operation. Clinical work was basically left out of the standardization debate altogether. Professionals should be on guard for possible coercion and 'superficial schematism' (Anonymous 1929):

The American system is in part based on coercion, and this is already troublesome to us. But, additionally, it is formulaic in many respects. The coercion can be seen in how it [the patient record system] was set up and implemented, the formulaic character is shown in the activities themselves, as is clearly illustrated by the stringent monitoring of both the medical staff's visits and their performance.

(Schoute 1925)

Whereas the American College of Surgeons decided to require standardized record keeping on the basis of its study of hospital records, a committee of the Dutch Medical Association (NMG) arrived at a very different conclusion on the basis of its comparative study of Dutch hospital records. A brief news item on this Dutch study appeared in the *Journal of the American Medical Association*:

The committee relates that in an examination of the books of the sixty-four hospitals in the Netherlands chaotic differences were found between the data recorded and the methods of compiling them in the different hospitals. Their records therefore cannot be compared, and thus are not a source for dependable statistics. The committee deplores this, and makes some suggestions which would remedy this state of affairs. In the first place, however, it deprecates any attempt to force uniformity in hospital records. The liberty of each institution to record and publish what seems to be important must not be interfered with. But certain data should be recorded, and these the committee thinks should be called to the attention of every hospital with the request to conform to the suggestions. The committee adds that the suggestions have been restricted to what is absolutely necessary, so as not to add to the *beslommeringen* of the hospital direction. (This useful and untranslatable Dutch word *beslommeringen* means 'to involve in all sorts of difficult affairs'.)

(Anonymous 1916)

Just like the College of Surgeons, the Dutch medical professional organization was confronted with vast differences in reporting methods in Dutch hospitals. In contrast to its American counterpart, however, it argued that the liberty of hospitals and physicians should not be encroached upon. Consequently, it merely issued a request to those involved to comply with minimal standards.

This episode from the early history of the paper record during the 1910s and 1920s illustrates that the construction and implementation of a technology implies a transformation of the practice in which it is functioning. The patient-oriented record system made it necessary to hire new clerical personnel, rearrange hospitals, and set up a new division of roles between physicians and nursing staff. What at first seemed to be just a minor organizational effort at improving medical reporting turned out to involve a far-reaching process that led to large-scale organizational transformations, including changes in the tasks of established professionals and even the invention of new professions. This process, however, works its way in two directions: during the implementation process, the technology is transformed as well. The juridical role that the patient record acquired in the process caused a further institutionalization of record keeping procedures; yet it also created a new mental reality among those involved: the constant awareness that each note in the record might one day end up on the desk of a lawyer or judge. Moreover, differences between the health care systems of the United States and those of European countries caused the reporting of medical data to develop along different lines. In the Netherlands, for example, the position of the major medical professional organization contributed to a situation in which, for the time being, the responsibility for record keeping was left in the hands of individual physicians and individual organizations.

The history of the patient record can be characterized as a process of *negotiations*, in which both the technology and the practices involved are changed and become intertwined. In addition, the particular episode discussed elucidates that the development of the patient record was not simply in the hands of one actor. There were multiple driving forces at work that represented a variety of interests. The actual shape of a technology's developmental trajectory is rarely predictable or linear. The American College of Surgeons was actively engaged in the realization of patient-oriented records for two main reasons. First, it could thus strengthen its hold on hospitals and second, it wanted to establish accreditation standards so as to be able to distinguish 'fellow surgeons' from insufficiently qualified physicians. However, the Hospital Standardization Movement it initiated soon found other allies as well. The new medical record professionals, hospital boards, scientists – each had its own stake in further stimulating this standardization process. As a result, the technological development gained momentum as well as acquired a specific character – one that was different from the one envisioned by the College of Surgeons. For instance, the Record Department's 'custodians' began to check on the activities of physicians; incomplete records were marked as deficient and returned, while physicians who repeatedly violated the rules were hauled over the coals in public.

The issues brought to the fore during these developments had significant political implications. As we just claimed, technologies transform practices: professional groups receive new responsibilities, specific professions acquire a stronger social base, patients play an important part or not, and hospital boards and governments have new tools at their disposal to structure care arrangements or push them into a certain direction. The ambivalent response of the Dutch medical profession to the American developments involving patient records offers one illustration of this political dimension: to Dutch physicians, the influence of the hospital's executive board on the content of medical work was a haunting spectre, something they watched carefully.

Although in the standard view of technology development, standardization processes are pre-eminently seen as 'technical' matters, it turns out that precisely in these matters social and political issues play a major role. Standardization entails the aligning of a variety of individuals, organizations, and technologies – while each specific arrangement brings along its own social and political implications. For instance, the activities of the American Standardization Movement were also part of the political struggle for authority in hospitals. Who possessed the power to determine what hospitals would look like, or who was best qualified to head hospitals, laypersons with management skills or physicians blessed with the same skills? Strikingly, the College of Surgeons, despite its general standardization effort, was consciously refraining from seeking to standardize surgical procedures, since that would doubtlessly have been unacceptable to the surgeons involved. The College was mainly concerned about establishing minimum requirements for

23

training and facilities, not for surgical procedures or diagnostic guidelines: 'By certifying the surgeon as competent, certifying the surgery was unnecessary' (Stevens 1989). Yet, from the angle of European medical professionals, this form of standardization was already too drastic. In countries such as the Netherlands, efforts toward standardization were only aimed at the logistic and financial side of 'the hospital business'.

TERRA INCOGNITA: THE INTRODUCTION OF THE ELECTRONIC PATIENT RECORD

> The health care system has become an organism guided by misguided choices; it is unstable, confused, and desperately in need of a central nervous system that can help it cope with the complexities of modern medicine.
>
> (Paul Ellwood 1988: 1550, quoted in Dick *et al*. 1997: 52)

When in the late 1950s the digital computer was introduced in Western medicine, the patient record basically looked the same as fifty years before. Because of the increase in the amount of registered information, the number of health care providers, and the number of pre-structured forms to be filled out, the patient record had grown substantially thicker. Its basic format, however, had not changed along. As is still the case today, the information was mostly arranged by 'source'. The x-ray forms, the bacteriology results, the progress reports of the physicians, the blood test results, clerical information – everything had its own section in the record. Within each section, the pages were arranged in a chronological order. Even the criticism of the content of the patient record still sounded the same as fifty years earlier – only louder. Critics claimed that the 'progress of medicine' was impeded by the fact that the patient records were 'prejudiced, incomplete or noncomparable' and that they were catalogued, crossreferenced, and integrated only 'loosely' (Anonymous 1950a; 1950b). As a result, they could hardly be used for studies of the clinical progress of pathologies or for studies of the results of intervention strategies. As the historian Reiser suggests, the source-based patient record was rapidly becoming a 'dinosaur':

> it remained a pastiche of laboratory reports, X-ray reports, nurses' notes, social workers' notes, statements by patients, objective facts, and subjective narratives. [It was] the endpoint of the network of communications that bound together the specialties dividing medicine . . . [and a] fragmented almanac of [the patient's] total medical experiences.
>
> (1978)

In fact, one of the first functions people had in mind for the computer involved medical reporting:

> It could accumulate and store complex medical records, which could subsequently be interrogated and manipulated for research and retrieval of medical history.
>
> (Anonymous 1960)

Already in 1963 it was argued that EPRs were 'inevitable' and that possibly they would compensate for some of the shortcomings of paper records:

> the medical record is changing in bulk and character, and . . . the demands on the medical record system are increasing [due to] (a) the shift from acute infectious diseases to chronic disorders, (b) the increased life span of patients . . ., (c) the complexity of modern medical treatment, (d) scientific advances which have made it possible to observe more patient variables, and (e) the constant geographical migration character-istic of modern life.
>
> (Anonymous 1963)

How was the EPR introduced? Who were the important, steering actors in this development? In this section we will (rather patchily) outline the development of PICS from the 1960s up to the present. It is not our aim to provide an exhaustive historical account but merely to introduce a number of essential developments and actors as a context for the issues that will be discussed later on in this book.

The first computers actually implemented in Western health care practice were large, centralized mainframes for the financial and patient administration of hospitals. The design and development of these systems was strongly stimulated by the Medicare Program, set up in the United States in 1965. This programme required hospitals to provide extensive, aggregated patient care information. Such systems did not play a role in the working life of physicians and nurses: during the 1950s and 1960s, they continued to work with the familiar paper records. The first EPRs used by health care professionals were developed in the 1970s in US outpatient clinics and general practices. One example of such a system was COSTAR, devel-oped by the Massachusetts General Hospital. For each consultation, the physician was given a printout of the patient record, whereas during the consultation he would fill out a pre-printed form. Physicians themselves had no contact with the computer: clerical staff had to be present to produce printouts and to enter the data from the filled-out forms into the computer.

The much cheaper 'mini computers' that entered the market in the 1970s made it possible for hospitals and clinics to experiment with computerized forms of medical data processing. Small experiments started up, such as the *Artemis* project in Paris, which supported care and research for patients in the Hypertension Clinic of Saint Joseph Hospital in Paris, or the 'computer aided diagnosis' system that helped detect acute appendicitis patients in the Department of Surgery at the University of Leeds.

A project that started similarly small was the Nobin-HIS project, started in 1972 at the Dutch University Hospital of Leiden. This project was co-sponsored by the Dutch government. This computerized Hospital Information System (HIS) was aimed at streamlining the flow of information within the hospital, while a more general goal of the project was to develop an operating system specifically designed for hospitals. The Nobin-HIS project resulted in BAZIS, in which initially only university hospitals participated, though after 1980 general hospitals in the Netherlands joined as well. Each hospital that decided to purchase the BAZIS system was allowed to pass on its cost to its general nursing fee. In this way, a close connection was established between the software company, whose design was indirectly funded by government money, and the medical field:

> As a result of this whole scheme, a critical mass was generated: these first three university hospitals – Leiden, Rotterdam, Utrecht – were soon joined by Groningen and Amsterdam, and so forth. Critical mass was developed among the user group, for [BAZIS] was still a nonprofit foundation where they simply said: we need this system and it must be produced now. It became a joint effort which was not aimed at profits and in which the customers had a large say in how they wanted things done. This has created the situation that we in the Netherlands, in comparison to a lot of other countries, ended up with pretty advanced systems.
> (Prof. Schonk, Leiden University Medical Center,
> personal communication)

BAZIS products were unique for their time in that they were not primarily geared towards financial or administrative tasks: until 1976, university hospitals – in contrast to general hospitals – were not required by law to report their activities.

Already in the early 1970s the expectations regarding the potentially positive effects of computerized patient records were high. In the United States some even argued that the computerization of health care might lead to 'a significant improvement in the level of health of all Americans' (Kernodle and Ryan 1972). At the same time, though, many projects failed and it proved to be extremely difficult to apply systems that appeared successful in one location with equal success at another clinic. In fact, of all the systems mentioned so far, only the BAZIS system became a commercially viable system; its successor, HISCOM (currently part of the UK Torex Group), owns approximately 50 per cent of the Dutch HIS market. Whereas designing an EPR for an outpatient facility was already a highly complex affair, developing effective EPRs for clinical use turned out to be just impossible for the time being. Because of the many intertwined flows of information and the large number of health care professionals that could be involved with one patient, this task could not be carried out with the available means. As one commentator put it: 'With the 70s came a decade of somber realization that developing comprehensive Medical Information Systems was a more complex task than putting a man on the moon had been' (Collen 1995). The BAZIS-HIS was characteristic of the many Hospital Information Systems of that period: it consisted of a network of mostly 'dumb' terminals which could only be used to look up centrally stored data, such as those from the laboratory, radiology, or bacteriology departments.

During the 1980s, the decentralization of computer hardware and software continued. The new microcomputers, interconnected through networks, facilitated configurations that were again less costly. In the United States, the first commercial clinical EPRs were put on the market. Commonly, these systems were developed at local hospitals or clinics, after which they were bought up by industrial partners. In the United States, an actual market seemed to be emergent – and once again Medicare was a prominent factor. In 1983, Medicare introduced its Diagnostic Related Groups codes (DRG) that institutions had to use to be refunded for claims. This enabled the government to gain better insight in 'case mix and resource use' (Collen 1995).

In more centrally run health care systems, at this time, the responsible agencies were starting to launch their first initiatives. The UK NHS had several top-down programmes in place, trying to sell the benefits of ICT to the health care organizations and the professionals within the NHS. These systems were aimed at enhancing the use of data collection for managerial purposes, and yielded very little enthusiasm from the professionals, as it was not clear what the systems would bring to them. Furthermore, these initiatives were little integrated, and were seen as mainly benefiting NHS bureaucracy.

CASE STUDY

Developing IT for primary care

The UK situation: software for collecting data for secondary purposes
The development of IT for GP practices took a somewhat different trajectory than the development of IT for hospitals. In the UK GP practices acted as independent businesses and therefore the GPs were not in the same way targeted by the NHS initiatives of using computers for management purposes. Still, however, the development of an EPR for general practice was carried along by an interest in data recording for secondary purposes like chronic disease management.

In the late 1970s, the Royal College of GPs published a report suggesting that the Lloyd George record, the standard format of the paper record, should be improved. The potential role of computers was not mentioned. Local UK GPs, however, were already experimenting with getting computers into their practices. In the years to follow a number of small initiatives started up. Individual researchers, aiming at collecting information for clinical databases, often drove these initiatives: in the early days, researchers would collect disease registers on punched cards from GP practices.

One of the biggest systems at that time, the VAMP system (Value Added Medical Practice), was written and marketed by a GP. He involved other GPs by paying visits to their practices, offering them his system for a fee every year. Parallel to this he started and ran another company that would buy the data they produced. This meant that basically the GPs were offered a free system.

Another system that similarly introduced free computer schemes was the Meditel system. Participating practices were provided with a multiuser computer system on the condition that the general practitioners agreed to collect and provide comprehensive data about morbidity, drug prescribing, and side effects. The data were sold to the pharmaceutical industry, and used for clinical trials (Benson 2002).

In the late 1980s VAMP and Meditel covered nearly 2,000 practices (20 per cent of all English practices). In spite of this the collection of standardized data from general practices using the systems eventually collapsed because the quality of the data collected was lower than had been expected. Still, these schemes had a great impact on shaping further developments in UK computing for primary care. An interviewee explains how the computers used in the late 1980s were all set up for filling in data for secondary purposes:

> In the 1990s some GPs began using computers for administration. That really came in with the fundholding, which came here in the nineties, but the computer systems were set up before that. They were set up with the idea that they would, you know, eventually provide a way of recording all GP data. Diagnostic data, information about tests as well as prescribing data and information about the patients. So there were fields there for blood pressures, fields there for putting in weights, fields there for putting in smoking habits . . . all sorts of informational things.

One political initiative that pushed the development of an EPR along was the fundholding enterprise. In the early 1990s under the Margaret Thatcher government the funder–provider split was removed, and GPs were requested to administer finances for their patients' use of some secondary care. GPs who wanted to become fundholders needed computer technology to handle this. In addition, they had to report on these activities to the health authorities, which similarly required increased registration and information handling.

The National Service Frameworks programme, launched in 1998, set out to 'establish performance milestones' (NSF website) against which progress within an agreed area could be measured. To have the audit programs work, GPs had to increasingly use diagnostic codes (Read codes) when filling data into their EPRs. The coded information would subsequently be transformed into publications that would outline guidelines for treatment within specific areas (such as cancer, child care or diabetes).

Within the last five years, GPs as well as voices within the government have argued for a change of classification system. The Read codes, it is argued, are too specific to be used for collecting high quality data for the above-mentioned purposes. The NHS has looked towards the United States for a classification system with a more hierarchical structure. Presently, work is being done to integrate the SNOMED classification in the UK GPs computer systems as the main classification for data registration.

The Dutch situation: the problem-oriented medical record in action
In the beginning of the 1980s, small informal groups of Dutch GPs began to experiment with newly bought personal computers. Their first initiatives were mainly directed at handling their financial administration and the processing of bills. In 1985, the two major Dutch professional GP organizations established a special taskforce on automation in general practice. This taskforce was to lead the automation of the GPs practices. The GP organizations explicitly aimed at developing an information system that would benefit the entire profession, and that would develop into a comprehensive General Practitioner Information System (GPIS) (including financial administration, but also a fully fledged EPR).

Initially, however, the efforts of the automation taskforce were primarily geared towards the automation of financial transactions, because in this area the practical gains seemed most obvious. Bills 'which otherwise had to be produced at night and over the weekend' no longer had to be handwritten, but would be produced by the computer more or less automatically. This would save much time and free general physicians from doing boring clerical work (Esch, LHV, personal communication).

From the beginning, however, the so-called 'medical module' of GPIS was also an important focus of attention for the professional organizations. User groups were established to ensure the continuity of both the software and the contacts with the software producer, while the automation taskforce took the initiative to write a Reference Model in which the basic requirements of a GPIS were formulated. The addresses where bills were to be sent to had to be unambiguously clear, it had to be possible to include the patient's medical history, and it had to be possible to mark individual records with the electronic equivalent of the 'coloured tabs' they had used for their paper records. Following Lawrence Weed, the patient record was to be *problem oriented*. This meant that all data, action plans and progress notes were to be organized around the problem(s) of the patient rather than kept in mere chronological order (or, as in hospitals, by organizational function).

On the basis of the first and later developed Reference Models, the existing software packages were tested and certified. The GP association commissioned a report on the projected quality improvements GPIS would have for its members and the health insurance companies. After its assessment of the report, the Dutch government decided to provide a subsidy to general physicians who purchased a certified GPIS as of 1 July 1991.

Part and parcel of the problem oriented record was the SOAP structure (Subjective, Objective, Assessment, Plan), according to which the GP should categorize his entries. In addition, entries like 'diagnosis' and 'medication' could all be coded. This structure was meant to discipline a GP to treat each problem or symptom according to the same procedure and register data accordingly; structured data were required for research purposes, but also to afford basic functionalities such as allergy warnings and so forth.

In practice, however, much of the record consists of free text entries. There are great variations between practices as to what extent they organize their data entry according to the SOAP structure, and whether or not they code diagnoses, for instance. One problem has been that GPs feel it takes too much time to register data this way, not the least when 'insignificant' problems such as small infections are at stake.

While the Dutch GPIS 'diffused' into Dutch GP practices very rapidly during the 1990s, the success story has turned into a near-disaster during the last few years. Due to sharply increased development costs, high existing functionality and uncertainty about future directions for development, many vendors have left the highly fragmented and small Dutch GPIS market. This has left the Dutch GPs with unsupported, often 10–20 year old systems, with no clear perspective what the future will bring. Some observers hope for international convergence in GPIS development, others see more future in integrated information systems for integrated health delivery organizations (that is to say: no more separate GPIS). Still others plead for Open Source GPIS development. What the future will bring is as yet difficult to predict.

The Danish situation: scaling up a local initiative
Just like in the UK and in the Netherlands, developing an EPR for Danish general practice has been closely connected to standardization of GP work. In Denmark in 1984 the Danish GP Association (PLO) decided in principle to support an intensification of ICT in general practices. Quite detailed specifications were developed for what the systems should look like, and several GPs were active in this work. The vision, primarily, was a GPIS that would make the financial administration of GP practices easier and – later on – enable electronic transfer between

different ICT systems embedded in the different health care sectors. The GP Association developed a system called Apex, which was offered to all GPs.

One of the immediate benefits for the health authorities in supplying electronic support for administration was that the GPs would begin to settle accounts electronically. This saved much administration for the state driven health insurance (Sygesikringen). As a result several of their staff members were laid off in the mid-1980s. To stimulate electronic accounting GPs were also offered a one-time amount of 1,350 Euro. The GPs were pleased with the possibility of using ICT for administration as well. Like the Dutch GPs they were used to spending their evenings on bookkeeping. The electronic system saved time and it even helped them remember to bill 'small things' like phone consultations, which they would sometimes forget.

In the late 1980s the GP Association had to close down the Apex system, since it could no longer afford the cost of its maintenance. Its users felt it was 'heavy' and not very 'user-friendly', and its 'diffusion' had been disappointing. This kicked off several small projects, started by enthusiastic GPs who were eager to improve their EPRs. One of the successful initiatives was the FynCom project. Its participants aimed at developing a system that would enable GPs to send and receive lab results, specialist letters and prescriptions using the EDIFACT standard. One of the GPs, who was part of the project from its beginning, explains:

> In 1990 we got the 'informatics scheme'. It was about how the politicians wished to develop health care ICT until the year 2000. The scheme consisted of 120 pages and on page 117 it said that perhaps one could imagine that in year 2000 primary and secondary health care organizations would be able to communicate with each other. We had tasted blood and agreed that we could not wait for that long.
>
> (Interview, GP, 1101)

In 1994 the standards developed by the FynCom group were transferred into a new project called MedCom, whose aim it was to make the protocols work on a national level. At that time, the extended possibilities for data exchange implemented by means of a number of locally based pilot projects had become a major incitement for non-computerized GPs to start working with an EPR.

New possibilities of sending and receiving data also meant that the content of the EPR was suddenly experienced by the GPs as very unorganized; it was basically one ever-expanding 'toilet roll of text'. They needed some organizing principles in order to keep an overview of their notes. Simultaneously, as elsewhere in Europe, health authorities felt a growing need to monitor GP practices to be able to better control health care expenditure.

In the late 1990s diagnostic codes were integrated in updated versions of the GPIS available on the market. The classification used was the International

Classification of Primary Care (ICPC), which was developed to register not only end-diagnoses, but also, for instance, a patient's reasons for encounter (the Dutch GPIS uses the same classification). At present day health authorities are searching for ways to use data from GPs databases for research purposes. This is no easy task. First, GPs easily feel that they become subject to external control, and many do not feel it is their job to register for 'external' purposes. Second, comprehensive policy aimed at protecting patient privacy is felt to stand in the way of such external use of data. The ministry of health has now put forward suggestions to reinterpret the strict rule that patients must give a written consent before anyone can exchange patient information.

Recently, within the ministry of health, the problem-oriented medical record has been put on the agenda. The aim is to enable more detailed registration of chronic diseases and subsequent transfer of this data into clinical databases. A National Indicator Project launched to develop performance indicators has been initiated and the authorities hope that this will enable better use of the registered data.

The arrival of microcomputers also created the technical possibility to develop GP information systems. In the Case Study, we outlined the different trajectories that this development took in three European countries: the UK, Denmark, and the Netherlands. Especially in the early years, these developments were entirely local: in each of these countries, enthusiastic professionals started experimenting with the possibilities of computers for their worktasks. Accordingly, the different systems took off in completely different directions. UK systems focused primarily on aggregated data collection for clinical databases, and Dutch and Danish systems focused primarily on reducing administrative work load for the individual GPs. On the other hand, throughout the 1980s, the UK and Dutch systems were run by entrepreneuring GPs or small businesses, while in Denmark the national GP association coordinated this work until the downfall of its Apex system.

The 1990s saw a veritable explosion of new initiatives involving EPRs. In the United States, the Institute of Medicine published an influential report in 1991, *The Computer-Based Patient Record: An Essential Technology for Health Care*, in which it was argued that the EPR, as the cornerstone of a national health care information system, was going to be the crucial technology in health care in the years to come (Dick and Steen 1991). The report outlines a decade-long offensive: by the year 2000, 'the' EPR had to be generally accepted. In Europe the number of EPR initiatives was equally growing rapidly, in part as a result of major funding from a number of large-scale European Research and Development Programmes. At this point, some even metaphorically refer to the presence of a 'make 1,000 flowers bloom' mentality: countless local projects were funded with resounding names like HELIOS, GALEN and NUCLEUS. Similarly, many countries started national initiatives. In France and Germany, much effort was put into introducing 'health smartcards', facilitating the handling of medical claims (between patient, provider and payer) and, potentially, as a carrier for basic clinical information. In Norway, the five main hospitals cooperated, and obtained government funds to further the development of a common, integrated hospital information system, based upon an EPR.

The UK NHS put Information Management high on their agenda, and now started to stress the importance of optimizing information flows for the prime benefits of professionals and their patients. A core development in the 1990s was the NHS Net, which would be the 'NHS information highway' through which GPs, hospitals and community services could 'share information' and thus offer 'genuinely seamless care for patients'.[1] This 'NHS Net' is a separate, 'safe' electronic highway for health care providers; a feature only dreamed of in many other countries without centralized health ICT decision making.

Despite the explosion of initiatives, however, as the 1990s wore on, it was widely believed that Dick and Steen's estimation of ten years was too optimistic, especially since the majority of initiatives was only marginally successful or evaporated quite quickly. The Danish GP Association terminated its GP information system project, which had become too costly to maintain. The early, information collecting UK initiatives also died at the end of the 1980s. In both cases, enthusiastic individuals (often GPs) took over these initial attempts, and, as in the Netherlands, started to develop systems that were built by individuals (or small companies) for individual GP practices.

In fact, the realization that the technical, social and organizational complexity of EPRs in health care practices has been seriously underestimated is gaining terrain. So far, EPRs have not 'replaced' paper records at all: both modes of recording data exist side by side, and, not surprisingly, this situation has led to an increase in the number of clerical tasks. The ever growing stack of printouts has undoubtedly opened the eyes of those who not too long ago still dreamed of an office environment not cluttered with piles of paperwork. The NHS Net is cheered by the NHS Information Management authorities, but criticized by others as being an 'expensive way to get on the internet'[2] that all too often 'simply grinds to a halt' (Majeed, 2003: 690). It is riddled by privacy questions, disputes about obligatory, costly usage, and the nagging question whether its functionality would not have been realizable by drawing upon much cheaper, common Internet technologies and infrastructures. 'The first four decades of medical informatics,' as Collen soberly concludes, 'were ones of high expectations and frequent disappointments' (1995).

At the beginning of the twenty-first century, the overall 'penetration' of IT in health care organizations is considerable. Routinely, nurses and physicians encounter PCs or terminals, read medical patient information using a clinical workstation, or create discharge reports using voice-recognition software. With regard to the GP information systems, the UK, Denmark and the Netherlands are amongst the world's leading health care ICT users. Yet their success – informating individual practices – is now their largest problem: how to integrate GP informa- tion systems in the larger health care information flows? The overall situation is patchy and difficult to summarize. Hospital laboratories may have state-of-the-art information systems, while the physicians requesting tests do so by using tradi- tional paper forms. These physicians might be able to query the digital archives of their radiology department, but still receive the laboratories' results through ordi- nary mail. Effective coordination (between and within institutions, between and within countries) is virtually absent: individual hospitals go about their own ways, individual departments *within* hospitals go about their own ways, and different providers go about their own ways. The result is called 'island automation': depart- ments have information systems which only cater to their own needs, and these systems can hardly communicate with other systems (if at all), while in between other departments are situated without terminals altogether. Often, it is difficult or even impossible to integrate such independently developed systems within a larger HIS system – let alone that different HIS systems can talk to each other or to GP information systems, for example.

This situation becomes even more complicated because many hospitals are still dependent on HIS systems which date from the early 1980s. Such so-called 'legacy systems' are typified by poor user-interfaces, are monolithic and hard or impos- sible to couple to other information systems, and are increasingly difficult to main- tain. On the other hand, they have developed over long time-periods, have become an integrated part of an organization's functioning, and are very expensive to replace. In many situations, thus, more or less improvisatory connections are made to link legacy systems to more modern, state of the art *modules* that add to or take over part of the functions of the legacy system (ibid.). In this way, many Electronic Patient Records are now evolving: as a thin, graphic-oriented layer that looks very modern, but in fact lies on top of (a) decades old information system(s).

In 1997, the Institute of Medicine published an update of their report, stating that progress has not been all that successful. Health care organizations have invested less than they could have; governments have failed to take action on elim- inating legal obstacles (such as the requirement to keep a 'paper archive', or to have signatures 'in ink') or to supply the necessary funding, and the lack of stan- dards hinders further development. The developments between countries are hardly converging: due to the differences between health care systems, the preva- lence of locally developed legacy systems and the local ties of vendors, a 'global' EPR market is virtually non-existent.

In addition, many health care ICT development and implementation projects still fail. Health ICT constantly seems to promise more than it can deliver. EPRs are promised but not delivered, vendors discontinue support for existing systems, or implementation projects run to the ground. In France, the 1999 opening of the 'hospital of the future', *Hôpital Européen George Pompidou* in Paris, turned into a nightmare when the 'paperless environment' failed to function. The robots in the operating theatres appeared too complicated to use, the EPR was impossible to use, and critics calculated that trying to order medications through the system was 1,000 per cent slower than with the ordinary, paper-based systems. Overnight, paper-based records had to be printed and put into use, although the hospital had proudly been built without any archive space or other logistical support for paper records. In the Netherlands, meanwhile, millions of Euros were spent on developing a 'health card', using chipcard technology, which would provide an infrastructure for administrative (insurance) data, and develop further into a basic health care information carrier. After years of promises, technological problems and political fights about who would pay what, and who would do what for who, the project was declared 'dead' in 2002. Similarly, the UK has its infamous failure cases, such as the Wessex Health Authority Regional Information System, cancelled in 1990 after spending more than £20 million, and the national Hospital Information System projects, started in the 1980s that cost over £32 million and have yielded only minimal results. When one looks behind the cheers and high hopes that dominate conference proceedings, vendor information, and large parts of the scientific literature, the actual number of systems that are in use in multiple locations, have happy users, and effectively and efficiently contribute to the quality of patient care are still all too rare.

At the same time, the *need* for integrated EPRs has not reduced. To the contrary. In recent years, the US Institute of Medicine has published two reports that have had a lasting impact on ICT initiatives both in the US and in Europe. The reports *To Err is Human* (2000) and *The Quality Chasm* (2001) both argue that the quality of current US western health care is far below what may be expected. In the first report, the emphasis was on medical errors: the report argues that medical error qualifies as the eight leading cause of death in the US, vying with diabetes for the No. 8 position between pneumonia (6) and suicide (10). In the second report, the criticism runs even deeper: the US health care system not only scores poorly on patient safety, but on *all* dimensions of quality: effectiveness, efficiency, patient-centredness, timeliness, and equity. In many countries, these criticisms have been corroborated; internationally, 'patient safety' has become an international priority. In the UK, for example, the chief medical officer of the newly established National Patient Safety Agency estimates that '850,000 incidents and errors occur in the NHS each year'.[3]

Both reports stress the importance of health care ICT to prevent medical errors, and to improve overall health care quality. While the EPR is mentioned as a necessary 'backbone', emphasis is shifting more to *order entry* and *decision support*, as means to eradicate errors in human communication and reasoning. Through the electronic placing of orders (to laboratories, but also for medication, nursing actions and additional investigations) and reception of results, communication should become more streamlined, legible and traceable. Decision support has always been a long-term goal within Informatics, but it has been put back on the agenda now that the electronic data collection which is required for such systems to work is becoming more available. Through decision support, it is hoped, diagnostic and medication errors can be prevented, and cases can be more optimally monitored.

In addition to order entry and decision support, more novel technologies have given rise to high hopes. The emancipation of the 'consumer-patient' has led to a whole range of activities around *patient information systems*: systems that provide individual patients with information on their condition, but also – possibly – with access to their own medical records. *E-mail consultation* and other web-based medical services are being tested out, and the emergence of *telemedicine* promises to make medical work ever more efficient (and to thereby reduce the pressure on the already shallow job market).

CONCLUSION: THE NATURE OF TECHNOLOGY

This, then, is where we now stand: a clear need, even higher hopes and ambitions, a very patchy state of 'penetration' of ICT in health care practices, island automation, legacy systems, governments and professional bodies searching for direction, individual institutions and professionals taking more and more initiatives, a widespread tendency to reinvent the wheel, and an often neglected long history of problematic and failed implementations. This is the backcloth against which this book tries to give some insights, recommendations and tools to take up this challenge.

What have we learned so far? This chapter attempted to create some historical depth to the issues that will be discussed in this book. In addition, it attempted to give a theoretical framework with which to get a hold on these issues. As the history of (paper and electronic) patient records tells us, the implementation of a new form of medical reporting entails a social process in which both the practice and the technology are being shaped. The way in which health care is funded, for instance, has great influence on the form and development of the EPR. The increasingly stronger connection between patient record and hospital bill creates a growing need to actually link patient data and financial data. From the UK and Dutch perspective, however, American systems are overly finance-driven: every entry needs to be linked to a 'billable category', which creates an unnecessary nuisance for UK and Dutch physicians working with such systems. Similarly, the Dutch health care system does not contain the strong split between 'outpatient' and 'inpatient' medical care that typifies German health care, thus creating the need to fundamentally rework German hospital information systems before they can be 'applied' in Dutch health care contexts.

The interwovenness of technology and health care practice is such that it actually makes no sense to speak of the 'consequences' or 'impact' of information

---

BOX 2.1   THE DIGITALIZATION OF HEALTH CARE: CAUSE OR EFFECT?

Is the prevalence of numerical data in health care practices a cause or an effect of automation? The increasing computerization of health care practices significantly contributes to this phenomenon. The series of numbers coming out of the laboratory computers and the overall tendency towards coded data-storage contribute to a culture in which quantitative information is valued more highly than non-quantifiable information. At the same time, the increasingly central role of this type of data in health care practices creates an environment for which the computer-based EPR is well equipped. It is no coincidence that applications for Intensive Care Units (ICUs), where the flow of numerical laboratory data is considerable, belong to the more successful EPR-like applications. These applications commonly use spreadsheet-like constructions, whereby the laboratory data – generated by lab computers – are directly taken out of HIS in the ICU application. Put differently, the 'digitalization' of medical practices itself contributes to their further automation.

---

technology. The developmental processes are too complex for identifying such simple, causal lines. The need for a closer link between patient record and hospital bill is one of the incentives for introducing the EPR – yet, conversely, the link itself fosters the need. Once it becomes possible to link individual patient data to financial data, the tendency to refine financial administrative procedures will be difficult to counter. Similarly, the EPR does not simply 'cause' organizational change: it may stir up, hinder or deflect developments that were already in motion, for example, or trigger a change process that will thereafter interweave with many other ongoing developments. The changing professional role of the general physician, the shifting power of the insurance company, the changing job definitions of health care professionals, the role of the patient – all those issues are bound up with the introduction and development of EPRs, yet none is simply 'determined' by it.

The historical episodes discussed above also again illustrate the irregularity of the trajectories in which technologies are being shaped as well as the unpredictable interplay between the various driving forces involved. While Dutch general physicians were one of the world leaders in the application of EPRs only five years ago, for example, their systems' vendors are now massively ending further developments of these GPISs. In a small market, with highly demanding customers (the GPs), and others arguing that separate GPISs had become obsolete, newer generation GPISs seem simply too costly and risky to produce. Similarly, the early UK emphasis on market research and disease management has undoubtedly marked the subsequent development of newer UK GP information systems – the demise of these first systems notwithstanding. Twenty years later, UK GP information systems are strikingly different from their Danish and Dutch counterparts in their emphasis on making quite detailed registration on patients' medical and social history and life style factors.

Undoubtedly, the Danish and Dutch professional organizations of general physicians started out to tackle the issue in a strategic way. Both considered the EPR as a tool to protect and enhance the professional position of the physician (see also Chapter 4). Because of the well-designed GPIS, the Dutch general physicians strengthened their role as a central organizational node of the health care system, where patient data are gathered and stored – thus enabling their role of patient record coordinator. Yet the physicians' professional organizations were just one actor in the overall network. The Dutch government – later on followed by the insurance companies – decided to support GPIS because it anticipated that automated data processing would also benefit its own information needs. Moreover, an important explanation of the early success of GPISs is the Dutch and Danish 'gate-keeper' system that operates on the assumption that the relationship between patient and physician is a long-term one. As a result, these general physicians are more inclined to invest in systems that make it easier to keep track of their patients than, for instance, their American colleagues who work with much more fragmented populations of patients. In the Danish case, however, government support arrived too late – the Danish GP association already had let go of its EPR at the time the government started pouring resources into health care IT development. As a consequence, at the time that the Dutch GP information systems really took off throughout the Dutch GP population, the Danish development slowed down substantially for several years. Additionally, in the 1970s, Dutch general practice was strongly aimed at prevention, and was founding its 'scientific basis' through a strong call for population-oriented health care research – much like its UK counterparts. Thus, the conditions of Dutch family medicine were such that the advantages of the EPR – specifically the opportunities it offered for prevention and keeping track of groups of patients – were immediately evident. Yet unlike the UK, these systems were not primarily built for *these* purposes, which, undoubtedly, prevented an early demise as in the UK. All in all, in short, 'successful ICT development' is a more or less happy confluence of contingent developments and interests, which is highly unpredictable.

The downfall of Dutch GPIS was an equally contingent affair. The dust on this issue has not yet settled – many of the involved parties (GPIS user groups, vendors, government, GP associations) are still shifting the blame. Yet it is clear that the high functionality of the earlier systems had been developed over many years, in close cooperation between academia, GPs and (often small and local) vendors. When the underlying software technologies of these packages became too outdated, and when the pressure to make these systems more inter-operable became high, vendors realized that novel developments would entail a much higher investment, given the existing, high expectations about functionality, flexibility of use, interoperability, and so forth. Since neither government nor insurance companies were willing to significantly rise the GPs' fee for ICT investments, vendors (who had often been bought up by larger, often non-Dutch companies) cut their losses, and announced their withdrawal from this section of the market. At this moment, parties are frantically searching for solutions: new small vendors are trying to win a corner of the market, others are pleading for Open Source solutions,[4] while others state that GPIS systems are obsolete. According to them, the solution should be sought in *integrated* patient care information systems, co-used by GP, specialist and other health care professionals.

Health care IT, then, can be said to be thoroughly 'social' in three ways. First of all, the development and implementation of such technologies are processes of ongoing *negotiations*, involving many different stakeholders that fight for their positions, and their views on how things should be organized. Second, because the 'final' IT application is the outcome of these processes, it itself 'reflects' this coming-into-being (German systems with German bureaucratic regimes built into them; GP information systems with the autonomy of the GP built into it, and so forth). Third, and final, technology development is accompanied by social transformations: such processes yield changes in workflows, professional hierarchies and institutional boundaries. In our age, technology development still all too often tends to be considered as an autonomous or neutral process. Yet technology is one of the most actively constitutive forces in our contemporary society, while, paradoxically, at the same time many believe that it is either impossible or undesirable to subject its development to some form of social evaluation.

DISCUSSION QUESTIONS

1   The last paragraph states that 'GP information systems' in countries such as Denmark, the UK or the Netherlands can be said to have 'the autonomy of the GP built into it'. Explain what is meant by this remark, and give additional examples of health care IT applications that have cultural, social or organizational norms or roles built into them.

2   How many 'successful' health care IT development projects do you know? How many 'failures' are you aware of? What is actually meant by 'success' or 'failure' in these cases? Is there a gap between the public portrayal of the IT project and the actual performance of it?

3   How 'integrated' is the patient care information system that you are familiar with? What are the limits of this integration, and can you think of organizational, political and/or technical reasons for this?

NOTES

1   UK NHS policy document *Information for Health*, 1998, quoted in (Jones 2003).

2   UK GP, personal communication.

3   [http://www.nhs.uk/nhsmagazine/story316.asp]

4   'Open Source' (Linux being the most well-known example) is software that is not commercially owned, but 'open' for everybody to use, build upon and, through explicit and public procedures, even modify.

REFERENCES

Anonymous (1904) Hospital 'bedside notes' not admissible in evidence, *Journal of the American Medical Association* 43.

Anonymous (1912) The care of hospital records, *The Lancet*.

Anonymous (1914) Standardization in hospital records, *The Boston Medical and Surgical Journal* 170: 63.

Anonymous (1916) Improvement in medical statistics, *Journal of the American Medical Association* 66.

Anonymous (1929) Developing the record department in the small hospital, *Modern Hospital* 32: 88.

Anonymous (1950a) The next fifty years, *Journal of the American Medical Association* 142: 34–5.

Anonymous (1950b) Roadblocks to clinical research, *New England Journal of Medicine* 243: 677.

Anonymous (1960) Electronic data processing apparatus, *Journal of the American Medical Association* 173: 58–9.

Anonymous (1963) Electronic data processing apparatus, *Journal of the American Medical Association* 186: 146–7.

Atwater, E. C. (1989) Women, surgeons, and worthy enterprise: the general hospital comes to upper New York State. In D. E. Long and J. Golden (eds), *The American General Hospital*. Ithaca and London: Cornell University Press.

Auchincloss, H. (ed.) (1926) *Unit History System*. New York & London: Garland Publishing, Inc.

Benson, T. (2002) Why general practitioners use computers and hospital doctors do not – Part 1: incentives, *British Medical Journal* 325 (7372): 1086–9.

Bottomley, J. T. (1918) Hospital standardization – its meaning, *The Boston Medical and Surgical Journal* 179: 219–23.

Collen, M. E. (1995) *A History of Medical Informatics in the United States, 1950 to 1990*. American Medical Informatics Association.

Committee on Quality of Health Care in America (2001) *Crossing the Quality Chasm: A New Health System for the 21st Century*. Washington: National Academy Press.

Davis, M. M. (1920) New York dispensaries; book and record keeping. *Modern Hospital* 15: 131–4.

Dick, R. S., E. B. Steen, and D. E. Detmer (ed.) (1997) (first edition 1991) *The Computer-Based Patient Record: An Essential Technology for Health Care.* Washington, D.C.: National Academy Press.

Ellwood, P. (1988) Shattuck lecture – outcomes management: a technology of patient experience, *New England Journal of Medicine* 23: 1549–56.

Genevieve Morse, M. (1934) *Hospital Case Records and the Record Librarian*. Chicago: Physicians' Record Co.

Gilman, D. (1932) A successful check system for current case records. *Modern Hospital* 38: 63–4.

Huffman, E. K. (1972) *Medical Record Management*. Illinois: Physicians' Record Co.

Jones, M. (2003) Do IS have nationalities? 'De-scribing' electronic patient record systems in the UK National Health Service. *Scandinavian Journal of Information Systems* (in press).

Kay, S., and I. N. Purves (1996) Medical records and other stories: a narratological framework. *Methods of Information in Medicine* 35: 72–87.

Kernodle, J. R., and G. A. Ryan (1972) Computers in medicine. A look ahead, *Journal of the American Medical Association* 220: 1489–91.

Kohn, L. T., J. M. Corrigan and M. S. Donaldson (2000) *To Err is Human: Building a Safer Health System*. Committee on Quality of Health Care in America, Washington: National Academy Press.

Lewinski-Corwin, E. H. (1922) Medical case recording in hospitals, *Journal of the American Medical Association* 78: 604–5.

Majeed, A. (2003) Ten ways to improve information technology in the NHS, *British Medical Journal* 326 (7382): 202–6.

Mansholt, W. H. (1931) Wat kunnen Europeesche en Amerikaansche ziekenhuizen werderkeerig van elkaar leeren, *Het Ziekenhuiswezen* 4: 28–42.

Munger, C. W. (1928) Hospital case records and professional standing orders, *Modern Hospital* 30: 99–106.

Ornstein, S. M., R. B. Oates and G. N. Fox (1992) The computer-based medical record: current status, *Journal of Family Practice* 35: 556–65.

Reiser, S. J. (1978) *Medicine and the Reign of Technology*. Cambridge: Cambridge University Press.

Schoute, D. (1925) Stafvorming in Amerikaansche en in Nederlandsche ziekenhuizen, *Het Ziekenhuis* 16: 106–13.

Smith, D. (1990) *Texts, Facts, and Femininity: Exploring the Relations of Ruling*. London: Routledge.

Stevens, H. P. (1919) Case records and histories in the smaller hospitals, *The Boston Medical and Surgical Journal* 181: 324–9.

Stevens, R. (1989) *In Sickness and in Wealth: American Hospitals in the Twentieth Century.* New York: Basic Books.

Stokes, J. H., R. A. Kern and L. K. Ferguson (1933) What sixty-six hospitals think of the central unit record system, *Modern Hospital* 40: 87–92.

FURTHER READING

On the history of medical records

Anonymous (1929) Developing the record department in the small hospital, *Modern Hospital* 32: 88.

Reiser, S. J. (1984) Creating form out of mass: the development of the medical record. In E. Mendelsohn (ed.), *Transformation and Tradition in the Sciences: Essays in Honor of I. Bernard Cohen.* New York: Cambridge University Press, pp. 303–16.

Stevens, H. P. (1919) Case records and histories in the smaller hospitals, *The Boston Medical and Surgical Journal* 181: 324–9.

Weed, L. L. (1968) Medical records that guide and teach, *New England Journal of Medicine* 278: 593–600, 652–7.

On the history of health care IT

Bakker, A., and F. Leguit (1999) Evolution of an integrated HIS in the Netherlands, *International Journal of Medical Informatics* 54: 209–24.

Barnett, G. O. (1984) The application of computer-based medical-record systems in ambulatory practice, *New England Journal of Medicine* 310: 1643–50.

Barnett, G. O. (1989) History of the development of medical information systems at the laboratory of computer science at Massachusetts General Hospital. In B. Blum, I. and K. Duncan (eds), *A History of Medical Informatics.* New York: ACM Press, pp. 141–53.

Berg, M. (1997) *Rationalizing Medical Work. Decision Support Techniques and Medical Practices.* Cambridge: MIT Press.

Chessare, J. B. and K. E. Torok (1993) Implementation of COSTAR in an academic group practice of general pediatrics, *MD Computing* 10: 23–7.

Collen, M. E. (1995) *A History of Medical Informatics in the United States, 1950 to 1990.* American Medical Informatics Association.

de Dombal, F. T., D. J. Leaper, J. R. Staniland, A. P. McCann and J. C. Horrocks (1972) Computer-aided diagnosis of acute abdominal pain, *British Medical Journal* 2: 9–13.

Degoulet, P., C. Devriès, R. Rioux, J. R. Chantalou, E. Klinger, D. Sauguet, F. Aimé and P. Zwiegenbaum (1980) Hypertension management: the computer as a participant, *American Journal of Medicine* 68: 559–67.

Ellingsen, G., and E. Monteiro (2003) Big is beautiful: electronic patient records in large Norwegian hospitals 1980s–2001, *Methods of Information in Medicine* 42 (in press).

Hodge, M. V. (1989) History of the TDS Medical Information Systems. In B. Blum, I. and K. Duncan (eds), *A History of Medical Informatics*. New York: ACM Press, pp. 328–44.

Keen, J. (1994) Information policy in the National Health Service. In J. Keen (ed.), *Information Management in Health Services*. Buckingham: Open University Press, pp. 16–28.

Schoenbaum, S. C. and G. O. Barnett (1992) Automated ambulatory medical records systems. An orphan technology, *International Journal of Technological Assessment of Health Care* 8: 598–609.

van der Lei, J., J. S. Dusterhouf, H., Westerhof, W. Boon, P. V. M. Cromme and J. H. van Bemmel (1993) The introduction of computer-based patient records in The Netherlands, *Annals of Internal Medicine* 119: 1036–41.

Whitley, E. A. and A. Pouloudi (2001) Studying the translations of NHSnet, *Journal of End User Computing* 30–40.

On the history of medical work during the times described in this chapter

Howell, J. D. (1995) *Technology in the Hospital. Transforming Patient Care in the Early Twentieth Century*. Baltimore: The Johns Hopkins University Press.

Reiser, S. J. (1978) *Medicine and the Reign of Technology*. Cambridge: Cambridge University Press.

Starr, P. (1982) *The Social Transformation of American Medicine*. New York: Basic Books.

On the nature of (information) technology development and the 'politics' of technology

Beck, U. (1992) *Risk Society: Towards a New Modernity*. London: Sage.

Bijker, W. E. and J. Law (eds) (1992) *Shaping Technology – Building Society. Studies in Sociotechnical Change*. Cambridge: MIT Press.

Latour, B. (1996) *Aramis, or the Love of Technology*. Cambridge: Harvard University Press.

Porter, T. M. (1995) *Trust in Numbers. The Pursuit of Objectivity in Science and Public Life*. Princeton: Princeton University Press.

On standardization in health care work

Bowker, G. C. and S. L. Star (1999) *Sorting Things Out: Classification and its Consequences*. Cambridge: MIT Press.

Timmermans, S. and M. Berg (2003) *The Gold Standard: An Exploration of Evidence-Based Medicine and Standardization in Health Care*. Philadelphia: Temple University Press.

On failing health IT projects in medicine

Balka, E. (2003) Getting the big picture: the macro-politics of information system development (and failure) in a Canadian hospital, *Methods of Information in Medicine* 42 (in press).

Berg, M. (1999) Patient care information systems and health care work: a sociotechnical approach, *International Journal of Medical Informatics* 55: 87–101.

Beynon-Davies, P. (1995) Information systems 'failure': the case of the London Ambulance Service's Computer Aided Despatch project, *European Journal of Information Systems* 4: 171–84.

Ellingsen, G. and E. Monteiro (2003) Big is beautiful: electronic patient records in large Norwegian hospitals 1980s–2001, *Methods of Information in Medicine* 42 (in press).

Jones, M. (2003) Do IS have nationalities? 'De-scribing' electronic patient record systems in the UK National Health Service. *Scandinavian Journal of Information Systems* (in press).

Jones, M. R. (2003) 'Computers can land people on Mars, why can't they get them to work in a hospital?' Implementation of an electronic patient record system in a UK hospital. *Methods of Information in Medicine* 42 (in press).

Kaplan, B. (1995) The computer prescription: medical computing, public policy, and views of history, *Science, Technology and Human Values* 20: 5–38.

Timmons, S. (2003) Resistance to computerised care planning systems by qualified nurses working in the UK NHS. *Methods of Information in Medicine* 42 (in press).

Chapter 3

Health care work and patient care information systems

- Health care work is a professional activity, which is characterized by its interpretative, interactional and pragmatic nature.
- A paper-based medical record or patient care information system has two basic functions: it accumulates data and it coordinates activities and events.
- For these functions to become possible, workprocesses, data and decision criteria need to be sufficiently standardized.
- Electronic patient care information systems offer many exciting possibilities over paper-based medical records, yet require a concurrent additional standardization of workprocesses, data and decision criteria.
- These additional standardization requirements, however, seem to be at odds with the before mentioned nature of health care work.
- There seems to be a fatal paradox between the nature of professional health care work, and the standardization of this work required in order for the PCIS to fulfil its promises.

KEY TERMS

- Nature of health care work
- Patient trajectory
- Accumulation of data
- Coordination of events and activities
- Standardization of workprocesses, data and decision criteria

INTRODUCTION

In one of his classical works, the organizational sociologist Henry Mintzberg has argued that the *coordination* of worktasks is a fundamental necessity for an organization (1979). The activities of the individual(s) managing the organization's resources, to mention a simple example, have to be coordinated with the activities of the individual(s) using those resources. A very small organization can survive on mere 'coordination by feedback': the direct coordination of work through direct supervision or informal communication between the (few) employees. Larger organizations draw upon standardization and technologies to tackle their increased coordination needs. When worktasks are explicated and standardized, for example, the necessary coordination is 'programmed' into these specifications, and is then subsequently automatically ensured. Likewise, the invention of the 'record', the filing cabinet and cross-referencing and indexing systems made it possible for an increasingly complex organization to handle an increasing number of clients. Such records are highly efficient 'externalized' memories – making the continuous handling of one individual by many different organizational members possible without the need for constant face-to-face contact between those members.

Following Mintzberg, Lars Groth has argued that the revolutionary impact of IT is that it enables new coordination mechanisms, and thereby makes new forms of organization possible. As an example, he discusses the design of the Boeing 777: the first aeroplane that was fully designed using an integrated CAD/CAE (computer aided design/engineering) system. This software did away with much of the traditional model- and mock-up building: it could display each designed part as a 3D picture, and would automatically detect whether any two planned parts would occupy the same point in space. More significantly, it made it possible for *several thousand* engineers (in different geographical locations) to collaboratively work on one project 'in real time'. An integrated database connected all their workstations, so that each engineer could monitor and check upon the work on parts and requirements that would affect his own work (1999, pp. 310–12).

There would seem to be a great need for IT's enhanced coordination capacities in health care. The move towards integrated care, in which care processes are re-designed around patients' needs, breaking through traditional boundaries between professionals, professions and institutions, would seem to be much helped by even a fraction of the coordinating power that Boeing's IT unleashed. As we discussed in the previous chapter, the current development of PCIS aims to structure and support the 'core business process' of health care: the primary care process. Integrating patient record systems with order-entry, integral medication management, inter-disciplinary carepaths and quality control functionalities are all seen to be the way of the future.

Yet at this point, analysts such as Mintzberg and Groth have a great disappointment in store. IT can only bring true organizational transformation when the core worktasks are structured and interconnected in highly standardized ways. Boeing's engineers worked on clearly delineated subparts, following strict requirements and strictly delineated methodologies. The work of doctors and nurses, on the other hand, happens to be the organizational sociologists' prototypical example of the work of a *professional* that is too complex and variable to be standardized in this way. On the medical workfloor, the coordination of their work is achieved, first of all, through constant supervision and communication. In addition, every professional (say a nurse) knows what (not) to expect from another professional (say a surgeon), since their professional training equips them with standard sets of *skills*. IT can support skills somewhat through decision support, and the cooperation between professionals can be enhanced through IT communication tools. Yet, Groth predicts, IT cannot do much to transform medicine's core business. 'Handling patients' is too much of an interpersonal and essentially non-standard activity to become truly 'informated'. High aims for patient care information systems, therefore, are doomed to fail.

Such arguments about the limited potential of IT to transform health care work do not stand alone. Many authors have pointed at the phenomenon that health care work, what we will describe as the collaborative managing of patient trajectories, is essentially interpretative, interactional, and typified by the need to constantly react to contingent events. Medicine's object (a patient, his/her history and his/her affliction(s)), organizational conditions (many health care professions with different backgrounds handling patients while time and resources are scarce) and knowledge-base (rapidly developing, vastly expanding, but also patchy, sometimes internally contradictory) together make 'health care work' into an enterprise whose complexity will remain elusive to strict protocollization, detailed pre-planning or tight workflow approaches.

Does this mean, then, that there is not much future for integrated, process-oriented PCIS? Does this mean that we can make guidelines or modest decision support tools (that both merely 'suggest' the proper action path to the professional), or that we may optimize communications through telemedicine applications – but that we cannot draw upon IT's coordination powers to further integrated care? Or to integrate quality management in the primary care process? If that would be the case, this book could have been short indeed. In the following three chapters, we will show how such pessimistic conclusions are not necessary. First, however, we will address the specific nature of health care work: a thorough understanding of this work is crucial to be able to develop systems that may actually *support* it. Subsequently, we will briefly look at the operation of a current core 'information technology' in medicine: the paper-based medical record. This tool, including all the little forms and paper slips that are generated through it and end up in it, currently facilitates order-communication, medication management, and the integration of the activities of individual care professionals. Although obviously far from perfect, this paper-based PCIS is a proper starting point. Its long history and ubiquitous presence indicate that its information handling and work coordinating capacities *have* been successfully integrated in health care work. An analysis of this tool's functionalities – and the subsequent analysis of its (potential) electronic successors – will allow us to look more in detail at the active, crucial role these tools play in work practices and the large impact of these tools on those work practices. We will argue that many of the computer-based PCISs[1] that litter the cemetery of 'failed attempts' were *bound* to fail because the model of health care work inscribed in these tools clashed too much with the actual nature of health care work.

While this chapter will deal with the nature of health care work, Chapter 4 will focus on the nature of *information,* and its implications for health care information systems. In Chapter 5, we will return to the paradox described above: how the potentially crippling tensions between the nature of health care work, of information, and the demands of PCISs can be turned into a productive synergy. A synergy, we will argue, that so happens also addresses some of the core issues that are now troubling Western health care practices.

HEALTH CARE WORK: MANAGING PATIENT TRAJECTORIES

CASE STUDY

University Hospital, ICU, Thursday, 9:05 a.m.
Agnes, an experienced resident, is standing near the bed of a newly admitted patient, a young man who has just had brain surgery. Such patients are routinely admitted to the hospital's general ICU (in the absence of a neurological ICU) on their first day of recovery. Agnes is standing at a computer terminal which displays the EPR of this unit; there is one terminal for every ICU bed. Soon it is clear to her that the patient's condition is stable, which means that he is expected to be moved to the neurological Medium Care Unit within 24 hours. John, one of the ICU nurses, joins Agnes at the computer terminal and asks her: 'Shall we only check the basics? Let's not go through the entire admission protocol and only

look at the glucosis, potassium, and so on.' 'Okay,' Agnes responds, while keeping her eyes fixed on the screen. John then asks her: 'And what about tomorrow morning? Same story? Only the basics?' Agnes looks up and says to him: 'Yes . . . only do what is indicated. In this patient's case, it would be nonsense to follow the standard admission protocol. Let's also cancel the ECG and the x-ray.' John nods approvingly and walks on.

Regional Hospital, Neurology Ward, Tuesday, 4:00 p.m.

Caroline, a nurse, comes into the nursing unit for the evening shift, sits down behind one of the two terminals, and types her password to log into the EPR system which was recently introduced in this hospital. She says there is an emergency admission and while Theo, another nurse, is busy with the particular patient, she wants to enter this patient's data into the EPR. Caroline looks at the patient's papers, opens the windows she needs, and copies the information from the papers into the EPR. As her beeper goes off, she stands up, and goes to see the patient who called her.

When a little later Caroline is busy once again entering patient data into the system, Theo enters the room. They were notified of a new emergency admission and Caroline and Theo talk about which room the new patient will be put in. This is no easy decision, for the new admission involves a terminal patient who is likely to die within half an hour. Since this patient is already on his way to the ward, they have no time to waste. Caroline asks Peter, a nurse, to make coffee for the patient's relatives. After the patient is handed over to them, Caroline and Theo ride him into a room, accompanied by some of the relatives. Theo stays with them, while Caroline, on the family's request, will try to call a pastor. The phone rings once again: another relative of the terminal patient wishes to talk to one of the family members present. Caroline returns to the patient's room to catch one of the relatives and she leads him into one of the unoccupied consultation rooms, so that he has a little more privacy for his phone conversation.

The ward physician comes in and asks Karen, a nurse in training, which family and which patient he will meet and where they are right now. Meanwhile, Peter is busy responding to all the patients who call for his attention. Every now and then the printer sitting behind the counter can be heard spitting paper (medication lists, schedules of new tests, new medication orders), but for some thirty minutes no one pays attention to it, until Caroline picks them up, checks them, and puts them on the medication cart.

4:45 p.m.

The terminal patient has died. Theo takes the bereaved family into another room and waits with them for the arrival of the pastoral worker. While Caroline is busy answering a phone call about another patient, Peter and the ward physician come in with questions on various patients. Next, the pastoral worker arrives and asks

where he can find the relatives of the deceased patient. Caroline takes the medication cart and asks Peter to help her administer the medication, while she asks
Karen to start passing out the evening meal.

What is at the heart of the work of physicians, nurses and other health care professionals is the *management of patient trajectories*. A patient's complaint or request
for medical help involves a trajectory in time that is partly shaped by the work of
the health care professionals who aim to positively influence this trajectory (Strauss
et al. 1985). A core feature of this work is that it is a social, collective process.
Only rarely do individual health care professionals determine the management
of a specific patient trajectory on their own: 'how to intervene' is decided in
formal meetings, at random encounters in the hallway, and in the continuous
flow of phone conversations. Even in the case of an individually operating general
physician, a home care nurse or a medical specialist, the intervention is decided
in interaction with the patient and – through the patient record, letters or immediate contacts – with colleagues and other care professionals. Seldomly, a patient's
trajectory is decided on the basis of individual contacts or consultations alone. In
particular in the case of chronic or complicated medical complaints, the course of
the trajectory may constantly be changed or adjusted from various sides. The final
minutes of the terminal patient described above take shape in part in the interaction between various nurses, the ward physician, and the patient's relatives.

The interactions continually cross professional boundaries. Also, not one of the
individuals involved has full control of how exactly one event is followed by the
next, or how, in other words, the trajectory unfolds. This is equally true of the way
the decision process is shaped in the first case study. The brief dialogue between
John, the nurse, and Agnes, the supervising physician, is characteristic of the way
in which health care professionals function in hospital departments. John proposes
to check the basics only, to which Agnes readily agrees, and she takes his suggestion one step further by deciding to also cancel the ECG and the x-ray. Frequently,
decisions are the outcome of formal meetings, written communications or brief
verbal exchanges. As such, 'decisions are collective acts, not individual acts'
(Anspach 1993).

In these interactions, a broad range of considerations can play a role. The
management of patient trajectories is not only moulded by medical concerns:
trajectories and decisions 'are shaped by the social context in which they are made'
(ibid.). This seems evident in terminal cases; typically, in such situations social
considerations are given priority over medical ones. In order to make it possible
for the patient to die in a dignified manner, for instance, no new infusions or other
interventions were ordered. Yet it is important to underline that concerns about
the preferences or desires of the patient or the opinions of relevant colleagues
constitute an important component of health care work in general, as is true of

economic considerations or issues related to workload or organizational priorities. Such considerations are not 'secondary to' or a 'bias in' the interventions of physicians and nurses: they are part and parcel of the work of health care professionals. They are, then, constitutive of the patient trajectory, as much as the medical/ nursing information and the professional decision criteria. The suggestion of John, which resulted in a departure from the standard admission protocol, can only be understood in terms of the need to save costs, a concern for avoiding unnecessary work, or the consideration not to burden the patient with inessential interventions. And the actions of Agnes and John can only be explained in light of the fact that both are seen as experienced professionals who have the authority and credibility to depart from the standard protocol without prior consultation.

An important aspect of health care work is the *contingent* and *emergent* character of the evolution of patient trajectories. In the case of the neurological ICU patient, the actual policy (few blood tests, no ECG, no x-ray) was directly produced by the conversation between John and Agnes – it is unlikely that either one of them had planned this particular approach in advance. Agnes responded to John's remark and the specific content of their exchange led to their reinterpretation of the protocol. If Agnes had not run into John by accident, she probably would just have routinely asked for the standard list of tests. This phenomenon is typical of health care work: the management of patient trajectories is not a matter of making detailed plans for action for individual cases. The complexity of patient trajectories makes this impossible. The wide range of considerations that may come up at any point and the great number of parties involved in the interactions imply that each patient trajectory is best understood as 'an in-course accomplishment' (Lynch 1985). It cannot be anticipated how long a terminal patient is going to live, what the exact reaction of the relatives will be like, or what the arrival of another emergency admission will do to the workload. Especially in cases of long-term chronic disease, the actual patient trajectory takes shape through the many ad hoc decisions and improvised interventions of the patient and his or her caregivers.

Our description of health care work could be read as a critique: after all, it appears to suggest that the work of health care professionals is not primarily guided by a scientific logic. Our emphasis on the provisional and pragmatic dimension of health care work could be interpreted as yet another sign of the limited rational and scientific character of that kind of work. This, however, would be a mistaken conclusion. The decision not to adhere as strictly as possible to the ICU admission protocol in our case study above is not a sign of irrational intervention. A protocol is just one tool that may contribute to a proper coordination of patient trajectories. Expertise, protocols and intervention strategies are but a few of the considerations that play a role simultaneously. Amidst ringing phones, emergency admissions and daily meetings, physicians, nurses and other health care professionals seek to manage patient trajectories by assigning tasks to others, by making short-term decisions and by questioning whether organizational routines and

51

protocols should be followed or not. The contingencies that shape patient trajectories and the ad hoc responses to such situations are what health care work is all
about. Concluding that its pragmatic character and its intertwining of 'social' with
'medical' considerations would stand in the way of the rational essence of that
work is 'very much like complaining that if the walls of a building were only gotten
out of the way one could see better what was keeping the roof up' (Garfinkel
1967). What is at stake here is a fundamental feature of work in a vast array of
contexts, ranging from basic factory labour to sophisticated academic work.

THE ROLE OF THE RECORD IN HEALTH CARE WORK

CASE VIGNETTE

Regional Mental Health Care Centre, Eindhoven, the Netherlands, Monday morning

Anton is the programme manager in charge of one the psychiatric care
programmes in the Eindhoven region. In his programme, a multidisciplinary team
is responsible for indication, referral and outlining patient care plans. The actual
care is provided in so-called 'care units' on the basis of these plans. Anton is
receiving a phone call about a client he is responsible for. While on the phone, he
searches for this client's data in Iris, the mental health care patient record that
was developed in Eindhoven. He finds the letter he is looking for and reads part
of it on the phone.

Meanwhile, a psychiatric nurse is coming in with a patient record under her
arm. She tells Anton about Mrs Meijer who ran out of Seroxat, medication she
had been using for two weeks. Most nights she has difficulty sleeping through
the night and she also feels quite nervous. Anton and the nurse decide that
the woman should try Seroxat for at least one more month, supplemented with
Seresta if needed. During their talk, Anton opens Mrs Meijer's patient record in
the computer and writes out the prescriptions. Just as he is ready to print them,
the phone rings again: someone who wants to make an appointment. Phone in
hand, Anton first finishes up the printing and with a few clicks of the mouse
he switches to his electronic agenda. While deciding on a date and time for the
appointment, the nurse walks in again with the printed prescriptions, which
Anton signs.

Protagonists of electronic patient records have vehemently criticized paper records
for their limited accessibility and their general incompleteness. The information in
paper records would be vague, ambiguous, incomplete or hard to extract from

its chaotically arranged and illegible handwritten pages. Bleich, for instance, uses harsh words:

> The medical record is an abomination. . . . [I]t is a disgrace to the profession that created it. More often than not, the chart is thick, tattered, disorganized, and illegible; progress notes, consultant's notes, radiology reports, and nurses notes are all co-mingled in accession sequence. The charts confuse rather than enlighten; they provide a forbidding challenge to anyone who tries to understand what is happening to a patient.
>
> (Bleich 1993)

Upon closer inspection, though, this view of the role and problems of the (paper) patient record is seriously flawed. The conception of the record as a 'container' filled with bits of information, that, when added up, would result in a complete picture of the patient trajectory cannot be supported. Patient records do not provide a mirror of medical work: they are *tools* used in doing the work. Patient records fulfil two, closely intertwined functions. First of all, they *accumulate* the data gathered during the course of a patient trajectory, resulting in the powerful 'external memory' that a paper file provides. The progress notes, written down in chronological order by the professionals while they circulate through the shifts, afford the experienced reader a fast and efficient overview of the central key developments, actions and problems. Likewise, blood test results are accumulated in tables (generated by laboratory computers, or filled in by the ward secretary) that allow the reader to overview the patterns of increase and decrease in values through time, and to compare these fluctuations with the fluctuations apparent in other (blood) test results.

The record's accumulation function consists of two elements. First of all, it is obvious that the record is the place where data are gathered (where the data elements 'accumulate'). Doctors, ward secretaries and nurses constantly write in the record, or paste notes or computer prints in it. Second, and less immediately obvious, the *way* the record organizes these data elements is important. The table with its built-in ease of comparison, and the progress form with its built-in chronology and standard headings add structure to the data entered: the data are put in a specific historical sequence, or in a specific context with other relevant blood test results. By collecting the data in this way, by providing for this specific sequence and context, the record's form *enhances the information content* of these data: the blood test result becomes part and parcel of a whole array of data whose overall evolution is vastly more informative than each individual measurement. In pre-structured intake forms, for example, the pre-set headings of the intake form – 'complaints', 'history', 'objective findings', 'conclusion' and 'policy' – suggest the classic reasoning process with which a doctor moves from 'patient problem' to 'action plan'. Yet the order in which professionals enter bits and pieces of information on the form

53

generally does not follow the temporal sequence suggested by the form. Part of the professional's skill is to *translate* the patient's stories and his actions into this neatly structured reasoning process, leading from 'complaints' through 'objective findings' to 'policy'. When such a form is re-read later, this implied and familiar reasoning process structures and speeds up the reading process, and the isolated data entries are interpreted in this framework. Even the paper forms in use in most current health care practices, then, can be said to *process* data. By structuring data entry, and by placing data elements in specific contexts and sequences, tables, progress forms and intake sheets make an important step in the transformation of the 'raw data' that is entered into 'information'.

In addition, through structuring and sequencing the *work* of professionals, PCISs *coordinate* activities and events at various locations and times. Standard headings on the progress notes structure the questions that physicians ask and the examinations that they perform, and make the notes of doctor A comparable to any other doctor using this form. Likewise, structured forms that are used by several people, at different moments (such as order-forms, checklists and so forth), help to link their activities without the need for 'face-to-face' or real-time interaction.

These forms link their worktasks by making clear who is responsible for what and when, and by indicating when one actor has done something and when another's action is requested. Rather than having to arrange by him/herself that a series of examinations (blood tests, x-rays) is performed on a patient, a doctor can simply write these requests on examination-request forms. More often than not, these forms not only play a vital role in getting the right request to the right department (and getting the result back to the right patient!): by providing automatic copies (already carrying the appropriate codes) for the financial departments, the doctors' work is automatically coordinated with billing activities as well. Through devices as simple as check lists and structured forms, then, doctors' activities are coordinated with each other, with other health care professionals and with supporting services without the need for any explicit coordination work by any of these actors.

The patient record is a 'reiterative, cumulative manuscript' (Hunter 1991): medical professionals constantly produce new summaries of their progression reports, in which they condense the details of the previous trajectory in a few, brief sentences. These sentences follow the standard narrative patterns as well. From the perspective of the current situation, they represent the relevant elements of the pre-history in a logical sequence. A series of blood pressure measurements is summarized as 'stable blood pressure', the complex situation of Mrs Meijer is concluded by prescribing Seresta and more Seroxat, and the brief conversation between John and Agnes on their handling of the protocol will never end up explicitly in the patient record at all. Later on, such summaries, conclusions and silences are condensed once more in new letters and notes, whereby the recorded patient trajectory is rearranged on the basis of the new situation.

These observations seem to underscore Bleich's harsh criticism of the status of patient records: medical professionals leave out details, rewrite events, and rearrange linear chronologies. This criticism, however, starts from the assumption that patient records must be carbon copies of patient trajectories. Yet when the production of medical notes and data is understood as part of the management of a patient trajectory, rather than as the *reporting* of this work, it becomes clear that it is very useful to describe patient trajectories in terms of established narrative patterns. The reductions, summaries, simplifications and standardizations found in the accounts of individual patient trajectories are 'needed to produce an account ordered enough to enable action or to communicate what is going on' (Gooding 1992). In such accounts, all that appears to have little or no importance for colleagues is discarded, highlighting only those details that are believed to be relevant.

This reconsideration of the role of the patient record leads us to a revaluation of the merits of the paper patient record. Advocates of EPRs, as we have seen, are generally depreciative of paper records, yet in the eyes of experienced medical professionals they function more effectively than is generally assumed. Even thick, substantial records create less problems when tracing specific information because medical professionals have 'effective strategies for limitation of search space by perception of positional and textual features' (Nygren and Henriksson 1992). Regarding these features, these authors argue, a paper patient record is superior to a computer screen. Paper records contain many informational 'cues', like coloured pages (which enhance fast tracking of information), their size (which provides instant information on the length or complexity of the patient trajectory), the various handwritings, the ink colours and types of pencils, the post-it notes, underlinings, arrows, markings and so on. The speed with which experienced medical professionals know how to zoom in on relevant parts of the record is striking, Nygren and Henrisson suggest, and the information quantity 'covered by a glance is enormous'. A nurse from the neurology ward of a regional hospital put it as follows:

PRACTITIONER'S PERSPECTIVE

With paper records you had a better overview, now you really have to go and search the various windows. The care plan is conveniently arranged, but for writing down notes things used to be better. . . . The night shift wrote in red, the day shift in blue, and the evening shift in green. You would just open up a folder and you could continue to write right away. On the left side, there was a nursing problem and to the right the plan, so you could easily see what had changed and what had been done . . . even if you had been gone for three days.

Such experiences are by no means exceptions. Some functionalities of paper just cannot easily be matched: you can take paper records along easily, put them next to you while interacting with a patient, or you quickly leaf through them and make a brief note. Conversely, it is harder to type and look at the screen when interacting with other medical professionals or patients, while the interactions also tend be interrupted more.

More importantly, still, paper-based records deserve merit for constituting the most widespread and successful information system in health care. They have been around for at least a hundred years (see Chapter 2), and they have co-evolved and adapted to the changing contexts of Western medicine to a surprising degree. Its functions are a *sine qua non* for the ongoing work in current Western health care practices. The paper PCIS's accumulating function makes it possible for one health care centre to provide care to thousands of patients, each of whom can be seen by dozens of professionals at different moments in time. Only through some type of system that is (relatively) easy and uniformly accessible, and that gathers all (or most of) the relevant information on a patient is any remote sense of 'continuous' or 'integrated' care thinkable.

The coordination function is similarly pivotal for Western medical work. The structured forms, check lists and protocols in the record afford highly complex decision making processes by professionals, and make complicated and high-risk treatment modes such as multi-organ surgery or chemotherapy regimes possible. Likewise, these same devices make it possible for a (growing) assembly of professionals to align their (increasingly complex) activities around a patient with each other without having to every time coordinate this work themselves.

Importantly, the PCIS can only fulfil these functions when the professionals working with the tool *align themselves to the demands of the tool*. These simple paper sheets and forms only become a powerful IS when the people working with these sheets and forms abide by their rules: relevant work and record keeping routines have to be *standardized*. They have to follow the pre-set classifications that the sections of the record offer lest their entries will not be retrievable at some later date, and they have to let the record structure and sequence their activities for the coordination to be indeed achieved. Simultaneously, patient trajectories are standardized: groups of patients are described in similar concepts, and 'processed' through standard sequences of activities using identical forms and checklists.

Interestingly, due to the specific nature of health care work, this is a highly skilled activity: *producing* the standardized bits of workflow and information is in itself not a 'standard' task at all! The professionals have to do the work of articulating the preset workflows in the checklists and forms to actual worktasks, whose details always vary, and which are structured by many more pressing issues and needs than could have been foreseen. Likewise, they have to do the work of 'fitting' accounts on and details of specific patient trajectories into the pre-set structure of standard forms and fields. Professionals, then, have to constantly balance the demands of the tool with the demands of the actual worktasks, and find ways to (re)align the two when contingencies have made a 'standard' application of a form or classification category impossible.

As a final point, we should not forget that the information handling and coordination functions are never performed only by the PCIS. The handling of information and the coordination of work tasks is a *joint* achievement of professionals, artefacts such as the patient record, and organizational structures. The professionals are not only responsible for writing into and reading from the record. They are themselves rich sources of memory (for themselves and for each other), and they also themselves spend much time ensuring that their activities are and remain coordinated. A doctor often gets a 'complete picture' of a patient by browsing the PCIS, which activates her own memory, or by asking colleagues or nurses who have dealt with this patient. Likewise, an enormous amount of activities are coordinated through phone calls, meetings and other forms of person-to-person coordination. Finally, organization science has taught us that the way the organization is structured is itself a major element in the coordination of the work activities that take place in these organizations. The coordination of doctors' tasks with nurses' work, for instance, is partly achieved through the forms, partly through their direct interaction, but also partly through the existence of organizational routines, including the specific hierarchical nature of their interaction.

ROLE OF ELECTRONIC PCIS

CASE STUDY

Regional Mental Health Care Centre, Eindhoven

In the Eindhoven region, the care innovations and mergers that took place during the 1990s have co-evolved with the development of a PCIS to support these new modes of health care delivery. The various outpatient mental health care facilities in the region have merged with the local general psychiatric hospital. Currently, the regional mental health care system is organized around six 'care circuits' (including, for instance, 'Emergency Care' and 'Complex Chronic Care'), while so-called 'case-managers' are in charge of coordinating the care provided to clients. This may often involve various circuits, several kinds of care, and a variety of institutions. Charles is employed as case-manager of the circuit 'Complex Chronic Care'. He says about his job: 'The case-manager is basically the intermediary between individual clients and the system. He makes sure that clients get the help they need. Thus the case-manager has a guiding role in the client's care programme. When a client goes into a crisis, I can hire care from 'crisis and intervention' for as long as needed. If necessary, the client is institutionalized and then I maintain close contact with the staff of the ward involved, but also with the client's family doctor and relatives. When, after some time, the client is ready to go back home, I make sure he gets psychiatric home care. I also check with the client if he or she might be interested to join a special programme on how to plan their day. Case-managers function as the primary care provider for individual clients and they coordinate all care provided to them.'

The PCIS (called Iris), specifically designed for this project, is geared towards the needs of the case-manager and it facilitates the collaboration between the various (mental) health care professionals and institutions. Iris strongly emphasizes communication: it contains a module for e-mail, a shared electronic record on each of the clients, and an electronic agenda for each of the employees. E-mail can be used for requesting prescriptions. With the help of the agenda's 'repeat function' it is easy to set up appointments between client and care provider. By clicking on icons, medical staff and other personnel – depending on their authority level – can check, enter, change, or search for data in the system.

Regional General Hospital, Neurology Ward

The Kardex system is an easy, widely used system for medication distribution. It mainly consists of a brief form (the medication order) with two carbon copies. The first part of the order form (yellow slip) is for the pharmacist, the second part (pink slip) for the physician's patient record, and the third part (white slip) goes into the medication folder (Kardex), in which nurses indicate whether or not medication has been administered. Initiating, stopping or changing medication is all done by filling out a medication order form. Officially this has to be done by physicians, but in practice nurses are frequently the ones to fill out the forms, with physicians signing them after the fact. (Or, alternatively, nurses have little piles of pre-signed, empty medication slips.)

MEDICATION ORDER				0675021/01/0188	
Age	Ward	Medication and strength		OR	TIME
				IV	
	Start date			IM	
Length				SC	
	Stop date	Dose		EXT	
Weight	Patient name		Name and signature MD	R	
				V	
	Hospital Nr.			HH	

Figure 3.1 *Medication order slip* (translated from the Dutch original).

In this hospital the Kardex system was in use for a long time, but the recent introduction of the PCIS has radically changed the procedure for distributing medication. If during his ward round a physician decides to change the medication of a patient, start with new medication, change the dose, or discontinue the medication altogether, he writes a quick note in a small notebook, while the nurse makes a note on the care plan (the computer-generated printout that is used during the ward round). After the ward round, the physician is supposed to enter the changes into the computer, whereas the nurse will check whether the physician has indeed entered the changes.

When the physician uses the EPR to request new medication, this shows up at several places at the same time. In the nursing unit, a new medication order is printed, which the secretary puts on the table. After that, it is checked by a nurse who puts it on the medication cart. The nurses of the night shift will put the requested medication on the cart to be distributed the next day. Furthermore, the new medication is automatically added to the care plan, while the pharmacy also receives a copy of the new medication order.

Forty-five minutes before the medication has to be distributed to the patients, the PCIS prints a list of 'ordered medication' in the nursing unit. The secretary or a nurse will put this list on the medication cart. For each patient, it shows the medication, dose, application method, frequency, date and hour of first administration, and the code of the physician who prescribed it. On the right side of the page, next to the list of patient names, there is a column with the abbreviations 'GIV' and 'NGIV', short for 'medication given' and 'medication not given'. At the proper time, the nurse – medication order list in hand – makes a round of all the rooms with the medication cart and for each patient he marks off either GIV or NGIV. When additional medication is given, this is marked, with a pen, in between the printed lines. After finishing the medication distribution, the nurse sits down behind the computer screen, opens the window he needs, and clicks on the appropriate spot if medication is administered to a particular patient.

The coordinating function of the patient record may take on a new and more dynamic role as a result of the introduction of PCISs. In the example above, the hospital's PCIS signals to the nurses that medication needs to be handed out, prints out an order list, and informs the pharmacy about the prescribed and administered medication. Thus the system does away with a number of manual tasks (like selecting, sending, and processing the Kardex slips), while it also serves as a memory aid to the nurses (it prompts them automatically that it is time to hand out medication). Finally, it offers various direct opportunities to monitor medication orders and automating stock records. Yet the PCISs more powerful functions put new demands on the work of the health care professionals. For example, the electronic medication orders have to be filled out accurately. In the old days the Kardex slips were handled manually, which enabled nurses and pharmacy staff to double check unclear or left out information, and to complete the missing information. Automated processing requires the information to be precise and complete, because otherwise the pharmacy's stock management may be hampered or the medication order list cannot be printed at the right moment.

The active, coordinating function of the PCIS also enables the close collaboration between the client's case-manager and the mental health care professionals working at a variety of locations. In this situation, too, the PCIS can only fulfil its coordinating role if all the electronic agendas and patient records are accurate and kept up to date in the same, standardized fashion. Here again, it is true that additional possibilities offered by the PCIS demand an extra effort on the part of the health care professionals who use it. They have to generate the conditions under which the PCIS's potential can be optimally exploited.

The computational powers of IT can change the coordination function of the record in four ways:

- it can *track* events and *send messages* to trigger these, and so coordinate them more powerfully (e.g. controlling whether a medication order has been executed, for example);
- it can *sequence and structure activities more powerfully* (e.g. by not letting a professional proceed to a next step before a previous step is completed);
- it can make *synchronous coordination* possible (the speed of electronic communication makes possible the simultaneous coordination of activities (by people and/or other artefacts) in different geographical sites (e.g. through a multimedia connection));
- it can facilitate *coordination between more locations and/or more entities* (once an infrastructure is installed, all the above mentioned functions can be distributed over larger numbers of recipients).

These more powerful coordinating functions of a PCIS can only properly articulate with professionals' activities if the latter become more strongly aligned to the record's demands. That is to say: more powerful functions require more standardization of

- workprocesses (meticulously following the structuring of the PCIS and keeping one's electronic agenda in precise order);
- data (agreement on terminology, coding and precise completion of records);
- decision criteria (adequate synchronous coordination and reminder systems require agreed upon decision criteria between system designers and (distributed) users).

On all these levels, increased standardization is a *sine qua non* for the PCIS's coordinating activities to work.

RETURN TO THE PARADOX: INTERMEDIATE CONCLUSION

The work of health care professionals centres on the management of patient trajectories: the monitoring or redirecting of the course of a patient's disease or problem. This is a social, interactive process in which a wide array of interests and concerns come to bear. Consequently, the actual form of a patient trajectory is impossible to predict, as is true of the developmental trajectory of a PCIS itself (cf. Chapter 2). Patient records fulfil two interdependent roles in this work: they accumulate inscriptions and they coordinate activities. The PCIS may fulfil these roles in a more active way. This implies, however, that health care professionals have to adjust themselves more to the demands of the EPR: their work becomes more standardized. Such adjustment is not problematic in itself: every introduction of new medical technology brings along a transformation of medical practices (cf. Chapters 2 and 4). In addition, to *produce* the standard data, decision criteria and work processes required is a highly active task of the health care professional (see also the next two chapters).

Yet the core question that was raised at the beginning of this chapter was whether the professional work of doctors and nurses *can* be standardized without hampering the very quality of that work. After all, as we argued earlier (p. 51), health care work has a thoroughly contingent and emergent character. Bluntly standardizing data, decision criteria and work processes would undo health care professionals' capacity to adequately adjust their skills to individual patient cases – or so many would argue. We saw, however, that paper-based PCISs also already require much standardization of data, work processes and decision criteria – and that such tools have fulfilled rather powerful functions in health care practices over the last century. So, *some* standardization is not antagonistic to health care work, at the very least. But where does the 'cut off point' lie? At what point does the added standardization pressure become so heavy that the PCIS can no longer function?

There are many examples of PCISs that failed because their function required a level of standardization of work tasks that was impossible to produce. Clinical pathways, for example, often structure and sequence the work of nurses and doctors in such detail that the central importance of articulating such general pathways to individual trajectories is denied. The latter becomes noise upsetting the smooth flow of the preset categories of trajectories rather than the core activity typifying health care work. It is then up to the professionals to constantly 'repair' the cracks and fissures that this causes in the flow of their activities. This generates the working failures of so many IT applications: the technology creates difficulties in '"good working practices" . . . because it is insensitive to the contextual reasons for the existence of those practices' (Button and Harper 1993).

As another example, many medication systems run into problems because they require the physician to issue and enter a medication order *before* nurses can follow up on it, and hand out the medication. Yet, as is already suggested by the case study on p. 58–9, in reality the boundaries between these tasks are rarely strictly demarcated. In fact, frequently the experienced nurses are the ones who take the initiative to change a patient's medication. Similarly, it is no exception that in emergency situations medication has already been administered before it is entered into the patient record. The Kardex system allows for such deviations from the protocol: experienced nurses may already fill out a form and have it signed, or a form may be filled out and processed afterward (after administering the medication). A medication system that would make it impossible to administer medication that is not yet officially entered into the system would seriously obstruct the proper course of medical work, rather than facilitate it. Allowing such pragmatic interpretation of professional and legal requirements is not paramount to being 'sloppy' or 'irresponsible'. Rather, a careful consideration of how medication systems may enhance the quality of work and patient safety may necessitate building in easy to use 'work around' routines for nurses that doctors may formally 'sign' *after* the fact.

Unfortunately, many PCISs rely too heavily on abstract, rationalist models of medical work: a more empirically based perspective on medical work – as introduced in 'Health care work' (p. 48) and 'The role of the record' (p. 52) – is only recently gaining strength in debates on PCISs. It is still an all too common notion in the standard literature on PCISs that health care work ought to be structured like a rational scientific process with clearly delineated tasks and steps. Traces of this view abound in PCISs: tasks are divided into subtasks that can only be carried out in a pre-programmed sequence. The common result of this overly rationalist approach is that health care professionals have to put in a lot of extra work merely to compensate for misapprehensions in EPR design.

How, then, *can* PCIS be made to interweave synergetically with health care work? How can the paradox of systems that have to 'kill' health care work in order to truly work be avoided? Before answering this question in Chapter 5, we will now turn to the nature of health care information in health care work and information systems.

DISCUSSION QUESTIONS

1   Patient care information systems (PCIS) are seen by many to provide an answer to current problems of information handling and coordination in health care work. What kinds of problems would be amenable to amelioration through PCIS, and what problems would not? Think of an example of a well-founded and a poorly-founded PCIS project, and give arguments for your choice.

2   Does the depiction of health care work given in this chapter undermine or underwrite the need for more 'Evidence Based Medicine'? Why?

3   Discuss examples of proper standardization of data, workprocesses and decision criteria in health care work, and of improper (or impossible) examples.

NOTE

1   From now on, we will use the term PCIS to imply a *computer-based* information system, except when explicitly noted.

REFERENCES

Anspach, R. R. (1993) *Deciding Who Lives. Fateful Choices in the Intensive Care Nursery*. Berkeley: University of California Press.

Bleich, H. L. (1993) Lawrence L. Weed and the problem-oriented medical record, *MD Computing* 10: 69–72.

Button, G. and R. H. R. Harper (1993) Taking the organisation into accounts. In G. Button (ed.), *Technology in Working Order. Studies of Work, Interaction, and Technology*, London: Routledge, pp. 98–107.

Garfinkel, H. (1967) *Studies in Ethnomethodology*. Englewood-Cliffs, N.Y.: Prentice-Hall.

Gooding, D. (1992) Putting agency back into experiment. In A. Pickering (ed.), *Science as Practice and Culture*, Chicago: University of Chicago Press, pp. 65–112.

Groth, L. (1999) *Future Organizational Design: The Scope for the IT-based Enterprise*. Chichester: Wiley.

Hunter, K. M. (1991) *Doctor's Stories. The Narrative Structure of Medical Knowledge*. Princeton: Princeton University Press.

Lynch, M. (1985) *Art and Artifact in Laboratory Science. A Study of Shop Work and Shop Talk in a Research Laboratory*. London: Routledge and Kegan Paul.

Mintzberg, H. (1979) *The Structuring of Organizations*. Englewood Cliffs: Prentice Hall.

Nygren, E. and P. Henriksson (1992) Reading the medical record. I. Analysis of physicians' ways of reading the medical record, *Computer Methods and Programs in Biomedicine* 39: 1–12.

Strauss, A., S. Fagerhaugh, B. Suczek and C. Wieder (1985) *Social Organization of Medical Work*. Chicago: University of Chicago Press.

FURTHER READING

On the nature of health care work

Anspach, R. R. (1993) *Deciding Who Lives. Fateful Choices in the Intensive Care Nursery*. Berkeley: University of California Press.

Berg, M. (1997) *Rationalizing Medical Work. Decision Support Techniques and Medical Practices*. Cambridge: MIT Press.

Hunter, K. M. (1991) *Doctors' Stories. The Narrative Structure of Medical Knowledge*. Princeton: Princeton University Press.

Strauss, A., S. Fagerhaugh, B. Suczek and C. Wieder (1985) *Social Organization of Medical Work*. Chicago: University of Chicago Press.

On the possible clashes of information technologies with the nature of work

Brown, J. S. and P. Duguid (2000) *The Social Life of Information*. Cambridge: Harvard Business School Press.

Forsythe, D. E. (2001) *Studying Those Who Study Us. An Anthropologist in the World of Artificial Intelligence*. Stanford: Stanford University Press.

Star, S. L. (ed.) (1995) *The Cultures of Computing*. Oxford: Blackwell.

Suchman, L. (1987) *Plans and Situated Actions. The Problem of Human–machine Communication*. Cambridge: Cambridge University Press.

Chapter 4

The contextual nature of information

KEY TERMS

- Contextual nature of health care information
- Primary and secondary purposes of data
- Accumulation of data

INTRODUCTION

Successful design, implementation and utilization of information systems in health care starts with a thorough understanding of the practices in which the systems are planned to function. In the previous chapter, we discussed the nature of health care work and the role of paper-based and electronic information systems in that work. In this chapter, we will discuss the nature of health care information, to illuminate problems and potentials in the design and utilization of PCISs. In government reports on electronic patient records, and in much of the medical informatics literature, the PCIS is often seen to afford the utilization of data gathered in the care process for *secondary* purposes: administration, financial management, research and so forth. Since the information gathered by the nurses and doctors that are managing the patient's trajectory would no longer be 'imprisoned' in the immutable paper pages of the traditional record, many additional users could draw upon this information. The Council on Scientific Affairs of the American Medical Association, for example, states that 'users [of the record] can be grouped into seven categories: providers, patients, educators, researchers, payers, managers and reviewers, and licensing and accrediting agencies and professional associations' (1993). All such users desire more detailed, more timely and more comprehensive information about the inner workings of health care – and all have high expectations about what the EPR could bring them.

The secondary utilization of information has achieved much attention since it touches upon the privacy of patients and the accountability of health care professionals. The first point will not be discussed here; we will come back to this issue of accountability in Chapter 5. Much less attention has been paid to another issue: is the secondary utilization of health care data possible, and what does it take to make it possible? In the views of much of the literature and reports on health care information systems, this secondary utilization becomes feasible as soon as the information technology (IT) connections are in place: it is simply a matter of selecting *which* information to transport to *where*. In such a view, medical information is conceptualized as the 'givens' about a patient that are 'collected' and then 'stored' in the record. Similar to much discussion about 'information super-highways' in general, 'information' is depicted as a commodity: a substance that is present in the world, that is transferable, and independent of its vehicle. It consists of autonomous, atom-like building blocks, which can be stored in a neutral medium. In this chapter, we will argue that this 'commodity' view of medical information is fundamentally mistaken. Rather, *information is always entangled with the context of its production*. We will discuss the implications of this rephrasing of the notion of 'information' for the PCIS, and argue that the disentangling of information from its production context is possible, but that it entails *work*. We will argue for the following 'law of medical information': *the further information has to be able to circulate (i.e. the more different contexts it has to be usable in) the more work is required to disentangle the information from the context of its production.* The question that then becomes pertinent is who has to do this work, and who reaps the benefits.

THE CONTEXTUAL NATURE OF INFORMATION

CASE STUDY

University Hospital, ICU, Thursday, 9:05 a.m.

Agnes is still standing by the bed of the newly admitted patient. The paper record from the operating theatre's anaesthesiologist lies next to the terminal of the ICU's PCIS. This system, for both nurses and physicians, has almost completely replaced the paper record. (The system is a commercial product from a US-based firm, specifically tailored to this ICU by two specially trained nurses and an anaesthesiologist.) The nurses have already copied the relevant medication from this list into their 'worklist' (one of the PCIS's 'forms'). Agnes looks at the PCIS's worklist, and subsequently looks at the 'intensive care list'. This is a form designed as a spreadsheet, covering one day, listing temperature, blood pressure and pulse graphs, and rows with respiration parameters, medication, fluid intake and loss, and so forth. These are all on the same page, in the same temporal format, so that interrelated changes are rendered visible. Some of these data are gathered automatically, but have to be validated by a nurse (such as temperature and blood pressure); some of these data have to be manually entered by the nurse (such as the different forms of fluid loss). Agnes then opens the 'progress notes' (a pre-structured form where the relevant clinical information is gathered). This form consists of sections such as 'cardiac', 'pulmonary', 'abdomen', 'extremities', which are subsequently split up in separate fields as depicted in Figure 4.1. The fields show the most recent entries made; each new entry erases the previous one from the screen (without erasing it from the computer's memory). Figure 4.1 also shows the section 'cardiac' as Agnes encountered it.

Having listened to the heart and the lungs, she clicks at the cardiac section, reads the blood pressure monitor, and types '135/70' in the field *Tension*. She types 'S1 S2' in the field *Rhythm* and 'none' in the field *Murmurs,* leaving the rest of this section empty. The section 'extremities' remains empty, and in the section 'pulmonary' she only jots the abbreviation for 'normal breathing sounds' in the

Cardiac

Heart rate: ____ Rhythm: ____ Murmurs: ____

Tension (sys/dias): ____ mmHg CVD: ____ mmHg PWAP: ____ mmHG PAP (sys/dias/mean): ____ mmHg

Remarks: _____

Figure 4.1 *Section 'cardiac' of the electronic Progress Notes form. PAP = pulmonary arterial pressure; PWAP = pulmonary wedge arterial pressure; CVD = central venous pressure.*

field *Auscultation*. She selects '2+' in the field 'pupils' (indicating the pupil's reactivity), after taking this value from the intensive care list. She writes the same medication list as the nurses have already copied in the 'orderlist' (the form where nurses are supposed to find what diagnostic tests have to be performed, and what medications have to be given).

We will elaborate three ways in which information is entangled with the context of its production. First, data are always produced with a given *purpose* – and their hardness and specificity is directly tailored to that purpose. In the case study, for example, Agnes is dealing with a routine case. Such cases routinely spend 24 hours on the ICU and are then transferred to the neurological Medium Care unit. These patients are very stable compared to the average ICU patient, and they have been investigated thoroughly before and after surgery. The data she gathers are for monitoring purposes only, and given the non-problematic status of this patient, there is no reason to expect any non-routine event to happen before transferral to the neurological ward. This is why her data gathering is so cursory: she copies the value for the pupils' reactivity from the nursing notes, listens only briefly to the heart and lungs, and skips much of the data that the pre-structured form requests.

If medical information is seen as a series of context-free givens, then it can only be concluded that Agnes has performed an incomplete examination, has produced an incomplete record, and has unduly relied on nursing information to create an entry in the medical section of the record. Yet if the contextual nature of information is acknowledged it becomes clear that within this concrete practice, the handling of this patient is perfectly adequate. All those involved in the care of patients on this ward are familiar with such patients: this is not a haemodynamically unstable patient who needs 'intensive monitoring'. Experienced co-workers *know how to read* such 'cursory' data. They will deduce from the empty fields that the heart and breathing rate were normal (if necessary, these data can be found in the nursing intensive care list anyway), and that there were no problems with the extremities that would be relevant for them. And they will deduce from the nature of this case that Agnes has just briefly checked the heartsounds; since the patient has been thoroughly investigated before, she has not listened for a faint murmur that she might have heard if she were on a diagnostic quest. Similarly, she has only auscultated the anterior side of the chest, so to spare the inconvenience – for both patient and staff – of having to turn over this patient to listen at his back. Given the severe constraints on residents' time (they are responsible for the day-to-day care of all ICU patients, amongst others), everyone considers it a sign of *good practice* to be brief where brevity is wise, and to trust experienced nurses at those points where their skills and know-how surpasses the capacity of less experienced residents. To search meticulously for faint murmurs in a patient such as this would be considered a wrong priority, or, worse, a sign of not knowing how to distinguish what matters clinically from what does not.

First, then, medical information is entangled with its context of production in that the meaning, hardness and significance of a piece of information cannot be detached from the specific purpose for which that information was gathered. A second way in which medical information is contextual is closely linked to this first phenomenon. An image of medical data as 'atoms', as isolated givens, overlooks how medical data *mutually elaborate each other*. To conceptualize the broad range of medical data on a patient as bits and pieces of an emerging *story* is much more apt than to consider them as a heap of facts. The above case can again illustrate what is meant here. The empty entries around the fields 'rhythm' and 'murmurs' *transform the meaning* of the entries in these fields much like a new event in a story can bring a new meaning to its evolving plot. In this situation, the empty entries indicate the routine nature of the event, and the non-problematic, stable cardiac status. Consider how the meaning of the data-item 'murmurs: none' would change if the entry after 'remarks' would read 'now three days after valvular surgery'. Not only would the significance and poignancy of the data item change drastically, but we would then suddenly and reasonably expect the 'rhythm' and 'murmur' information to be the result of a meticulous investigation.

Examples from this same phenomenon abound. Take the following notes, written by an experienced registrar, from a record of a young, female leukaemic patient from the oncology ward of an academic hospital:

PE: Nodes –

       Spleen –

For an (already rather knowledgeable) outsider, the only information that seems to be recorded is that in the *physical examination*, no enlarged lymph nodes or an enlarged spleen were felt. An insider, however, would know this ward's working routines, would be familiar with the specific demands of this particular medical situation, and would note that this is this registrar's first own entry in the record. Having this background information, this insider would read this as central information on the core indicators in the staging for chemotherapeutic treatment: both an enlarged spleen and enlarged nodes are important signs in staging leukaemia. In this situation, this was a very efficient way of communicating between each other – clear to everyone involved. In a different clinical situation, this information might have meant something completely different. If the patient would have been older, and suffering from another chronic leukaemia, 'Spleen –' might have been taken to indicate that the physician had confirmed that the spleen had been surgically removed. Or, in the context of a patient who had been suffering from swollen axillar nodes, 'Nodes –' would indicate that the physician had looked at *these* nodes and found that the swelling had disappeared.

The mutual elaboration of medical data also evolves over time: the *temporal* dimension is as crucial to medical information as it is to a story. In the course of a patient's illness trajectory, data items are constantly reinterpreted and reconstructed. Consider the following sequence of blood pressure measurements in the post-operative patient mentioned above: at 6 a.m., 120/70; at 9 a.m., 125/75; at 11 a.m., 115/65. If all other clinical signs would remain unchanged, then this series of readings would most likely be read as a 'stable blood pressure'. But if the 1 p.m. reading would be 100/50, then the 11 p.m. reading would be reinterpreted as the beginning of the decline. At many medical wards, medical work is characterized by this ongoing (re)interpretation of the tendencies in graphs and tables: is this temperature going up? Is this haemoglobin level stable? Again, medical information is not a timeless collection of unchangeable entities, that retain their essence once captured in a record.

So far, then, we have seen two ways in which medical information is entangled with the context of its production: medical data are tied to the purpose of their generation and they are part of an evolving array of medical data which continually reshapes their meanings. The two are closely related: doctors are aware of the constantly evolving nature of the data they produce, and they generate their data accordingly. When Agnes checked upon this patient the next day, she did not change the entry for the blood pressure she had entered the day before ('135/70'), although the monitor now read '125/65'. For all practical purposes, and in this particular, stable patient, this was not a difference worthy of registration. Agnes does not intend the 'S1 S2' and 'none' entries to stand for an in-depth scrutiny of this patient at that particular time. Rather, those marks are intended to convey an ongoing monitoring process, in which, at this particular moment, nothing noteworthy has changed or is expected to change within the next monitoring episode.

The third way in which medical information is inextricably context-bound is that 'physicians [and other health workers] typically asses the adequacy of medical information on the basis of the perceived credibility of the source' (Cicourel 1990). That is: whenever a physician takes a specific piece of information into account, s/he will assess that information in the light of who or what generated it. When the supervising senior physician at the ICU encountered Agnes's progress notes during his rounds later the same day, he just nodded and moved to the next patient. Agnes is an experienced resident, who has been 'around' for a while, and whose capacities are trusted. The very same entries would have been judged quite differently if they had been made by a junior resident: he would most likely have been scolded for his incompleteness, and the senior physician would have rechecked the patient's condition.

This judging of the value of information happens whether the source is a human or a machine. Physicians develop a sense of the trustworthiness of the apparatuses they work with, and they learn to more or less trust the x-rays produced by their x-ray department, or the blood tests performed by their lab. Similarly, in the ICU, the EPR is linked to some of the monitors: measures like the blood pressure, the pulse and the temperature are automatically displayed in the intensive care list's spreadsheet. Yet nurses have to 'validate' this data: they have to check if the data registered makes sense. The temperature-probe might be loose, for example, or the patient might be inadvertently closing off the air-tube for the automatic blood pressure measurement. Until they are validated in this way, these values are displayed in italic. For each automatically registered data item, nurses judge the adequacy of its source. Recursively, when others later scrutinize the intensive care list, they can check the name of the nurse who validated the data in *their* evaluation of the worth or quality of the data.

PATIENT CARE INFORMATION SYSTEMS: MAKING INFORMATION MOBILE

CASE STUDY

University Hospital, ICU

The fluid balance is an important parameter on the ICU. Patients in critical conditions easily either dehydrate or 'overfill' (leading to oedema, hypertension and potential heart failure). The section 'fluid balance' in the EPR is set up as a spreadsheet: it lists fluid 'gone in' (infusions, fluid nutrition products, glasses of water) and fluid 'gone out' (urine, drains). It automatically calculates the totals per time unit, per day, and the 'total fluid balance': the total balance for the whole period the patient has been at the ICU (see Figure 4.2). The fluid balance should be zero: as much fluid should 'go in' as 'out'.

Producing the fluid balance is a complex activity. Every two hours, nurses have to check how much urine has been produced, how much fluid has been drunk, and whether the infusions are running well. They enter these values in the appropriate cells in the spreadsheet. The PCIS calculates how much fluid will be given through infusions – these infusions are entered in another part in the record – and it puts the outcome of these calculations in the spreadsheet. The nurse has to validate these values, since the infusions might be running too fast, or be stopped unexpectedly. Until s/he has done so, the value is shown in italic. The computer then adds the columns, and calculates the cumulative totals.

Main menu ↓	Functions ↓	View ↓			Print ↓			Enter Data			

	Interval: 2uur	09nov99 1600	1800	2000	2200	10nov99 0000	0200	0400	0600	0800	1000	1200
Vital Graph	NaCl 0.9%	10	10	10	10	10	10	10	10	10	10	10
	Glucose 5%											
	Nutrison Stand.	126	126	126	126	126	126	126	126	126	126	126
Vital Values	Urine Cath	10	90	70	120	170	60	40	60	110	60	60
Swan Ganz	Gastr.Intest.Mcs.											
	Gastr.Intest.Feac.					0						0
												0
Resp. Param	Infusions Total	130	140	150	160	170	180	190	200	210	10	10
	Med IV Total			100		100				100		
	Med per os Total											0
	Med PS Total											0
Intake	Urine Total	520	610	680	800	970	1030	1070	1130	1240	60	60
	In Total	1089	1225	1461	1597	1833	1969	2105	2241	2477	136	136
	Out Total	520	610	680	800	970	1030	1070	1130	1240	60	60
Output	Day Cumulative	+569	+615	+781	+797	+863	+939	+1035	+1111	+1237	+76	+76
	Cumulative Total					~+28734						~+28810
Fluid Balance												
Lab												
Medi cation												
CVVH Param.												

Clinical Chem results available at 10:06 nov 10 '99 | Mo. Nov 10 '99   11:22

Figure 4.2 *A screen print of the fluid balance of the ICU PCIS. The rows indicate the different means fluid can go 'in' or 'out'. The last four rows are the totals. The total fluid balance is listed once a day (8:00 a.m.), and on the current time.*

General Physicians Unit, Brabant, The Netherlands

The Dutch GPIS makes it fairly easy to code diagnoses, complaints and medication data. If a physician wants to prescribe the antibiotic amoxillin, he opens the window for requesting medication. This window consists of two fields. The lower one lists the medication the patient currently uses or has used. By double clicking the name of a drug the data are copied to the upper field. When a physician wants to prescribe a specific drug for the first time, he enters its name. By typing 'amox' a field appears with names of drugs that begin with these four letters (including their proper doses). Selecting from a standard list means that the drug is coded: one, standardized term is used to refer to this drug. In the same way, complaints and diagnoses may be coded, so that every 'diabetes' case can be easily found. These physicians make use of the International Classification of Primary Care (ICPC).

On the basis of these codes, the GPIS may call the physician's attention to side effects of specific drugs or allergies. When 'amoxillin' is entered in the EPR of a patient who at an earlier visit was coded '01' (which indicates a penicillin allergy), the EPR automatically generates a warning that the amoxillin prescription may cause an allergic reaction.

The general physicians may also initiate preventive activities with their EPR.

For influenza vaccinations, an 'influenza module' may be used, which, following the GP's professional association's guidelines, creates a file of all patients in the physician's EPR who are eligible for an influenza vaccination. The module selects patients on the basis of relevant ICPC codes (like 'diabetes'), medication (like Ventolin, used for asthmatic diseases) and age.

In this general practice, the list selected by the influenza module consisted of 1,000 patients (out of a total of 6,200). For each member in this risk group, the module has entered an 'IM' code on the electronic card. The physicians of this practice also checked the list by hand. In some cases a patient did not truly belong on the list (for instance, because he had used Ventolin just once to treat a severe bronchitis), or some patients were wrongfully omitted from the list because not all patient records were completely updated and coded yet. The influenza module, of course, could not identify these cases. Gerda, the doctor's assistant, therefore produced a new list, which she linked to the influenza module. All patients on the new list received the 'IS' code on their record and were sent a letter telling them they were eligible to receive a preventive influenza vaccination. A total of 1,057 letters were sent off and during a period of two weeks Gerda vaccinated some 1,000 patients. Afterwards, she used the influenza module to code patients who had received the influenza vaccination 'IV+'. Those who had not responded kept the 'IS' code. These patients were invited by phone, so that they could still have their vaccination.

We saw in the previous chapters how the *accumulation* of inscriptions is one of the roles that medical records play in medical work: health care workers write their notes in records, laboratory results accumulate there, and so forth. A core feature of the PCIS is that this accumulation can take a more active form: the record can start to make calculations with the data gathered in the record, trigger alarms or reminders, and aggregate data for research use, administrative purposes and so forth. An electronic PCIS could change the accumulation function in four ways:

- It could *draw upon larger databases* (the ability of IT to access 'records' in a (distributed) database is incomparable with the effort it takes to physically access a paper-based medical record).
- It could perform *more powerful operations* on these data (an integrated PCIS could synthesize, e.g., overviews of workload, monthly 'throughput' overviews, and run checks on data entered – to spot incomplete records, for example, or to flag incompatible drug combinations).
- It could *more easily allow for changing the logics of the information handling* (whereas in the paper-based record, the information is always presented

per patient and by source, an electronic PCIS could facilitate searching the database by disease-category, by year of admission, by treating specialist and so forth).

■ It could *make real-time information handling possible* (the PCIS could perform all the above mentioned operations in real-time: give immediate feedback upon the entry of a wrong medication, for example).

In the previous paragraph, however, we have argued that medical information is fundamentally context-bound. What are the implications of this observation? Does this imply that data can only be used within that context? To start answering this question, let us look at the case studies above. The way the fluid balance actively calculates with and aggregates entered data is a basic but illuminating example of the way IT can enhance the accumulating role of medical records. The computer automatically transfers information from other locations in the record to the fluid balance and it adds columns and totals. This more active role affords a more precise measurement of the fluid balance. Before the coming of this EPR, the fluid balance was calculated only once a day; now there is a continuous, up to date fluid balance available. This function also saves time: the daily calculations had to be done manually, and took about 15 minutes per patient. Yet to afford this active accumulating function, the nurses have to be more meticulous in their routines: they have to follow a similar action sequence every two hours (check urine, enter values, validate values), and they have to ensure that all values are entered correctly, precisely and error-free. If they fail to do so, the computer's totals will be unable to calculate totals, or it will produce erroneous figures.

A critical investigation of Figure 4.2 could lead one to the conclusion that these totals are wrong anyway. The total fluid balance of this patient is more than 28 litres positive – a fatal condition. The reason for this phenomenon was simple. Notwithstanding all the precise procedures that contributed to the calculating of the fluid balance, the loss of fluid through respiration and transpiration were not taken into account: the instruments that would be needed to measure these values were too cumbersome and expensive for daily, routine use. Since an 'average' patient loses about 1–1.5 litres of fluid through respiration and transpiration, however, this implies that patients that are about 1–1.5 litres positive per day are 'in fact' rightly balanced. The judgement whether '0.75 litre positive' constitutes a negative fluid balance depends on a judgement of the psychological condition of a patient, his physical condition and the temperature of his surroundings. In the case of a tense patient that has spent his day lying in the sun, for example, '0.75 litre positive' might count as a negative fluid balance. Although this is a very significant 'fudge factor' (the total fluid that goes in and out per day is only a few litres!), the fluid balance is adequate for the purposes of this ward's needs: the uncertain transpiration and respiration values hardly ever constitute a problem. The values are indicative and useful, and clinical knowledge and experience to interpret them is always available. A more precise fluid balance is not worth the investments that would have to be made.

In a similar way, the built-in warnings and the influenza module of the general physicians' PCIS supported the work of the doctors and their assistants. The automatic generation of warnings or reminders may reduce the chance of error, while the automatic selection of risk patients, as well as the automatic processing of letters to those in this category, enables a vaccination campaign of a much larger scale than would have been possible without this particular module. Yet, here too it is true that the PCIS can only fulfil these functions effectively if physicians code their patients' complaints and diagnoses according to the rules and if assistants carefully monitor any changes in the 'IS', 'IM', and 'IV+' codes. Moreover, physicians have to check the module-generated list patient by patient and the meaning of each warning has to be assessed individually. This, however, does in no way lower the usefulness of the influenza module: it is simply less work to check the list manually than to keep the data files updated and flawless so that any manual checking would become superfluous.

Here as well, then, we see that data are bound to the context of their production. The fluid balance functions adequately as long as it is used and interpreted by experienced users, who can relate the always positive figures to their clinical experience and other information at hand. Outside of this context, these figures would be absurd: read at face value, we would have to conclude that this was an ICU where medical miracles (or lethally inadequate care) were the order of the day. The fluid balance, Agnes' data, the empty fields and the 'IM' codes are data that are richly and adequately meaningful within the context of their use – yet they are meaningless, faulty or even patently absurd outside this context.

For this reason, attempts at aggregating primary medical information – for secondary utilization, or for advanced functions within the care process – are problematic. As one commentator put it: 'we may aggregate nonsense as effortlessly as we aggregate fact' (Levitt 1994). This insight has been translated into a *First Law of Medical Informatics*: 'Data shall be used only for the purpose for which they were collected. If no purpose was defined prior to the collection of the data, then the data should not be used' (van der Lei 1991).

If data are nevertheless transported outside the context of their immediate use, things indeed often go wrong. In one health care practice, for example, medical specialists wanted to process electronic bills by automatically linking them to the health care activities recorded in the PCIS. Previously, doctor's assistants used to keep track of all the medical interventions on separate lists. The PCIS designers, quite logically, expected that the PCIS could process such a list automatically. However, after the introduction of the PCIS it turned out that not all interventions were entered into the computer. Activities that were part of standard routines, for example, were often not separately entered. The effect was that earnings threatened to go down drastically – which is why the idea of an automatic link was quickly abandoned.

This does not mean that the utilization of health care information for research, for generating bills or alarms is impossible. Far from it: the *disentangling* of information from their primary care contexts, the making 'mobile' of data, is a core component of health care work. What starts as an utterance understandable only within the direct context of its production, has to be made 'transportable': understandable elsewhere, and recognizable outside of the specific conditions of its generation. This disentangling, however, is *work*. The fluid balance totals will have to be adjusted, and details will have to be added or explained so that the information becomes useable in the *new* context of use.

This is a crucial point: work is required to make data suitable for accumulation. We might phrase this as a second 'law of medical information': the more active the accumulation will be, the more work needs to be invested. Information technology can help in this work: it can facilitate coding, for example, or automatically code free text. Yet this can only facilitate the required work – it cannot obviate its necessity. In order to create data that can be added, subtracted and treated as 'equals' by the ICU PCIS, then, nurses have to follow meticulous routines in data gathering and validation. If one would have wanted to use the fluid balance totals for additional calculations, or if one would have wanted to compare patients or draw upon these totals in other contexts, the transpiration and respiration factor would have to be dealt with in a systematic fashion. This would necessitate an additional investment: installing additional equipment to measure respiration and transpiration, or manual corrections on every total by experienced nurses or doctors. Similarly, if one wanted to compare total numbers of patients requiring an influenza vaccination per region, for example, general practitioners and assistants alike would have to meticulously keep and maintain the codes.

Just like work processes need to become more standardized to make PCISs work, then, health care information needs to become more standardized for the additional accumulation powers of PCIS to come true. The level of standardization achieved by the pre-structured forms and fields in today's paper medical records is generally insufficient for these aims. The entries that professionals make in these records are mostly made for the purpose of the proper unfolding of the primary care process. The notes and orders are meant to be read and understood by colleagues and other 'insiders'. For these purposes, communicating in shorthand, omitting issues that are 'self-evident', and dwelling upon local dialects is the rule rather than the exception. The need to be meticulous, elaborate, to code data entered or to use even more pre-structured forms is a demand that is inevitable when electronic PCISs are developed – but that should not be taken lightly.

A central issue is the question where this additional work is to be done, and where the benefits end up. In the case of the fluid balance, the nurses have to invest time and effort in additional, meticulous routines. Yet they themselves are the ones who profit most: they gain more time than they invest, and they now have a more precise fluid balance at their disposal. Likewise, general practitioners who use their PCISs to code data for their own research purposes, or to facilitate screening activities and the generation of automatic reminders invest a bit of work from which they themselves benefit. In hospitals, separate 'record administrators' often do the coding of DRGs or ICD codes for administrative purposes, and research assistants do the translations between patient record and clinical trial form. They disentangle the data from different contexts, fill in gaps, interpret unexpected phrasings and outliers, and translate all this into a single 'code' that has all the characteristics of a commodity. In this case, the work of those who manage the patient's trajectory is not affected: the work to 'commodify' information for use by administrators is delegated to an additional group of people, specially assigned to this task.

Yet just as the skill and tacit knowledge that comes to play in the work of these coders is often overlooked, the task to produce data for secondary utilization by others than the primary care givers is often unthinkingly delegated to those primary care givers. Too often, current PCIS designs implicitly or explicitly make them responsible for the production of standardized, 'transportable' data. They have to fill in long, coded forms, to write elaborate explications, and to be – from their viewpoint – overly complete.

One way in which this friction plays up is in the discussion on 'free text'. Some information specialists see the multiple use of free text in patient records – in the progress reports of physicians, in the observations of nurses, in radiology reports, in reports on ultra-sound scans – as a shortcoming of health care practices. After all, quantifiable information is the apex of scientific accomplishment. Everything that can only be captured in vague phrases is therefore less scientific and hence subject to perfection: 'The kinds of information that are currently stored as free text have not generally evolved to as mature a state of evolution as that which is currently stored as structured formats' (McDonald 1992).

This assumption, however, rests on a misconception. The coding and quantification of information are methods for taking information out of the context in which it is used. Yet this does not imply that 'coding' and 'quantification' render this work itself more scientific. This is by no means necessarily the case. The use of free text and local dialects are actually highly functional for an optimal and flexible performance of common tasks by a joint team of professionals: more 'standardized' information generally is *less* informative in such circumstances. Coded data often can hamper the ongoing work because the nuances and details – which are so crucial in the management of patients' trajectories – tend to disappear behind the 'generic' codes. Likewise, health care professionals run the risk of losing their general overview of the situation as soon as they are exposed to an overdose of isolated 'items' or to too much standardized prose. For primary users of a patient record, a summary of three lines in the 'conclusion' section of an observation form is much richer in information than three lines of preprinted, checked off standard formulations. The way in which a medical problem is described generates a wealth of information for the experienced medical professional. What is emphasized in the free text? What is qualified in a subordinate clause? What is omitted? To what extent does a formulation depart from standard narratives? This is no mysticism or computer phobia, but a reflection of the fact that making data transferable requires different demands – and at times even opposite demands – than the efficient use of data in their immediate context of origin. Ideally, in the latter case, data are rich in specific detail, low on information that users already know, and tied to each other in a narrative sequence. By contrast, the perfect transferable data are coded, independent from each other, and ridden of any 'couleur locale'.

The accumulating function of PCIS, we conclude, has definitely acquired a new dimension since the arrival of information technology. More active accumulation creates entirely new options for using patient records, but making information more cumulative requires more work as well. If medical data seem to have universal qualities, then this is the result of much effort and not a natural, intrinsic quality of these data. As soon as data are accumulated so as to make them more accessible to third parties it is important to start asking critical questions. Adding this new task to the workload of health care professionals who tend to be over-burdened already will doubtlessly take away more of their time – precious time which might be spent on other tasks, such as the care for the patient.

CONCLUSION

In this chapter we discussed the contextual nature of health care information. Health care information should not be conceived as some sort of substance or raw material that can be 'harvested' and 'transported' freely at the risk of privacy concerns only. Rather, information is always tied to the context of its production: inscriptions only become 'information' if they are placed in a specific context. At the same time, records accumulate information, we already argued in the previous chapter. This implies not just a passive 'collecting' of inscriptions: it implies actively adding structure to the data inscribed in it. If the paper record would just *gather* the information without smartly organizing and integrating it in meaningful wholes, the information would again be impossible to retrieve and assimilate in the short and dispersed spans of time that typify most professionals' working days.

Paper records, it seems, have probably been criticized all too harshly within medical informatics. In the previous chapter, we already pointed out that health care professionals get much more out of paper records much faster than most critics would assume. Also, paper has use-features – easy to handle, easy to anno-tate, high information load per cm^2 – that are still hard to beat with electronic means. In this chapter, we encountered even more arguments why much of today's criticism on paper record keeping is at least too simplistic. The idea, for instance, that the level of completeness or the clarity of the record is a direct measure of the quality of the medical care is a misguided one. As the sociologist Garfinkel already claimed in 1967, there might be 'good organizational reasons for "bad" records'. For outsiders, most notes and remarks in patient records are indeed hopelessly incomplete and incomprehensible. For those directly involved, however, they are generally adequate. Health care professionals tend to include in their records only what is strictly necessary at that moment and in a given situation. They generally legitimately presume that insiders will recognize the particular situation and that on the basis of their local knowledge of such situations they will fill in the missing context and implicit details. A patient record is only comprehensible for those 'who know both the code and the cultural expectations that inhere in the situation it delineates' (Hunter 1991). Or, as Garfinkel put it: 'The folder contents much less than revealing an order of interaction, presuppose an understanding of that order for a correct reading' (1967).

An adequate interpretation of the meaning of medical data implies, in other words, that the specific clinical context in which that data is generated can be interpreted adequately. The patient record does not so much represent what has happened; it is a potentially very useful tool *in* that work. It presupposes that the reader will know what normally happens in comparable situations, and hence it supplies only a few data needed to establish the specificity of a particular situation. The conciseness and the seeming incompleteness 'works' because insiders, just like the participants in any conversation, understand the context in which medical professionals produce notes. They know what their tasks are, what will cause them worries regarding a patient, and what they will be looking for. In the busy context of medical work, succinctness is a form of saving time, both for the one who enters the information in the patient record and for the one who quickly tries to trace it. During their training and socialization process, interns and residents learn that brevity is a virtue – and with good reason. Lengthy and exhaustive narratives are even distrusted because they betray the author's inexperience.

Yet however much we can learn from the powers of paper records, it is obvious that the PCIS has the potential to enhance the accumulation power of these tools much further. With these greater powers, however, come greater demands on those that use these tools. Health care professionals now have to standardize their data input in order to allow the tool to aggregate the data. Using primary care data for billing, for research, for automatic fluid balances all requires more work to disentangle these data from their primary contexts. Crucial questions are who does this work, where the benefits end up, and whether the added standardization and time effort do not in fact *hinder* the ongoing work of health care professionals.

DISCUSSION QUESTIONS

1   Find and discuss pieces of information generated in the primary care process, and discuss the (im)possibilities to use this information for different, secondary purposes.
2   Similarly, discuss what extra detail, context, etc. has to be added to this information in order to be able to fulfil a role in a secondary context.
3   What do you think of the often heard ambitions to create 'paperless' hospitals or wards?
4   So-called 'natural language processing systems' attempt to 'code' information entered in free-text mode automatically, often without the user's intervention. Does this imply that the tension between the advantages of 'free text entry' and the requirement of standardization of terminology is resolved?

REFERENCES

Cicourel, A. (1990) The integration of distributed knowledge in collaborative medical diagnosis. In J. Galegher, R. E. Kraut and C. Egido (eds), *Intellectual Teamwork. Social and Intellectual Foundations of Cooperative Work*, Hillsdale, NJ: Lawrence Erlbaum Associates, pp. 221–42.

Council on Scientific Affairs of the American Medical Association (1993) Users and uses of patient records, *Archives of Family Medicine* 2: 678–81.

Garfinkel, H. (1967) *Studies in Ethnomethodology*. Englewood-Cliffs, N.Y.: Prentice-Hall.

Hunter, K. M. (1991) *Doctors' Stories. The Narrative Structure of Medical Knowledge*. Princeton: Princeton University Press.

Levitt, J. I. (1994) Why physicians continue to reject the computerized medical record, *Minnesota Medicine* 77: 17–21.

McDonald, C. J. (1992) Physician's needs for computer-based patient records. In M. J. Ball and M. F. Collen (eds), *Aspects of the Computer-based Patient Record*, New York: Springer, pp. 3–11.

van der Lei, J. (1991) Use and abuse of computer-stored medical records [editorial], *Methods of Information in Medicine* 30: 79–80.

FURTHER READING

On the nature of information and task-oriented communication

Agre, P. E. (1995) Institutional circuitry: thinking about the forms and uses of information, *Information Technology and Libraries* 14: 225–30.

Garfinkel, H. (1967) *Studies in Ethnomethodology*. Englewood-Cliffs, N.Y.: Prentice-Hall.

Garrod, S. (1998) How groups co-ordinate their concepts and terminology: implications for medical informatics, *Methods of Information in Medicine* 37: 471–6.

Gregory, J., J. E. Mattison and C. Linde. (1995) Naming notes: transitions from free text to structured entry, *Methods of Information in Medicine* 34: 57–67.

Harper, R. H. R., K. P. A. O'Hara, A. J. Sellen and D. J. R. Duthie (1997) Toward the paperless hospital?, *British Journal of Anacsthesia* 78: 762–7.

Nunberg, G. (1996) Farewell to the information age. In G. Nunberg (ed.), *The Future of the Book*, Berkeley: University of California Press, pp. 103–38.

Chapter 5

Meeting the challenge

Integrating quality improvement and patient care information systems

Marc Berg and Cé Bergen

KEY POINTS OF THIS CHAPTER

- Given the financial resources and individual skills that go into current Western health care systems, there is a 'quality chasm' between what they should deliver, and what they actually deliver.

- Information technology is seen by many to be a *sine qua non* if we want to close this gap, yet the standardization of health care work that this requires may render this 'solution' to be fatally contradictory to the nature of health care work and information.

- This chapter outlines, in a few principles, how this paradox can be avoided, and how a real answer to the quality challenge can be provided:

  - standardized care paths need to be formed for the majority of patient trajectories;
  - care processes need to be carefully unravelled, and work activities need to be redistributed over the different professionals and the patient;
  - standardization is necessary, but only where it enhances competencies and quality;
  - 'flexible standardization' is not a contradiction in terms
  - the success of a redesign of the care process according to the first two principles is crucially dependent on the opportunities given to the professionals to skilfully integrate the demands of the care paths and the PCIS in their workpractice.

KEY TERMS

- Quality chasm
- Standardized care path
- Redistribution of workactivities
- Flexible standardization
- Care process redesign

INTRODUCTION

In 2000 and 2001, the US Institute of Medicine published two reports that set a new tone in the ongoing calls for health care reform. In the first report, 'To Err is Human: Building a Safer Health System' (Kohn *et al.* 2000), the Committee on Quality of Health Care in America claimed that medical errors (such as administering wrong drugs, or failing to execute a planned intervention) are a leading cause of death in the United States. Critique was raised against the precise figures listed, and the exact definitions of 'error', yet the overall argument of the report was not substantially contested. The US health care environment was not the 'safe environment' that one would expect it to be. One year later, the same committee published *Crossing the Quality Chasm: A New Health System for the 21st Century*, in which the insights of the first report were generalized to the claim that the overall quality of US health care services was far below standard. Given the amount of resources spent and the motivation of the average health care professional, the Committee argued, there is a huge chasm between what the overall quality delivered by the system *should* be and what it actually is. The Committee discerned six dimensions of 'quality':

1 *Safety* ('patients should not be harmed by the care that is intended to help them').
2 *Effectiveness* (the care given should be evidence-based, and optimally directed at the individual's medical needs; practice variations should be due to differences between patient situations, not to individual preferences of professionals).
3 *Patient centred* (care should respect patients' values, preferences and expressed needs; patients can and should be much more involved in the planning, organization and delivery of their own care; services should be organized and integrated around the patients' experience, to maximize physical and emotional comfort; information, communication and education should be central).
4 *Timeliness* (waiting times and delays before and during care delivery should be minimized. 'Any high-quality process should flow smoothly.').

5 *Efficiency* (care should be directed at getting 'the best value for the money spent'. Waste through inefficient processes, inefficient utilization of resources or the execution of non-effective interventions should be reduced.).

6 *Equity* (health care should be universally accessible, and the quality of care received should not depend on individuals' personal characteristics such as 'gender, race, age, ethnicity, income, education, disability, sexual orientation, or location of residence').

In an unusually critical tone, the Committee charges that the current US health care system fails miserably on all these levels. It is highly fragmented, 'a nightmare to navigate', 'bewildering' and 'wasteful'. Any journey through it includes many 'steps and handoffs that slow down the care process and decrease rather than improve safety'. All in all, 'our attempts to deliver today's technologies with today's medical production capabilities are the medical equivalent of manufacturing microprocessors in a vacuum tube factory' (2001, 28–30).

This already rather damning conclusion is further aggravated by the fact that the demands on the health care system will increase substantially over the coming years. Technological and scientific developments in fields such as genomics will not slow down, the Committee argues, and this will significantly add to the complexity of health care delivery. In addition, the incidence of chronic conditions increases rapidly with the rise in life expectancy and medicine's increasing ability to 'control' diseases even if it cannot 'cure' them.

> Meeting this challenge demands a readiness to think in radically new ways about how to deliver health care services and how to assess and improve their quality. Our present efforts resemble a team of engineers trying to break the sound barrier by tinkering with a Model T Ford.
>
> (Chassin *et al*. (1998) quoted in Committee on Quality of Health Care in America (2000) pp. 23–4)

It is generally acknowledged by quality advocates that the Committee's overall insights are applicable to most Western countries. The issue of 'equity' might be less significant for other countries, where lack of health insurance is not such a major issue as in the United States. On the other hand, when increasing numbers of patients pay high fees to private clinics to 'bypass' waiting lists in the UK or the Netherlands, 'equity' is at stake there as well.

According to the Committee, information technology is a *sine qua non* for Western health care to make the required quality leap. Information technology can help prevent errors, and help link together currently fragmented care delivery systems. It can truly transform Western health care practices – to make the jump from 'tinkering with a Model T Ford' to 'breaking the sound barrier'. This statement, however, seems to be at odds with the paradox that we described in Chapter 3 and 4: the more powerful the desired PCIS functionalities, the more standardization (of work processes, data and decision criteria) is required. Against the Committee's high hopes, critics would argue that the possibilities of ICT in professional work are fundamentally limited. The increased standardization requirements, after all, will soon start to be counterproductive for the quality of these professionals' work.

In this chapter, we will outline a way out of this paradox. We will describe how PCISs *can* be interwoven synergistically with health care work, in such a way that the standardization paradox is avoided, and a real answer to the quality challenge is provided.

REDESIGNING HEALTH CARE DELIVERY PROCESSES

Let us discuss a simple, relatively innocent, but real example: the experience of one patient in a Western health care system. This example happens to be taken from the American context (Timmermans and Berg 2003), but it is sadly universal in its implications.

CASE STUDY

When Ruth found out she was pregnant, she went to her primary care physician for a referral to a neighborhood birth center. She had to schedule the appointment with her physician during work hours, quite inconvenient because she did not want to let her boss know she was pregnant. On the day of the appointment, she first registered with the receptionist and then saw her physician. The primary care physician confirmed the pregnancy with a urine test, similar to the one Ruth used to find out she was pregnant, and then wrote the referral letter. Ruth called for an appointment with the birth center and was able to secure a spot on a Saturday morning. She presented herself with the referral letter to the birth center's receptionist who placed the letter in a file folder she retrieved from the archive behind her. Ruth met with the midwife, answered a ten page long list of questions to assess any risk factors during pregnancy and underwent a physical exam. Ruth would have preferred to answer the survey at home because she would have been able to consult with her own mother about her family's reproductive history. The midwife ordered that a blood sample be drawn and, according to the new hospital policy, suggested that she undergo a genetic test for cystic fibrosis. The receptionist prepared the referral forms and sent Ruth to the blood laboratory in the nearby hospital. Ruth again registered in the main hospital and then waited for a phlebotomist to draw the blood. Because it was a Saturday, the phlebotomist was unable to draw the blood for the cystic fibrosis genetic test. Ruth would have to come back during the week. In this example, even though pregnancy check ups are routine events, all steps need to be planned and executed one at a time, resulting in an inefficient use of time of patients and health care providers and a chance for misunderstandings and sub-optimal care. Because it was too difficult to take time off work and after weighing the risks, for example, Ruth decided to forgo the cystic fibrosis genetic test.

Now, imagine an outpatient clinic where the receptionist contacts a patient to figure out the reason of the visit. Relying on a simple decision support system, integrated in the PCIS, the receptionist determines whether the patient qualifies for a pre-defined standard care path. If the patient qualifies, the receptionist accepts the electronic ordering of a number of blood laboratory tests, suggested by the PCIS, and asks additional questions. (Alternatively, Ruth could have answered the questions used to assess the pregnancy risks from home, on the clinic's website.) The patient subsequently has her blood taken, and when she sees the physician the latter already has all the results and other data available in the PCIS.

The information system could also contain standardized care paths for more highly trained health care providers, for example in the form of pre-defined therapeutic interventions that can be activated with a click of a mouse. When presented as 'templates' that can be easily modified, they structure the professional's work in a helpful way: allowing fast access to routine action-paths, while fully retaining the flexibility to adjust these paths to individual trajectories when necessary. In Ruth's case, one adaptation would be that she intended to give birth in a birth center and work with midwives instead of in a hospital with an ob-gyn as is typical in the US.

The planning of all the links in the chain can be further supported via collaborative agenda systems, to plan as many activities as possible in a convenient time frame. Instead of spreading four different visits over several weeks, a pregnant patient could visit a primary care physician, nurse-midwife, phlebotomist and genetic counsellor in one morning and end up with a care plan at the end.

There are many variations possible to this simple example, within or between health care organizations, more or less integrating 'care' and 'cure', and more or less organized around specific patient categories or groups. In many instances, the patient may play a central, active role in the care process. Diabetes patients, for example, would be able to monitor and adjust their own therapeutic regimes to a far greater extent than currently routine.

What are the fundamental principles, found in these examples, which make a synergy between health care work and PCISs possible, so that the challenge of twenty-first century health care can be met? And in such a way that health care organizations become more attractive working environments for the (scarce) health care professionals as well? Health care providers, we argue, can only do this if they are ready to radically *redesign currently existing health care delivery processes.* We will discuss five principles in turn.

Standardized care paths need to be formed for the majority of patient trajectories. As argued earlier (see also Chapter 3), a core characteristic of individual patient trajectories is their unpredictability. Not only is every individual case different in its symptoms, its severity and its reaction to treatment: patients also happen to have individual desires, needs, complications, social histories and so forth. As a consequence, the delivery of health care is traditionally organized to meet this need for high flexibility: every patient follows his or her own trajectory, which is decided upon on a step-by-step basis. You see a doctor, who decides, for example, that tests need to be done. These tests are subsequently arranged for you, and upon the evaluation of their results, the next step to be taken is decided upon and organized.

This step-by-step organization of health care work may result, in principle, in a health care trajectory that is optimally geared to the individual patient's needs and desires. As a corollary, this organization also affords the individual health care professionals a relatively large autonomy over their own work processes. The gynaecologist, organized in an organizational unit with other gynaecologists, decides when to receive a patient and how to deal with her just like the surgeon does for his patients, the x-ray department does for its clients, physiotherapists do for their patients and so forth.

Yet in the highly specialized environments of current Western health care, this mode of organization now rather results in a very fragmented experience. The lack of coordination between the individual steps and decisions has become deeply ineffective, as we have argued above. In addition, it has also become very inefficient (for both health care provider and recipient). Outweighing the pros and cons of a decision and organizing the next step to be taken every time anew takes up much time. In addition, the lack of overview over the use of all the required facilities (nurses, specialists, laboratories, MRI equipment) guarantees a suboptimal utilization of these facilities.

The result of these modes of organizing the work is a high variability in the course of patient trajectories, even between physicians within health care institutions, and the subsequent impossibility to be transparent about the care processes in the health care institution (let alone its outcomes). This variability and lack of transparency (and consequent inability to learn from and improve upon their own approaches) is painful even to those that are critical of the ideals of evidence-based medicine.

Given all these problems, the basic organization of health care work as a one-by-one, step-by-step processing of individual patients' problems needs to be revisited. Indeed, on the level of the individual patient trajectory, every trajectory is unique, and no predictions can be certain. Yet on the *aggregate* level, of *categories* of patients – such as 'heart failure', or 'monitoring of diabetes type II' – what has to be done, and how patients will react *is* predictable. As a rough guiding figure, one can say that 70–80 per cent of the patient flows in any given health care sector can be made predictable enough to warrant the production of care paths. Within these care paths, 70–80 per cent of the steps and decisions can be explicated. These paths are multidisciplinary: tying in the activities of doctors and nurses, of different specialties, and explicating a central role for the patient whenever possible. When one organizes these categories around the problems with which patients present themselves to the health care organization, 'care paths' emerge that form a radical departure from the traditional, specialty- and capacity-oriented organization of health care organizations.

In this way, it is no longer necessary to fill in individual care trajectories again and again, for every single patient. This saves much unnecessary and routine coordination work, and affords cooperation that is simultaneously multidisciplinary *and* patient-centred *and* guideline-based. In addition, it allows the planning of care paths from beginning to end, including the necessary people, skills, space and technologies. In turn, and here some core logistical principles can be used, planning the utilization of resources in this way implies that the different professional groups and services (that used to live happily side by side) have to give up much of their individual autonomy in order to create truly integrated 'chains' of care. Rather than planning their own days of work, for example, a radiology department will have to allow other professionals to plan work for them. Using a properly equipped PCIS, Operation Room, radiology and Intensive Care utilization can all be planned to a rather high degree – thus preventing the now all too current problems of Intensive Care overuse, Operation Room under use, cancelled surgical interventions and so forth. The principle of 'predictability at the aggregate level' even includes the planning of *emergencies*. Whilst being the archetype of unpredictability at the level of the patient, it is actually quite easy to measure how many outpatient contacts and how much of the OR's time, for example, is taken up by emergency care – and to plan for this (see Box 5.1 for a more detailed specification of some of these logistical principles; see also Vissers (forthcoming) in this series).

This, in turn, helps to reduce unnecessary waiting times, and optimizes the utilization of a health care institution's (often scarce) resources. Needless to say, having explicated what it is that a health care institution does for 70–80 per cent of its patients is a leap forward towards more transparent care delivery processes – which makes it possible to start thinking about further improving these processes' outcomes.

It is of utmost importance that these standardized care paths do not remain mere agreements between professionals, written down in a guideline that is subsequently stored in a handbook or even a protocol database on a health care

BOX 5.1 SOME LOGISTICAL PRINCIPLES UNDERLYING THE NOTION OF WORKING WITH STANDARDIZED CARE PATHS

Patient trajectory is leading; capacity planning follows

The planning of capacities is secondary to the planning of patient flows. Only by explicating this, and by ensuring that this principle becomes crucial in the hospital's basic operations, can we break free from the traditional focus on optimizing the utilization of available (and scarce) *resources* rather than optimizing the 'handling' of a patient's trajectory. Of course, such a principle may be seen as rather costly, but when combined with the principles below the ultimate benefits far outweigh the costs of planning by patient flow.

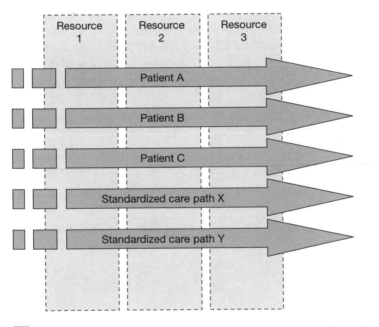

Figure 5.1 *Main ordering principle: the optimization of the patient trajectory.*

Order acceptation and work preparation

'Order acceptation' is the principle that a placed order has to be actively accepted by the receiving party. In this way, a filter is built into the process that prevents poorly specified orders to be able to hamper a smoothly running work process.

'Work preparation' is the logistic principle that a work activity has to be prepared as much in advance as possible before the actual work is started. If this would be done thoroughly, for example, many repeat outpatient visits would be avoidable.

Categorizing work activities and separating them where logistically relevant

Categorizing different kinds of work and handling these separately can reduce the variation within the work processes and thereby enhances the predictability of these work processes. This, in turn, affords the preplanning of the individual steps of these processes. Often, four kinds of work are distinguished:

■ *Urgent.* A separate handling of 'urgent' cases prevents the disturbance of the other work.
■ *Diagnostics/triage.* A standardized care path usually starts with a diagnostic or triage phase, which can be organizationally separated. Often, one separate diagnostics/triage care path can lead up to a host of several different standardized care paths. Also, of course, the outcome of this work activity can be that the patient should be treated as a 'special' (see below).
■ *Standardized care paths.* The multidisciplinary protocol, embedded in the ICT and work arrangements handling 80 per cent of patient trajectories.

Figure 5.2 *Increasing predictability of work activities by distinguishing different kinds of work.*

■ *Specials.* This is the handling of the 20 per cent of moments, at any time during a patient's trajectory, where integrated planning is not possible. In addition, this is where those 20 per cent of patients end up for whom there is no standardized care path to begin with. Due to co-morbidity, specific histories or needs, patients may be unwilling or unfit to enter a standardized care path. What is crucial is that this category 'specials' is not treated as the 'rest category' for whom *less* effort is made to provide optimal care. And, simultaneously, the activities for these patients should not disturb the planned activities within the standardized care paths.

Using the Flight Control model for standardized care paths

The 'Flight Control' model implies that no plane will be allowed to leave until all the steps of its trajectory (including landing and disembarking) are arranged. The health care equivalent is that no admission or intervention is allowed until its subsequent steps (including post-admission home care or nursing home admission, for example) are arranged. This is the complete opposite, of course, of the traditional step-by-step approach to patient care. If full planning is not possible, the burden of organizing next steps, including ensuring continuity between the steps, only falls on the patient if s/he so desires.

Introducing three levels of planning

- *Strategic planning*, with a time horizon of one or several years. Here, the expected yearly demand on a resource is matched with the yearly available capacity of that resource. It is here that decisions will have to be made about the yearly number of admissions for resource-intensive interventions: while patient trajectories are logistically primary to capacity planning, the *overall* capacity available sets the limits for patients admissions.
- *Tactical planning*, with a time horizon of 1 to 3 months. Tactical planning has a 'roll forward' character: it becomes progressively more detailed and fixed when the time slots are nearer to the present. Tactical planning is done monthly. The main purpose is to prevent disturbances in the execution of planned care. Tactical planning implies also:
  - keeping *'white spots'* in your agenda for (different types of) urgent care (the amount of time reserved necessary can be predicted on the basis of historical data);
  - *opening up time slots for specific capacities* (diagnostic interventions, but also beds, nursing capacity) to be planned by those responsible for a standardized care path.
- *Operational planning*, with a time horizon of 1 to 4 weeks.

institution's database. Rather, they have to be *embedded* in the supporting PCIS, the paper forms and the organizational arrangement between departments. For two decades now, reformers and professional bodies have argued for the introduction of guidelines that would outline what the preferred (evidence-based) action is to be taken at any relevant decision point. Yet the overall impact of all this work has remained limited: guidelines are yet one additional input to the already over-whelmed health care professional, easily ignored, or never even read. There are many reasons for this, such as a lack of 'fit' between practical needs and evidence-based assumptions, and a lack of attention to the practical obstacles to implemen-tation and to the required organizational change. In addition, most guideline proponents perceive guidelines to be a tool to transport optimal knowledge to the professional's *head*: educating the doctor as to the most preferable action in a given situation. Yet given the abundance of information already overflowing pro-fessionals, it may be much more useful to embed the guideline in the material and organizational environment in which they work. In this way, their activities are *prestructured* through pre-defined order sets, suggested medication or referral options, and so forth.

Care processes need to be carefully unravelled, work activities need to be redistributed over the different professionals and the patient, and the PCIS should be drawn upon to (help) make this redistribution and subsequent interrelation of tasks possible.[1] Making standard-ized care paths should begin with a rethinking of current, often historically grown modes of working. Just standardizing and building ICT support for what one already does is meaningless: one then 'standardizes' modes of work that may be suboptimal. In addition, one then suboptimally draws upon the powers of a PCIS, which do not lie in copying what its paper predecessors already did (see Chapters 3 and 4). Often, (specialized) nurses or other health care workers can perform initial diagnostic or therapeutic tasks, so that the physician is freed from tasks that do not require his/her specialized expertise. Given the shortages in both qualified personnel and other resources that typify Western health care practices, such a redistribution of tasks is the only way to manage the still increasing demand for care. Eye check ups for diabetes patients, medication optimization in heart failure patients, cardiovascular prevention: these are just some examples where a re-distribution of tasks between doctors, nurses and/or paramedics makes effective and efficient care possible for more patients.

Redistributing and reorganizing tasks and standardizing care paths are mutually dependent. The former is an ideal way to start standardizing care paths, but stan-dardizing care paths is also the only way in which a properly redesigned care path becomes possible. First of all, it is only through standardizing *decision criteria* (what patients may be handled by the nurse; what should the optometrist do in case of doubt), *data* (what data should be registered, using what terminologies and in which detail) and *work procedures* (what actions that should be done by who in what sequence) that a task redistribution becomes possible that enhances the quality of the delivered care rather than threatens it. In the example above, the receptionist is supported by protocols or computer-based decision support systems that have been made and validated by the physicians who hold final responsibility. The care process, in addition, is shaped so that the chance of errors is minimized: whenever uncertainty arises, the patient drops out of the 'standard' category, and is seen by a qualified physician immediately.

Second, it is only through explicating and formalizing what each individual care professional does that these individual tasks can be properly connected through the PCIS and the work arrangements (see also Chapters 3 and 4). The PCIS may afford the required access to each other's data, and may help link each other's tasks through electronic ordering, or by sequencing and dividing tasks over different individuals. (For example, having a senior physician check the work of a junior physician, or automatically generating billing information when orders are entered.) This is only possible, however, when an individual using the PCIS abides by the decision criteria, terminology and work procedures that are formalized and explicated in the PCIS. As we argued in Chapters 3 and 4, more powerful ICT functionality requires more alignment of the professionals' activities with the PCISs' demands. If the PCIS alerts a physician about a task that now has to be done, he or she should be able to trust that the activities that led up to this alert were indeed properly executed as agreed. If the PCIS should support health care workers in making decisions, in addition, the health care workers have to use the basic algorithms and terminology the PCIS draws upon to properly interpret its advices. Only by 'preprogramming' into the PCIS which patients have to be dealt with how, can more coordination tasks be delegated to the PCIS.

A keen redesign would also maximally reduce the need to disrupt each other's ongoing work activities to announce or request something (see Chapter 6). For every outsider observer, this incessant flow of interruptions is astonishingly inefficient – yet a health care professional's working day is often more typified by the constantly ringing phone, beeper and colleagues dropping in than by the ability to actually concentrate on the work that needs to be done. On the one hand, these constant interruptions are part and parcel of the 'unpredictable' nature of health care work, and cannot (nor should) thus ever be completely avoided (see further). Yet smartly restructuring the task divisions, and using the PCIS, may importantly reduce such interruptions. Tasks can be made more independent when optimally sequenced, and, moreover, those later on in the process can be more fully informed through the PCIS about the steps that went before. In addition, more asynchronous modes of communication (more informal such as e-mail, but also highly structured such as through a care path's template) can be used to facilitate communication.

Ideally, the redesign should be based on information about the 'performance' of the care path (in terms of health outcomes, efficiency, patient satisfaction, safety

93

and so forth). Also, once in place, the effect of the new organization should be equally measured. This improvement process should, in principle, be continuous: new data analysis leading to new innovation needs, requiring new redesigns and new measurements, and so forth. This is the principle of continuous quality improvement, or performance management (see Walburg forthcoming). Having standardized care paths greatly facilitates these processes of continuous improvement. Data registration becomes more uniform (since the care paths are more alike), and may also become more extensive (see also below). In addition, the standardized care paths themselves form the framework for the interpretation of the gathered data: they are, after all, guidelines that link the data that would otherwise remain difficult to integrate. Finally, these guidelines can also suggest proper outcomes to monitor, and/or performance levels that may be taken as target for the professionals.

Standardization is necessary, but only there where it enhances competencies and quality rather than reduces it. In the alternative scenario, receptionists' and nurses' tasks are highly standardized. Yet they received new tasks and responsibilities in the care process: supported by decision support techniques (including detailed guidelines) they were allowed to take up a central role and take over some of the specialists' tasks. The quality of the delivered care is guaranteed by those professionals who helped design the decision support techniques and take care of patients that fall outside the standard modules.

The specialists' work, on the other hand, is only standardized when they enter the patient in a standardized care path – and even this form of 'programmed co-ordination' can be modified at will. The simple decision support programmes and practice guidelines that afford a new role for the receptionist and streamline the care process, would generate an unworkable level of standardization for more highly trained health care providers. Specialists would continuously need to overrule the system's advice, spend too much time on trying to work with (and around) the system, and might eventually lose their motivation. The history of medical information systems has shown that the road towards autonomous or 'intelligent' decision making systems has been a dead-end street (Collen 1995). It makes more sense to search for the optimal synergy between professionals' knowledge and the system's capacities rather than have them compete. It makes more sense, in other words, to build 'intelligence' into the care process than into the standardized information technology.[2]

In redesigning care processes, thus, standardization should be localized in only some specific parts of the health care process (e.g., routine diagnostic tests, repeated aspects of therapeutic trajectories, recurring triage moments, etc.). In other aspects of the health care process, possible variation should be embraced. This ensures that competencies and quality are maximally optimized throughout the entire health care process. Highly trained specialists would focus primarily on

94

the patients who fall outside the standard trajectories, on the linkages between the 'standardized' elements of the care process, and on fine-tuning the individual diagnostic and therapeutic tasks.

In this way, it would also no longer mainly be the 'most highly trained professional . . . with the greatest opportunity cost [who ends up] in the data-entry role' (Massaro 1993). When the health care process is restructured so that the secretary, nurse practitioners and the patients themselves enter data in a standardized way, a much more 'complete' file becomes feasible without any individual care professional carrying too large a burden. When the follow-up is subsequently appropriately reorganized as well, clinical outcomes may be registered, and aggregated data may be used for feedback to the overall group of professionals involved in the health care process. Through such standardization, moreover, subsequent information handling or coordination tasks by the patient care information system are made possible — such as alerts or reminders, semi-automatic letters, and so forth (McDonald *et al.* 1984; van der Lei 1993).

'Flexible standardization' is not a contradiction in terms. An important characteristic of standards is their flexibility. In the alternative scenario the specialist could easily deviate from the standardized care path and make adaptations. The extent that the care path or PCIS allows for deviation and improvization is crucial. Flexibility implies that the system is not more detailed than required, not more stringent than necessary, not more imperative than usable. A flexible PCIS or care path can be smoothly integrated in daily health care work. It implies not detailing thirty steps when three suffice; no choice of five thousand diagnostic categories when four hundred are sufficient. It implies, as illustrated above, that it should be possible, at each moment, to modify a standardized care path for an individual patient, or to take the patient out of the path. At that moment, the patient becomes one of the 20 per cent of patients that will be dealt with in the traditional fashion: step by step, with decisions taken at every turn, to optimally fit this specific patient's problem.

Flexibility also implies that the standard can be easily revised and adapted to local demands or to new scientific insights. Compared to Danish GP systems, for example, the coding schemes used in British primary care systems are easily adaptable, rendering the entire system more meaningful and acceptable to GPs (Winthereik in press). In addition, it should be possible to adapt standard care paths to newly emerging insights, for example based on feedback from aggregated health data tabulated from the support systems themselves.

This might sound obvious and simple but it is not. The importance of local adaptability, for example, clashes with the demand that a standard is just that: *standard*. Everywhere applicable, everywhere similar. And simple, pragmatic standards that do not standardize more than necessary might lead to an unwieldy patchwork of overlapping and contradictory standards. Many standard developers abhor such disorder, and much effort is spent on attempts to develop (inter)national, all-encompassing models in which data, decision criteria and work processes are ordered in formal, unequivocal and universal ways. Both within several European countries and at the European level, many resources have been wasted at attempts to create the 'ultimate' model of the health care process. Likewise, much work has been – fruitlessly – invested in the quest for a modern Tower of Babel to resolve the vagueness and multiplicity of medical language. Such standards are inevitably very elaborate and complex, and contain a logic opaque to everyone except the designers themselves. Because these standards are so far removed from daily practice, they become difficult to implement and lead to manifold frictions in the care work. And once those standards are implemented, finally, they are very rigid and hard to change. Any proposed change to the complex whole has to be carefully investigated for its consistency and logic; any such proposition has to follow a long trajectory of (inter)national consultation rounds and committee meetings.

The success of a redesign of the care process according to the first two principles is crucially dependent on the opportunities given to the professionals (and other users) to skilfully integrate the demands of the care paths and the PCIS in their work practice. Even for simple triage situations as described above (the outpatient clinic secretary categorizing a pregnant patient), decision support systems, when left to their own devices, are remarkably ineffective. Worried patients end up worrying more, and the tool's answers more often than not fail to answer the question as the patient phrased it. To translate between patient and tool requires interpretation by the secretary – and knowledge about what the tool's purpose is, and what the meaning of the pre-set categories is. Similarly, paramedics responsible for a diagnostic 'pre-trajectory' should be able to react properly to a patient whose situation is such that a test is unlikely to provide clinically relevant information. It requires much skill to act appropriately in such situations: knowledge about the test's purposes, and clinical skills to realize its inappropriateness.

For the potential synergy between the PCIS and professional work to emerge, then, the tool's coordination tasks should not be seen as self-sufficient. In the common parlance of 'intelligent agents' and 'computerized care paths', this imperative is easily forgotten. Yet we already concluded that constantly bridging the needs of the patient or the work situation and the tool's or care path's demands is a highly skilled activity. It is crucial that the secretary, the paramedics and other users are supported in this task: through formal training, but also through the opportunity to constantly learn from and interact with the other actors in the 'care chain'. Such 'lateral connections' between individuals that hold seemingly independent positions in the formal 'workflow' are essential to facilitate this articulation work (Brown and Duguid 2000). This comes down to facilitating physical access to each other, and enhancing unstructured modes of communication such as e-mail or telephone. This implies not being too rigid when trying to reduce interferences: when the care path or PCIS controls the work process so rigidly that the receptionist is no longer in touch with the specialist, then the former will fail to grasp just what the triage aims to do. Their tasks may be formally separated: according to a workflow diagram, these two individuals need not be in direct personal contact with one another. But without adequate and unstructured contacts between the two, they lose the opportunity to inform and learn from each other. These are simple things that may seem insignificant in the light of the larger organizational changes that the PCIS and care paths bring. Yet they make the difference between being able or not to integrate the functionality of these standardizing tools in the ongoing flow of work. Thereby, they make the difference between an innovation that clashes with that flow of work, and an innovation that lifts professionals' work to a higher level.

CONCLUSION

In this chapter, we greatly increased the stakes. This was nothing more or less than a highly ambitious – yet necessary – requirement specification for the redesign of care delivery at the level of the actual care processes. This redesign is necessary because it is the only way to ensure high quality of care without sacrificing one dimension (say 'effectivity') to another (say 'efficiency'). It is ambitious, because concrete, successful examples of similar attempts are hard to find in Western health care practices. A *systematic* approach such as proposed here is rare. This is not surprising: the cultural and organization changes that this would yield are enormous, and great efforts would have to be invested in standardizing care paths, introducing process-supporting ICT, and restructuring care trajectories.

Without a redistribution of tasks, however, redesigning care paths cannot go very far. Without ICT, also, the more ambitious goals remain unreachable. Without proper standardization of care paths, finally, thorough redesign is impossible, and quality systems can only stumble along. How can we realize these ambitious aims? In the following chapters, constituting part II of the book, we will attempt to give you some more practical 'do's' and 'don'ts' with which to address the information management challenge in your work environment.

DISCUSSION QUESTIONS

- Do you feel the terminology of 'the chasm' between the quality delivered and the quality *potentially* delivered by the health care system is useful?
- Given the existence of the quality chasm, generate a list of five ICT priorities that your health care organization should set.

- Given the existence of the quality chasm, generate a list of five ICT priorities that your countries' health care system should set.
- Find and discuss a case where the principles discussed here are (explicitly or implicitly) put to practice. What are the lessons learned, and does this case indeed deliver what it promised?

NOTES

1 See Chapter 1 on the difficulties of *making* these organizational changes, or the impact of these 'redistributions' on professional relations and so forth.

2 Thanks to Mario Stefanelli for this phrasing.

REFERENCES

Brown, J. S. and P. Duguid (2000) *The Social Life of Information*. Cambridge: Harvard Business School Press.

Chassin, M. R., R. W. Galvin and the National Roundtable on Health Care Quality (1998) The urgent need to improve health, *Journal of the American Medical Association* 280:1000–5.

Collen, M. E. (1995) *A History of Medical Informatics in the United States, 1950 to 1990*. American Medical Informatics Association.

Committee on Quality of Health Care in America (2001) *Crossing the Quality Chasm: A New Health System for the 21st Century*. Washington: National Academy Press.

Kohn, L. T., J. M. Corrigan and M. S. Donaldson (eds) (2000) *To Err is Human: Building a Safer Health System*. Committee of Health Care in America, Institute of Medicine, Washington: National Academy Press.

Massaro, T. A. (1993) Introducing physician order entry at a major academic medical center: I. Impact on organizational culture and behavior, *Academic Medicine* 68: 20–5.

McDonald, C. J., S. L. Hui, D. M. Smith, W. M. Tierney, S. J. Cohen, H. Weinberger and G. P. McCabe (1984) Reminders to physicians from an introspective computer medical record. A two-year randomized trial, *Annals of Internal Medicine* 100: 130–8.

Timmermans, S. and M. Berg (2003) *The Gold Standard: An Exploration of Evidence-Based Medicine and Standardization in Health Care*. Philadelphia: Temple University Press.

van der Lei, J. (1993) Experience from computer-based patient records for computer-assisted decision making, *Methods of Information in Medicine* 32: 14–15.

Vissers, J. (forthcoming) *Health Operations Management.* London: Routledge.

Walburg, J. (forthcoming) *Performance Improvement in Health Care.* London: Routledge.

Winthereik, B. R. (2003) Achieving localization in an information system for primary care: codes, classifications and accuracy, *Methods of Information in Medicine* 42 (in press).

FURTHER READING

On the health care quality chasm and attempts to meet this challenge in general

Berwick, D. M. (1998) The NHS's 50 anniversary. Looking forward. The NHS: feeling well and thriving at 75, *British Medical Journal* 317: 57–61.

Committee on Quality of Health Care in America (2001) *Crossing the Quality Chasm: A New Health System for the 21st Century.* Washington: National Academy Press.

Kohn, L. T., J. M. Corrigan and M. S. Donaldson (eds) (2000) *To Err is Human: Building a Safer Health System.* Committee on Quality of Health Care in America. Washington: National Academy Press.

Millenson, M. L. (1997) *Demanding Medical Excellence. Doctors and Accountability in the Information Age.* Chicago: University of Chicago Press.

On health care redesign

Batalden, P. B. and P. K. Stoltz (1993) A framework for the continual improvement of health care: building and applying professional and improvement knowledge to test changes in daily work, *Joint Commission Journal on Quality Improvement* 19: 424 47.

Berwick, D. M. (1998) Crossing the boundary: changing mental models in the service of improvement, *International Journal for Quality in Health Care* 10: 435–41.

On using IT in health care redesign

Eccles, M., E. McColl, N. Steen, N. Rousseau, J. Grimshaw, D. Parkin and I. Purves (2002) Effect of computerised evidence based guidelines on management of asthma and angina in adults in primary care: cluster randomised controlled trial, *British Medical Journal* 325: 941.

Kuhn, K. A. and D. A. Giuse (2001) From hospital information systems to health information systems. Problems, challenges, perspectives, *Methods of Information in Medicine* 40: 275–87.

Quaglini, S., M. Stefanelli, G. Lanzola, V. Caporusso and S. Panzarasa (2001) Flexible guideline-based patient careflow systems, *Artificial Intelligence in Medicine* 22: 65–80.

99

Stefanelli, M. (2002) Knowledge management to support performance-based medicine, *Methods of Information in Medicine* 41: 36–43.

On using information for measuring 'performance'

Freeman, T. (2002) Using performance indicators to improve healthcare quality in the public sector: a review of the literature, *Health Services Management Research* 15: 126–37.

Marshall, M. N. and R. H. Brook (2002) Public reporting of comparative information about quality of healthcare, *Medical Journal of Australia* 176: 205–6.

Marshall, M. N., J. Hiscock and B. Sibbald (2002) Attitudes to the public release of comparative information on the quality of general practice care: qualitative study, *British Medical Journal* 325: 1278.

Chapter 6

Designing interactions

Enrico Coiera

KEY POINTS OF THIS CHAPTER

- In contrast to the dominant, computational view of decision support, the conversational view emphasizes the sharing and interpretation of information as a social and interactive process.

- The communication space, including all the interactions between professionals during a working day, is largely ignored by informatics. Yet it is in need of support: it is interruption-driven, has poor communication systems and poor practices.

- Information technologies (such as a decision support system or an EPR) require formalizations of information processes for them to operate, while communication systems (such as a telephone) do so much less.

- Proper design for the communication space requires balancing the need to formalize with the benefits of supporting informal communications.

- 'Common ground' is a concept which helps to decide when to opt for informational and when for communication solutions. Two communicating agents always share a 'common ground' of background knowledge that does not require explication.

- Creating common ground (between people or between people and IT) costs time. Yet in the absence of a pre-established common ground, this needs to be established when performing a task, which is risky and expensive.

KEY TERMS

- Communication space
- Computational and conversational view of decision support
- Common ground
- Interaction space
- Interaction design

INTRODUCTION

> In the next fifty years, the increasing importance of designing spaces for human communication and interaction will lead to expansion in those aspects of computing that are focused on people, rather than machinery. . . . The work will be rooted in disciplines that focus on people and communication, such as psychology, communications, graphic design, and linguistics, as well as in the disciplines that support computing and communications technology. . . . Successful interaction design requires a shift from seeing the machinery to seeing the lives of the people using it.
>
> (Winograd 1997)

Traditionally information systems are designed around an idealized model of the task that needs to be accomplished, and failure in system performance is explained away by blaming human social and cultural 'barriers' to technology adoption. In this world, the barrier of human frailty always impedes the newly engineered system. The design of the computational machinery is the scientific high ground, and understanding the mess of implementation in the real world is left to 'soft' social science and happenstance.

But people are part of the system. The web of interactions needed to make anything work in a complex organization always involves humans solving problems with limited resources and working around imperfect processes. Designing the technological tools that humans will use, independent of the way that the tools will impact the organization, only optimizes local task-specific solutions, and ignores global realities. The biggest information repository in most organizations sits within the heads of those who work there, and the largest communication network is the web of conversations that binds them. Together, people, tools and conversations – that is the 'system'. Consequently, the design of information and communication systems must also include the people who will use them. We must therefore design interactions that reflect the machinery of human thought and communication, sometimes mediated by communication channels, sometimes in partnership with computational agents.

Interaction design is a newly coined discipline, focusing on constructing the ways people interact with objects and systems. The product of interaction design is almost entirely the quality of the user's experience. The effectiveness of a piece of software is not an internal attribute of the software, but emerges from the way the software is interpreted by users, and that interpretation is dependent upon the user's specific context, culture, knowledge and resources.

In this chapter, the *communication space* will be introduced as a major component of the overall interaction space for humans working in complex organizations. The gap between the current focus on interactions outside of the communication space and the overall interaction needs of humans will also be highlighted. A framework will be developed next, based upon the notion of bounded mutual knowledge, or common ground, that is shared between communicating agents. This will help us decide whether an interaction was best served by communication or information technology. Finally we will turn to the task of designing systems to support interactions, whether in the communication space or not and specifically look at how, through a formal theory of interaction design, we can design and implement technological systems to support individual interactions by modelling the wider interaction space within which individuals operate.

THE COMMUNICATION SPACE

The current decision-support paradigm in health informatics is a computational one. The computer sits at the centre of information systems that acquire, manipulate, store and present data to clinicians. Computational models of clinical problems allow computers to make inferences and create views on data, or perhaps prompt, critique or actually make clinical decisions.

In this computational paradigm, human information processes are shaped into a form dictated by technological structure. Yet as we have seen in the previous chapters, the development of technology is socially shaped. The value of any particular information technology can only be determined with reference to the social context within which it is used, and more precisely, with reference to those who use the technology. For example, in one study the strongest predictor of e-mail adoption in an organization had nothing to do with system design or function, but with whether the e-mail user's manager also used e-mail (Markus 1994). Further, a highly structured view of human processes sits uneasily with the clinical workplace. It is not just that people have difficulty accepting information technology in a social setting because their interactions are loosely structured. We know that people will treat computers and media as if they *were* people. Consequently, they superimpose social expectations on technological interactions.

So, should we recast the tasks of acquiring and presenting clinical information socially? In the computational paradigm, when faced with a decision problem,

103

clinicians turn to computer-based systems for support. However, if we examine what actually happens clinically, it is clear that people preferentially turn to each other for information and decision support. It is through the multitude of conversations that pepper the clinical day that clinicians examine, present and interpret clinical data, and ultimately decide upon clinical actions. In contrast to the computational view of decision support, this conversational view emphasizes social interaction within health care, and sees the sharing and interpretation of information as an interactive process that emerges out of communication. Rather than 'acquiring' and 'presenting' data in some mechanistic way, conversations are better characterized with the fluid and interactive notions of asking and telling, inquiring and explaining.

While there are few studies that have attempted to directly quantify the size of the communication space which contains the direct interactions between clinicians, we do know some fundamental issues. Rather than document sources, about 50 per cent of information requests by clinicians in the clinic is met by colleagues (Covell *et al.* 1985). Furthermore, about 60 per cent of clinician time is devoted to talk (Tange *et al.* 1996). Safran *et al.* reviewed the information transactions in a hospital with a mature computer-based record system, and still found about 50 per cent of information transactions occurred face-to-face between colleagues, with e-mail and voice-mail accounting for about another quarter of the total. Only about 10 per cent of the information transactions occurred through the EMR (1998).

Not only is the communication space huge in terms of the total information transactions and clinician time, it is also a source of significant morbidity and mortality. Communication failures are a large contributor to adverse clinical events and outcomes. In a retrospective review of 14,000 in-hospital deaths, communication errors were found to be the lead cause, twice as frequent as errors due to inadequate clinical skill (Wilson *et al.* 1995). Further, about 50 per cent of all adverse events detected in a study of primary care physicians were associated with communication difficulties (Bhasale *et al.* 1998). If we look beyond the raw numbers, the clinical communication space is interruption-driven, has poor communication systems and poor practices.

So, in summary, the communication space is apparently the largest part of the health system's information space. It contains a substantial proportion of the health system information 'pathology', but it is usually ignored in our informatics thinking. Yet it seems to be where most of the information in the clinical workplace is acquired and presented. The biggest information repository in health care lies within the people working in it and the biggest information system is the web of conversations that link the actions of these individuals.

POSSIBLE RESPONSES TO THE COMMUNICATION PARADIGM

How do we respond to the idea that information exchanges within the social communication space are primary, and that therefore this is where substantial informatics efforts need to be focused? There seem to be four plausible responses, depending upon how one views communication tasks and what technical interventions are considered to support those tasks:

1   *Identity: Communication tasks are replaceable with information tasks.* In this view, the problem is the size and behaviour of the communication space, and the solution is to transform communication interactions into information transactions. For example, we replace information-seeking questions that currently occur in conversation with queries to databases. The identity response implies a 1:1 correspondence hypothesis that all communication tasks are replaceable with computational tasks. It is similar to the so-called strong hypothesis in artificial intelligence that states that human intelligence can be directly simulated in a computational system. The strong hypothesis is a matter of on-going debate in the Artificial Intelligence community. For our purposes it should be sufficient to say that pragmatically we do not currently have the technology capable of transforming any arbitrary conversation between humans into identical human–computer interactions. Consequently for now we must dismiss the identity response.

2   *Exclusivity: Communication tasks are necessary and not replaceable.* This view emphasizes the necessity of communication, and considers the size of the communication space to be natural and appropriate. Communication tasks are essentially 'different' to the ones we currently support with information systems and consequently accomplish different things and need to be supported in different ways. For example, the informal and interactive nature of most conversations is essential since the types of questions we seek to answer might be poorly structured and only become clear through the act of conversation. The idea that a query to a database could replace a conversation is meaningless because the query only comes into existence as a result of the discussion. The exclusivity of communication response suggests that problems within the communication space arise because of the way we support those tasks, either ignoring them completely, or shoe-horning them into formal information technology solutions that misunderstand the nature and role of communicative interaction.

3   *Mixed: Some but not all tasks can be satisfied in either the information or communication space.* Attempting to find common ground between the previous identity and exclusivity responses, the mixed hypothesis suggests that some communication tasks should be replaced with information systems. For

105

example, information requests that occur frequently within the communication space such as for laboratory results or drug information could be gainfully replaced with information systems. The regularity of these requests permits them to be modelled accurately and serviced by a formal information system. The mixed response is probably the status-quo viewpoint in informatics thinking, albeit an implicit one since active consideration of tasks within the communication space is rare.

4   *Continuum: Communication and information tasks are related but drawn from different parts of a task space.* This view holds that while there are essential differences between what happens in an informal conversation or a formal information system transaction, these differences are simply those we find at different ends of the same continuum. Unlike the previous responses, the continuum view sees the whole information-communication task problem as a false dichotomy, in part perpetrated by technology. We see information and communication interactions as different only because we support them with different tools. While the telephone and the computer might rightly be seen as supporting one or the other type of task, a complex system like the Web begs classification, and can support both communication and information tasks. As a result, the continuum view aims to understand which specific task characteristics would indicate where along the technological continuum we look for solutions. However, to build tools tuned to the specific needs of information and communication tasks, we need to characterize this continuum more precisely. For example, is there some measurable parameter that we could measure in a clinical process that helps us decide when communication is better than computation? Without such precision, we are left to rely on rules of thumb or case lore, and have progressed only little beyond the mixed hypothesis.

Two implications arise from the above analysis. First and pragmatically, based on either the 'necessity of communication' response, or the mixed hypothesis, we need to recognize the importance of the informal transactions that occur in the communication space. Directly supporting communication between clinicians should substantially improve how our organizations acquire, present and use information. By recognizing that the communication space is an essential part of any organization's information systems we avoid depending solely upon the computational paradigm, which can end up shaping our view of how clinical decisions are made and cause us to ignore features of clinical practice that sit outside of it. Thinking only in computational terms, we run the risk of becoming focused exclusively on re-engineering all clinical work into formal behaviours suitable for computational treatment. Second, the 'continuum' view suggests that developing a richer understanding of communication tasks should help us more appropriately craft and target information and communication technologies for our organizational information needs. Both of these implications will now be examined in turn.

SUPPORTING CLINICAL COMMUNICATION

If we are to create processes and technologies that support the communication space, we first need to characterize the activities that occur within it, and understand where there is need for improvement. While much has been written about the dynamics of patient–clinician communication, very little is known about the way that clinicians communicate with each other. More pertinently, the studies of communication processes from the wider perspective of the clinical organization are almost non-existent. Perhaps the only shining exception here is the development of the structured clinical interview and problem-oriented medical record. These can be seen as communication innovations as much as information ones. They ensure that messages between clinicians are well formed and maximize the likelihood that critical information is 'sent' and 'received' via a reliable communication channel we call the medical record.

What we do know about clinical communication systems in an organization like a hospital is that they carry a heavy burden of traffic, and create an interrupt-driven workplace. Clinical tasks generate many communication requests, and inefficiencies in communication system design, technology and clinical behaviour lead to an apparently much higher level of interaction than is necessary.

It is only by delving into the details of the specific conversations that we can start to understand who is responsible for the high level of traffic across communication systems, and what the reasons for it are. In one analysis of a UK hospital, doctors were the highest generator of communication traffic, sending almost twice as many messages as they received (Reitman 1974). Further, doctor–doctor interactions made up over 40 per cent of the calls made by the doctors in the study, denying the truism that medical staff suffer constant interruption because of the actions of other clinical staff in the hospital.

Of concern is that the high level of interruption, whatever its source or reason, may lead to errors by clinical staff. There are well known cognitive costs associated with interruption, leading to diversion of attention, forgetfulness and errors. Further, interruption often requires rescheduling of work plans. The interrupt-driven nature of the hospital work environment thus has the potential to generate extra costs in staff time and efficiency.

There are many potential reasons for the high level of call traffic in an organization. Many are specific to the systems in place within particular organizations, but others are general characteristics of clinical work or human interaction. Some of the factors that have been identified in one study as potential causes of the high level of call traffic in hospitals include:

- *Synchronous bias*: People seem to favour interruptive communication mechanisms such as face-to-face discussion, paging or the telephone, rather than using less interruptive methods that may be available to them. This may be because in busy environments there is a need for tasks to be 'ticked off the list' once completed to reduce cognitive load. For example, asking someone directly to complete a task produces immediate acknowledgement that the hand-over has occurred, but asynchronous channels like e-mail, voicemail or notes are usually not designed to deliver the appropriate acknowledgement of message receipt and task acceptance.

- *Information seeking from humans*: The reliance of clinicians upon discussion to resolve information needs has suggested to some that this is in response to poor printed or computer-based information sources (Markus 1994). Another hypothesis is that communication is actually the preferred mechanism for information gathering. Clinical problems are often poorly defined, and clarification can be obtained through conversation. Thus, clinical staff may opportunistically interrupt each other because face-to-face discussion is highly valued but difficult to schedule, and any opportunity is avidly seized.

- *Poor directory information about roles and responsibilities*: Up to a quarter of calls in hospital may be associated with identifying the name of an individual occupying a specific role. This suggests that poor support for identifying role occupants contributes significantly to overall call traffic.

- *Failure to reason about the impact of individual behaviour*: Most clinicians operate to maximize their personal efficiency in serving their patients, but do not seem to reason about the consequences of their behaviour on the overall operational efficiency of their organization. However, the consequence of interrupting colleagues to satisfy individual needs may be a far more inefficient organization overall. This phenomenon is similar to everyone electing to drive a car rather than take public transport because the car is more convenient personally, but the overall impact is congested roads and slower transport times for all on the road.

While it is clear that much more research is needed to understand the nature of clinical communication processes, we can begin to outline the types of intervention that should lead to improved communications.

Non-technical interventions

While it is tempting to immediately suggest new technical solutions, there are a variety of powerful non-technical interventions that can profoundly alter the communication dynamics of an organization:

- *Alter communication behaviours*: Individuals can be encouraged to regard communication behaviours not as a personal style choice but as a professional skill. Educational programmes can emphasize the individual and systemic costs of interruption, and train staff to reason about the costs and benefits of different communication channels and services.

- *Alter communication policies:* Beyond educational interventions, organizations have some power to institute mandatory policies that constrain professional behaviour involving poor communication practice. For example, it might be reasonable to prohibit sending e-mail organization-wide unless strict criteria are met.

Technical interventions

With the merging of information and communication technologies into new classes of communication networks and devices, the opportunity to innovate technically to improve communication is enormous. When faced with a communication task, system designers have the opportunity to introduce a variety of different interventions:

- *Channels:* One of the simplest interventions is to improve organizational infrastructure by introducing new channels for staff. For example, introducing pagers, mobile phones, or e-mail offer new options for interaction amongst staff who might otherwise have difficulty contacting each other. When faced with apparent difficulties in information flows within an organization, one should remember that communication channels are prime bearers of information and are a part of the solution to information problems – the telephone is an information system too! For example, members of a clinical team may spend much of their day geographically separated. Providing team members with an asynchronous channel like a shared 'to-do' list on a wireless palmtop device would allow team members to track each other's activities, and prevent duplication of tasks as well as a check to ensure all team tasks are completed.
- *Communication services:* Communication channels can bear a variety of different services or applications on top of them. The telephone channel, for example, can bear voice, fax and e-mail services. Thus, if analysis of organization call traffic reveals that many calls are attempting to identify who occupies a specific role, or that errors occur because there is failure to contact an individual in a role, then a role-based call forwarding service might help (Coiera 1996). Teams of individuals can also be coordinated using complex role-based calling services. For example, calls to a medical emergency team can be managed by a system that uses knowledge of team roles to ensure that someone in each designated role is called and acknowledges receipt of a call. Such information-enhanced communication systems use specific knowledge about communication patterns and users to optimize the routeing and management of messages.

■ *Types of message:* Fine-grained analysis of communication traffic may reveal that certain classes of messages may benefit from automation. For example, computer-generated alerts can be sent to physicians to notify them of significant clinical events, with substantial clinical benefit (Sullivan and Mitchell 1995). Computer-based notification systems thus integrate with the communication infrastructure of an organization and offer a mechanism to extend the level of interaction between traditional information systems and clinicians. Sometimes, even simpler methods of 'sending' messages can help. For example, individuals in specific roles can be routinely interrupted with the same request from different individuals. Providing a page of information on a Web-based local directory with answers to these frequent questions could reduce the number of calls they receive.

■ *Agents:* The notion that some computational services can act as semi-autonomous proxies for their owners is now well established. Agents can be created that are responsible for creating, receiving or filtering messages. As with humans, there are interesting conflicts between the needs of individuals and organizations. For example, clinicians may wish to instruct an agent to filter certain classes of message they consider annoying, but organizational policy may wish to override such individual preferences when wider concerns are taken into account.

Typically, a communication system will introduce a bundle of new interventions into an organization, each with different effects. For example, introducing a computer-based notification system for alerts will have channel, service and message effects. The channel effect may be positive by permitting a shift of existing events from the synchronous to the asynchronous domain, reducing the number of interruptions. For example, rather than receiving pages from laboratories or the pharmacy, a clinician will instead receive e-mail that can be read at the time of the clinician's choosing. However the message effect of introducing a new communication system may be to generate new types of events in the asynchronous domain. This could increase the overall message load, with consequent increases in demand on user time and effort. Such systems thus have the potential to either harm or help, depending upon which of the effects dominates and the state of the local environment.

THE CONTINUUM OF INFORMATION AND COMMUNICATION TOOLS

The 'continuum' view suggests that developing a richer understanding of the connection between communication and information tasks should help in the design and blending of information and communication technologies. It is easy to

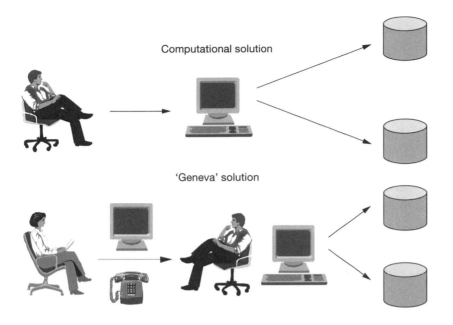

Computational solution

'Geneva' solution

Figure 6.1 *A voice-driven interface to an electronic medical record system can use a computational solution relying on speech technologies, or a hybrid approach using communication and information technology. One design solution developed at the University Hospital in Geneva allowed clinical staff to interact with the medical record via a telephone pool of trained operators.*

Source: Scherrer *et al.* (1990).

construct specific examples where a solution to a problem can be engineered using different mixes of computational or communication technologies. For example, to minimize the efforts of clinical staff in learning to use an electronic record system, one might utilize speech recognition and synthesis technologies. Alternatively, using a communication channel like the phone, and alternative structuring of processes and roles, staff can dictate notes and send orders via trained computer operators (Figure 6.1).

The challenge is to develop a set of principles that permit choices between such alternatives to be made rationally, and to guide the design and implementation of systems along different points of the continuum. From an informatics viewpoint, we can take a 'first principles' approach that regards all informatics tasks as model construction and application. It makes sense therefore to look at how models are handled within information and communication technologies.

In simple terms, we can say that information technologies require explicit formalizations of information processes for them to operate, whilst communication systems remain relatively informal to process models (see also Chapters 3 and 4). A telephone, for example, needs no model of the conversation that occurs across it for it to operate. In contrast, a computer system would need to explicitly model any dialogue that occurs across it. From this point of view, we can say that there is a continuum of possible model formalization available to us. For a given task, system designers make an explicit choice to model some or all of a process, based upon their perception of costs and benefits. When the choice is to formalize the process substantially we will sometimes find computational solutions are used. When the task is left informal, we should instead find that communication solutions are required.

Searching for a similar characterization of the continuum, one can turn to the literature in psychology and linguistics. While much communication research is focused on the specifics of conversational structure, some work does step back and look at the underlying notions of how much of a conversation has been explicitly modelled. In particular, the psychological notion of *common ground* is a strong match with the notion of relative formality of model construction.

Common ground refers to the knowledge shared by two communicating agents. For a conversation to occur, agents have to share knowledge about language as well as knowledge about the subject under discussion. We know intuitively, for example, that discussing a medical problem with a clinical colleague or with a patient results in very different conversations. While messages can be concise and much mutual knowledge can be assumed between colleagues, explaining an issue to a non-expert requires the main message to be sent along with the background knowledge needed to make the message understandable.

Unsurprisingly then, human agents communicate more easily with others of similar occupation and educational background, since they have similar experiences, beliefs and knowledge. Further, the more individuals communicate, the more similar they become. We can recognize sharing of common ground as a key reason that similar agents find it easy to converse with each other. Further, during the process of any given conversation, there are actually two separate streams of dialogue. The first is concerned with the specifics of the conversation, whilst the second is devoted to checking that messages have been understood, and may result in sharing of common ground when it is clear assumptions about shared knowledge do not hold. Thus building common ground requires mutual effort and consent between participating agents.

The notion of common ground holds whether we are discussing a conversational interaction between humans, or a human–computer interaction. For a computationally rendered information system, the system designer must create a model of what the user will want to do with the application. For their part, users will have to learn a model of how to operate the computer application. Where both computer and user share this common ground, the interaction should be succinct and effective. Where the user or system do not share mutual knowledge we run into difficulty. If the user lacks knowledge of the system's operation, the human–computer dialogue will be ineffective. Where the system does not model its context of use, it will be regarded as an inappropriate intrusion into the work place.

Building common ground incurs costs for the participating agents. For example, a computer user spends some time up-front learning the functions of a system in anticipation of having to use them for future interactions. Inevitably, not everything that can be 'said' to the computer is learnt in this way, and users also typically learn new features of a system as they interact with it for particular tasks. This means that agents have two broad classes of grounding choice:

- *Pre-emptive grounding*: Agents can share knowledge prior to a specific conversational task assuming it will be needed in the future. They elect to bear the grounding cost ahead of time and risk the effort being wasted if it is never used. This is a good strategy when task time is limited. For example, training a medical emergency team on how to interact with each other makes sense because at the time of a real clinical emergency, there is no time for individuals to question each other to understand the meaning of any specific orders or requests. Pre-emptive grounding is a bad strategy when the shared knowledge is never used and the time and effort in grounding becomes wasted. For example, training students with knowledge that is unlikely to be used when they face a task in the workplace is usually a poor allocation of resources. From first principles, the cost of pre-emptive grounding is proportionate to the amount of common ground an agent has to learn. For example, the length of messages increases, as does the cost of checking and maintaining the currency of the knowledge once received (Figure 6.2).
- *Just-in-time grounding*: Agents can choose to only share specific task knowledge at the time they have a discussion. This is a good strategy when there are no

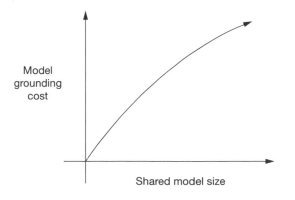

Figure 6.2 *The cost of pre-emptive grounding increases with the amount of knowledge agents share – the more we share, the greater the cost of telling and maintaining.*

other reasons to talk to an agent. For example, if the task or encounter is rare it probably does not make sense to expend resources in the anticipation of an unlikely event. Conversely it is a bad strategy when there is limited task time for grounding at the time of the conversation. For example, if a rare event is nonetheless an urgent one, preparation is essential. Thus pilots, nuclear power plant operators and clinicians all train rigorously for rare but mission critical events, since failure to prepare has potentially catastrophic consequences. Just-in-time is also a poor strategy if one of the agents involved in the dialogue is reluctant to expend energy learning. Thus computer system designers might face difficulties if they assume users are willing to spend time during the routine course of their day learning new features of their system, when the users are already over-committed with other tasks. The cost of just-in-time grounding is inversely proportional to the amount of prior shared knowledge between agents. For example, a message between agents with a high degree of common ground will be very terse, but the length (and thus cost) of transmitting a message to an agent with little common ground will be greater (Figure 6.3).

Any given interaction between two agents usually involves costs borne at the time of the conversation, as well as costs borne previously in pre-emptive grounding (Figure 6.4). For information system designers we thus have a space of choices in regard to the amount of grounding we expect of the agents who will participate in organizational interactions. At the 'solid ground' end of the spectrum, tasks will require agents to share knowledge ahead of time for the task to be effectively or efficiently completed. At the other end of the spectrum there is 'shifting ground', where it is hard or uneconomic to decide what ground should be pre-emptively shared. Thus, with 'solid ground' interactions, a user is expected

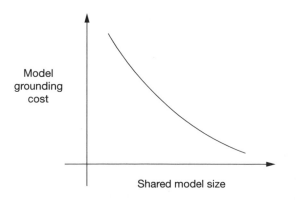

Figure 6.3 *The cost of just-in-time grounding decreases with the amount of prior knowledge agents already share about a task – the less we share, the more I have to share now.*

114

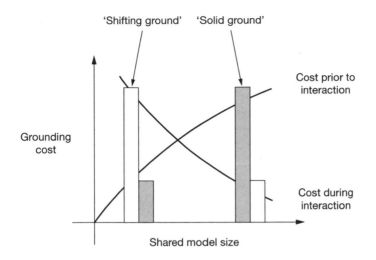

Figure 6.4 *For any given interaction, some of the grounding costs are borne at the time of the interaction, and some have been taken earlier. For an information system designer, this means that there is a spectrum of options in designing the interaction between computer and user.*

to have learnt most of the formalities of using an information system, or conversely the system is expected to have adapted to the needs of the users. With 'shifting ground', the information system is designed to handle interactions that require new knowledge to be exchanged at the time of interaction. This may be in the form of on-line help to the user, or acquiring data from the user.

WHEN IS CONVERSATION BETTER THAN COMPUTATION?

Common ground is a candidate for the 'continuum' parameter that links information and communication system design. It offers us an operational measurement that can be used to define the characteristics of specific interactions between agents, whether they are human or computational. Using it, we should be able to analyse the specifics of a particular set of interactions and make broad choices about whether they would be better served by communication or computational systems. It should also allow us to make finer grained distinctions about the dynamics of such interactions, for example with regard to the amount of grounding that needs to be supported within a specific human–machine conversation. With this in mind, we can now simply regard information models as part of the common ground of an organization and its members. We can choose to model any interaction across a spectrum from zero to a 'complete' formal description (Figure 6.5).

Further, the models we build of our organizational systems only have value when we interact with them through our information or communication systems. In other words, for computational tools to be of value, they have to share ground with humans. Users need to know how to use the system, and the system needs to be fashioned to users' needs. If an information system is perfectly crafted to model the processes of an organization, but not the resource constraints of those who will need to learn to use it, there is inevitability to the logic that predicts its failure. Consequently we should no longer consider information models in isolation but rather include the models that users will need to carry with them. Simply building an information model without regard to how it will be shared with those who interact with it ignores the complex realities of the workplace, and does not factor in the costs and benefits of using the model for individuals.

'Pure' communication tools such as the telephone can now be seen to be neutral to any particular conversation that occurs over them, and need no common ground with the agents using them. As such they are well suited to supporting poorly grounded conversations, when it is hard to predict ahead of time what knowledge needs to be shared. We thus favour the use of communication tools across 'shifting ground' with a high just-in-time grounding component. This may be because the interacting agents do not share sufficient ground or it may be that it is simply not economic to do the modelling. The information transacted is thus often personal, local, informal or rare. It is up to the agents having the discussion to share knowledge. The channel simply provides basic support to ensure the conversation takes place. Communication channels are thus used de facto when there are no computational tools to support the process.

Further, for highly grounded conversations, we know the agents will be able to have succinct conversations. One can predict that they will need lower bandwidth channels than would be the case if the message exchange were poorly grounded. Poorly grounded conversations in contrast will need higher bandwidth, since more information will have to be exchanged between the conversing agents. Building such common ground between agents may require the sharing of information objects such as images and designs.

In contrast, we favour computational tools when it is appropriate to formalize interactions ahead of time, and the users of the system are willing, able and resourced to build common ground with the tool (see, e.g., the standardized care paths discussed in Chapter 5). Such interactions occur over 'solid ground', having a high pre-emptive grounding component. The information exchanged in such situations is worth formalizing, perhaps because it is stable, repetitive, archival, or critical but rare. The computational system moves from being a passive channel to the interaction, to either modifying what is said, or becoming a conversational agent itself.

An information system designer also needs to take into account the common ground that is expected of the system users. For example, the voice-driven electronic record system in Figure 6.1 requires users to both understand their clinical task ground as well as how to operate the electronic tool. For complicated systems the resource implications of mastering both clinical task and tool ground can be unacceptable to users. In contrast, using operators to drive the computer system allows the clinical users to only master their clinical tasks, and leave mastery of the computational system to the operators. Thus, clinicians can devote most of their pre-emptive efforts to clinical tasks, and learn most about the specifics of the computational tool on a needs-only basis during interactions.

For computational tools, there are also choices to be made between the traditional process of information modelling prior to system construction, and a more interactive approach to building models. Thus, a system designer may try to model all the user needs prior to the construction of a system, or engineer some flexibility into the architecture that allows personalization of the interaction for specific users. For example, a system may gather data about the frequency of different requests from a specific user, and customize its behaviour to optimize for the most frequent requests of the individual, rather than the population as a whole. Such computational systems build common ground with their users in a 'just-in-time' fashion, as well as having pre-emptive modelling to cover the commonest features users will need.

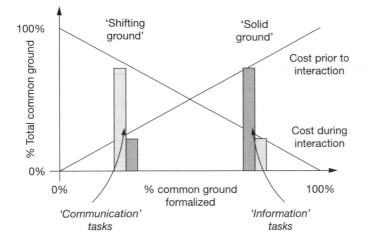

Figure 6.5 *There is a continuum of common ground between agents that defines how much of the interaction can be modelled formally ahead of time, and how much needs to be left informal until the time of the interaction. Computational systems work well when substantial modelling can occur ahead of time, whilst communication systems can be used when agents are unable to reliably model their interactions ahead of time.*

THE INTERACTION SPACE

Typically information system design occurs with a single task assumption that the user is going to be wholly focused on interacting with the system that is being designed. Such 'in vitro' laboratory assumptions do not translate 'in vivo' when individuals use systems in working environments. Since individual agents in an organization are working in a complex environment, they may at any one time be carrying out a variety of tasks and interacting with other agents to help execute those tasks. With the exception of environments where there is rigorous work-flow control, this means that we cannot predict what interactions will actually be occurring at the same time as any interaction we specifically design.

While we cannot predict every specific interaction that will occur in the real work environment, the design process can model the typical *interaction space* within which any new system will be introduced. The interaction space can be modelled to include the most important interactions that will be competing with the new designed interaction. Within the overall interaction space, the *communication space* forms a subset containing interactions that are informal person-to-person exchanges. We can also conceive of an *information space*, which by corollary contains those formally structured interactions that typically rely on information models and computational systems. We saw earlier that the notions of the communication space and information space are probably driven by a dichotomy in communication and information technologies, and that at a more abstract level, they actually are not separate spaces but form different ends of a continuum of explicit task modelling.

To construct the interaction space, we start with a general description of an interaction between two agents, which may either be human, or computational. An agent typically has a number of tasks that need to be carried out, and a pool of resources available to accomplish those tasks. An interaction occurs between two agents when one agent creates and then communicates a message to another, to accomplish a particular task. A *mediated interaction* occurs when a communication channel intermediates between agents by bearing the messages between them. For example, e-mail can be used to mediate an interaction between two individuals, just as can an electronic medical record, which is as much a service to communicate messages between clinical staff, as it is an archival information repository.

The first step in modelling the interaction space surrounding a new interaction we wish to design is to note which other agents will be local to the new interaction, and then to examine the likely effects of any interactions they might have on the new interaction. By doing so we enhance the chance that new interactions will succeed when they are eventually introduced into the intended interaction space. In general terms the impact of one interaction on another may be to (Figure 6.6):

- *Compete with another interaction as a direct substitute.* For example, a user could use an on-line database to seek information, or instead, use the telephone to call a colleague to ask for the same information. The human–human interaction mediated by the telephone competes with the database to meet the user's information needs.

- *Compete with another interaction for the resources of an agent.* An agent has limited resources and if they are expended on one interaction they may not be available to another. For example, an information system may be well received in 'in vitro' laboratory tests, but when placed in a work environment we may find the users have insufficient time to use the system, because of competing tasks. The new system is then 'rejected' not because it does not do what was intended, but because the impact of the real-world interaction space on its intended users was not modelled. Concurrent interactions can also subvert the execution of a designed interaction. For example, a user may be interrupted in the workplace and take up a new task, and not log off the information system they were using, causing a potential breach of security.

- *Create new information transfer pathways, through a combination of interactions.* Each interaction connects agents, and each new interaction enables novel conversations between agents. If these combinations are not factored into system design, then the introduction of a system may produce unexpected results. For example, consider the interaction between a human agent and an electronic patient record system or EPR. Computational agents that might co-exist with the EPR could include other applications like e-mail or a word-processor. If the design process fails to include these additional computational agents, then unintended interactions made possible via these other agents may subvert the original EPR design. For example, it may be possible for a user to copy a section of text from the medical record to a word-processor, where it can be edited, and then re-inserted into the EPR. However, since this interaction with the word-processor is not part of the original design scope, it may introduce problems. A user could inadvertently paste the text into the record of a different patient, and no formal mechanism would be in place to prevent this context-switch error. Similarly, text might be copied from an EPR that has been designed with powerful security features to prevent unauthorized access, and then copied into an e-mail message, which is insecure. In both cases, the co-existence of an unmodelled additional computational agent introduces interactions beyond the scope of the original system design, and permits behaviours which would be prohibited within the designed interaction, but which are permitted in the interaction space.

- *Support the new interaction by providing resources that are critical to its execution.* The designer of a medical record system usually focuses on sculpting the interaction between a single clinical user and the record. However, other human agents also populate the EPR interaction space. The EPR user is often not

119

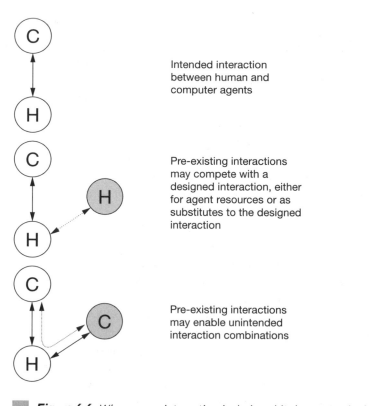

Intended interaction
between human and
computer agents

Pre-existing interactions
may compete with a
designed interaction, either
for agent resources or as
substitutes to the designed
interaction

Pre-existing interactions
may enable unintended
interaction combinations

Figure 6.6 *When a new interaction is designed it does not exist in isolation but is placed within a pre-existing interaction space. Other interactions that exist in the interaction space impact on the new interaction in a variety of ways, and if they are ignored in the design process, these may have unexpected consequences when the new interaction is implemented.*

the sole author of the content that is captured in the record, but is recording the result of a set of discussions with these other clinical colleagues. If the goal of designing an EPR is to ensure the highest quality data is entered into the information system, then it may be even more important to support the collaborative discussion between clinicians, than it is to engineer the act of record transcription into the system. Failing to model the wider EPR inter-action space means we may over-engineer some interactions with diminishing returns, when we could be supporting other interactions that may deliver substantial additional benefit to our original design goals.

CONCLUSION

This chapter has shown how we can approach the design of interactions within an organization by viewing them from the point of view, not of the technology mediating the new interaction, but of the people who are asked to use the new technology.

The communication space is the largest part of the health information space, and seems to contain a substantial proportion of the health system's information 'pathology'. Nevertheless, it has largely been ignored in our informatics thinking. Two implications of acknowledging the primacy of communication have been explored. First, there is an immediate need to support communication in our health care organizations, since this should lead to substantial improvements in organizational efficiency and effectiveness, as well as offering a genuine opportunity to improve patient care. To do this we need to develop a richer understanding of the specific communication systems within our health care organizations. With such an understanding, a variety of technical and non-technical interventions can be brought into play to improve poor communication processes. Second, interaction research is also important in evolving our understanding of the basic principles of informatics. Understanding the interrelationship between communication and information tasks may help us re-evaluate the role of technological support. Common ground is a powerful candidate concept that may help unify our understanding of information and communication in just such a way.

DISCUSSION QUESTIONS

- From your own work environment, give examples of how information or communication technologies support or interfere in the communication space.
- Give examples from your own work environment that fall in each of the four different areas cut out by the curves in Figure 6.4.
- The theory developed in this chapter explicitly addresses the issue of *design* of systems. In health information management, actual system 'design' is less and less common: increasingly, systems are bought 'out of the box'. Does this mean that this chapter is less relevant?

REFERENCES

Bhasale, A.L., G. C. Miller, S. E. Reid and H. C. Britt (1998) Analysing potential harm in Australian general practice: an incident-monitoring study, *Medical Journal of Australia* 169: 73–6.

Coiera, E. (1996) Clinical communication – a new informatics paradigm, *Proceedings of the American Medical Informatics Association Autumn Symposium* 17–21.

Covell D. G., G. C. Uman and P. R. Manning (1985) Information needs in office practice: are they being met?, *Annals of Internal Medicine* 103: 596–9.

Markus, M. L. (1994) Electronic mail as the medium of managerial choice, *Organisation Science* 5(4): 502–27.

Reitman, J. S. (1974) Without surreptitious rehearsal, information in short-term memory decays, *Journal of Verbal Learning and Verbal Behaviour* 13: 365–77.

Safran, C., D. Z. Sands and D. M. Rind (1998) Online medical records: a decade of experience, *Proceedings of EPRIMP*: 67–74.

Scherrer, J. R., R. H. Baud, D. Hochstrasser and O. Ratib (1990) An integrated hospital information system in Geneva, *MD Computing* 7(2): 81–9.

Sullivan, F. and E. Mitchell (1995) Has general practitioner computing made a difference to patient care? A systematic review of published reports, *British Medical Journal* 311: 848–52.

Tang, P., M. A. Jaworski, C. A. Fellencer, N. Kreider, M. P. LaRosa and W. C. Marquardt (1996) Clinical information activities in diverse ambulatory care practices, *Proceedings of the American Medical Informatics Association Autumn Symposium,* 12–16.

Wilson, R. M., W. B. Runciman, R. W. Gibberd, B. T. Harrison, L. Newby and J. D. Hamilton (1995) The quality in Australian health care study, *Medical Journal of Australia* 163: 458–71.

Winograd, T. (1997) The design of interaction. In P. J. Denning and R. M. Metcalfe (eds), *Beyond Calculation – The Next Fifty Years of Computing,* New York: Springer-Verlag.

FURTHER READING

On interaction design

Coiera, E. (2000) When communication is better than computation, *Journal of the American Medical Informatics Association* 7: 277–86.

Coiera, E. (2001) Mediated Agent Interaction. In S. Quaglini, P. Barahona and S. Adreassen (eds), *AIME 2001 – Proceedings of the 8th Conference on Artificial Intelligence in Medicine Europe,* Springer Lecture Notes in Artificial Intelligence No. 2101, Berlin (2001).

Coiera, E. (2003) Interaction design theory, *International Journal of Medical Informatics* 69: 205–22.

Crampton Smith, G. and P. Tabor (1996) The role of the artist-designer. In T. Winorad, *Bringing Design to Software,* New York: ACM Press.

Winograd, T. (1997) The design of interaction. In P. J. Denning and R. M. Metcalfe (eds), *Beyond Calculation – The Next Fifty Years of Computing,* New York: Springer-Verlag.

On the social shaping of technology

Berg, M. (1997) *Rationalizing Medical Work: Decision-support Techniques and Medical Practice.* Cambridge, MA: MIT Press.

Coiera, E. (1999) The impact of culture on technology, *Medical Journal of Australia* 171: 508–9.

Lorenzi, N. M., R. T. Riley, J. C. Blyth, G. Southon and B. J. Dixon (1997) Antecedents of the people and organizational aspects of medical informatics: review of the literature, *Journal of the American Medical Informatics Association* 4: 79–101.

Reeves, B. and C. Nass (1996) *The Media Equation.* Cambridge: Cambridge University Press.

On interruptions

Baddeley, A. D. (1986) *Working Memory.* Oxford: Oxford University Press.

Coiera, E. (2003) *Guide to Health Informatics. 2nd Edition,* London: Arnold.

Coiera, E. and V. Tombs (1998) Communication behaviours in a hospital setting: an observational study, *British Medical Journal* 316: 673–6.

Reason, J. (1990) *Human Error.* Cambridge: Cambridge University Press.

Technical communication support

Coiera, E. (1997) *Informality.* Bristol: HP Laboratories Technical Report HPL-97–37 970212, 1997 (available at http://www.coiera.com/publica.htm).

Coiera, E. and A. Gupta (1999) A communication system for organisations incorporating task and role identification, and personal and organisational communication policy management. US patent 5,949,866, grant September 7, 1999.

Scherrer, J. R., R. H. Baud, D. Hochstrasser and O. Ratib (1990) An integrated hospital information system in Geneva, *MD Computing* 7(2): 81–9.

Wagner, M. M., F. Tsui, J. Pike and L. Pike (1990) Design of a clinical notification system, *Proceedings of the American Medical Informatics Association Autumn Symposium,* 989–93.

On common ground

Clark, H. H. (1996) *Using Language.* Cambridge: Cambridge University Press.

Clarke, H. and S. Brennan (1991) Grounding in communication. In L. B. Resnick, J. Levine and S. D. Behreno (eds), *Perspectives on Socially Shared Cognition.* Washington: American Psychological Association.

Lazarsfeld, P. F. and R. K. Merton (1954) Friendship as social process: a substantive and methodological analysis. In M. Berger, T. F. Abel, C. H. Page and R. M. MacIver (eds), *Freedom and Control in Modern Society.* New York: Octagon.

Ramsay, J., A. Barabesi and J. Preece (1996) Informal communication is about sharing objects and media, *Interacting with Computers* 8(3): 277–83.

Rogers, E. M. (1995) *Diffusion of Innovations, 4th Edition.* New York: Free Press.

Part II

Information strategy, implementation and evaluation

Chapter 7

Information strategy

An introduction

Bert Huisman

KEY POINTS OF THIS CHAPTER

- Decision makers need strategies to coordinate and direct the disparate activities of organizations.
- Strategy is about making choices and managing alignment between functions of the organization.
- There is no generally accepted framework to derive (information) strategies from.
- The strategic application of IT in health care is primarily an effort of developing a vision and culture, process improvement, organizational development, and a network of aligned interests.
- Information strategy formation and implementation needs new methods for dealing with the complexity of the health care sector.
- These methods require health care organizations to invest heavily in the development of a professional, independent, open and flexible workforce, which is able to deal with multifaceted issues and developments.

KEY TERMS

- Strategy
- Information strategy
- Alignment
- Complexity of organizations, wickedness of problems
- Organizational transformation

INTRODUCTION

In Chapter 5, two simultaneous strategies were developed to deal with the tension between the demands for standardization of information systems and the nature of medical work, offering a way to move forward. The first strategy is to unravel care processes and to redistribute information handling and coordination tasks anew between the professionals and between the professionals and the information system. The second strategy is to grant the professionals the skills and resources to manage the tensions between standardization and the unpredictable nature of (the disease of) the patient. The chapter thus introduces two important notions. First, in order to come to grips with the complex problems described in Part I, it is necessary to have some kind of strategy. Implicitly, it is assumed that having a particular strategy will produce the outcomes for which the strategy was developed. Second, this strategy should encompass the redevelopment of hospitals' core processes, organizational structures and possibly context. Such a strategy would be considered to be ambitious by most knowledgeable observers and the effort and risk involved would only be worthwhile if an imperative need to change the outcomes of the hospitals' production (for example on the dimensions of quality and/or productivity) would be felt. We believe that in many countries and health care organizations this need for change is increasingly being felt. In this chapter we endeavour to increase insight into the potential of the concept of strategy as a means of achieving desired results in hospitals, thus laying the basis for systems development, implementation and standardization directions. Strategy in this sense is intended to be the beacon for the multitude of big and small decisions that will have to be made by a great number of people within and outside of the organization as the organizational change process unfolds.

Those with responsible positions (high or low hierarchically, elected or appointed) in health care are in need of coordinating insights and mechanisms, which will allow them to direct their organizations through complex change processes towards desired goals. Doing so, they will have to serve the interests of their stakeholders and fulfil their governance responsibilities, while also taking into account the specific characteristics of the industry as described in the previous chapters. Politicians, executives and managers[1] try to perform these tasks by deploying human and other resources to their organizations' best advantage. This is called *strategy*. Although the term has its origins in the military domain, it has been used in almost all areas of human endeavour where the complexity of decision making increased and leadership and coordination were needed.

Strategy, thus, is about setting goals, a course of action and allocating resources. For larger organizations, among which hospitals can be counted, the goals, actions and resources for one activity or department (such as the information management function) need to be synchronized with the goals and actions set for and the resources allocated to the other activities. This is called *alignment* or fit, which is an essential element of *strategy implementation*.

In this chapter, we will focus on recent issues in strategy and directions for information strategy formation and implementation in health care. We will do so by presenting the debate between theory and practice. We will also address the question whether health care and health care information management are different from other socio-economical activities from the strategy point of view, and whether they thus merit separate treatment. Next, we will distil general directions for new approaches to health care information strategy. In the next chapter, these issues will be filled in further in a series of concrete steps to take and issues to consider in developing an information strategy.

Because of the importance of the alignment of information strategy to an organization's overall strategy, we will start our discussion 'top-down'.

DO WE KNOW WHAT STRATEGY ACTUALLY IS?

In an article called 'What is strategy?' (Porter 1996), Michael E. Porter, perhaps the world's most widely read author on competitive strategy, distinguishes between strategy and the operational effectiveness focus, which dominated business until at least the mid-1990s. Although he does not address health care as such in this article, there are some lessons to be learned from his approach for this industry as well. Operational effectiveness is about productivity, quality and speed. In other words, do we perform similar activities better than rivals? Strategy, according to Porter, is about choosing to perform *different activities* than rivals or perform the same activities in a *different way*. Why do these approaches work out in a different way? If organizations try to compete on doing the same things better than their rivals, they actually compete on their ability to adopt best practices. It has turned out that many companies can become quite good at that game, thus collectively improving operational effectiveness in absolute terms. Relatively, however, this ability to adopt best practices does not help them much. It does not translate into a *sustainable competitive advantage*. Strategy is about choosing to perform (certain) activities other companies do not perform, or perform them in a different way. These choices make the company *different,* with the goal of creating a unique and

129

valuable position. Choosing to be different also implies choosing not to be every-thing to everybody.

Finally, as opposed to operational effectiveness, strategy is about what Porter calls fit (others would call this alignment). Whereas operational effectiveness is about performing certain individual activities better than rivals, strategy is about combining the disparate activities effectively. Strategic fit among activities is funda-mental to competitive advantage, and it is also crucial to the ability to sustain that advantage.

In order to implement the choice to be different and to create an effective fit, planning horizons should be longer than just a single planning cycle, but cover a decade or more. Strategy, according to Porter, is the core responsibility of general management and is about defining a unique position, making clear choices and tightening fit. It also includes communicating the strategy to managers and employees, in order to guide them in making day-to-day choices, which influence the character of the company and the fit between its activities. Of course, opera-tional effectiveness is essential to a company's survival, but it will not provide a sustainable competitive advantage.

The topic of 'strategy' derives from the battle field: in the fourth century BC, Aineias the Tactician already wrote about 'How to survive under siege'. Whether about military or business strategy, however, the common aim of the extensive literature on strategy is how to outdo your opponent or competitor. Another commonality in the longstanding tradition of strategy theories is that these works primarily pay attention to the formation and content of strategies, assuming a fairly unambiguous relationship between the strategy and the multitude of organ-izational transformations that will eventually lead to the achievement of the organizations' objectives. There are at least two reasons to be critical about this assumption. First of all, more than 24 centuries of discussion on the subject have not brought any agreement among practitioners, scientists and theorists about a common framework that can be built upon to derive strategies (De Wit and Meyer, 1998). Second, practice has learned that most proposed strategies result in un-expected and sometimes undesirable transformations and results. Given the nature of technological and organizational change described in Chapter 2, this should not come as a surprise: negotiations and contingencies typify any socio-technical change process of some scale.

As far as information strategies are concerned, they have the tendency to end up in information infrastructures that look more like puzzles than the well-orga-nized and properly aligned tools traditional views would like them to be (Ciborra, 2000; see also Chapter 8).

If an unambiguous relationship between strategy and result is assumed, choosing the proper theoretical framework is very important. This may explain the lively interest management 'gurus' can count on; as if they can provide a secret recipe that will give managers the key to certain competitive advantage. If, however, as we would propose, this relationship is ambiguous at best, the process of strategy formation, implementation and evaluation cannot be reduced to simple 'to do' lists or recipes for success. What is *less* important, then, is the exact theory or methodology an organization adheres to in developing its (information) strategy. What is *crucial*, on the other hand, is to develop organizational capacity which is able to deal with this ambiguity and to understand the organizational *characteristics* and *drivers* underlying the (need for an) information strategy. It is these issues that this and the following chapters will focus on.

CASE STUDY

Case I: On Alignment or Fit: The UK – NHS procurement strategy

The following is an excerpt from the report *Delivering 21st Century IT Support for the NHS, Summary of the overall procurement strategy, 26 July 2002*, of the Department of Health – *http://www.doh.gov.uk/ipu* – 9 May 2003.

In the United Kingdom, the National Health Service (NHS) aims to improve care and services. The current plan depends on transformations in quality, speed and capacity of the organisation. IT and the electronically stored information it handles are key enablers of some of this transformation. With modern IT, information can be captured once and used many times, working practices can be modernised and communications speeded up.

The National Programme for IT in the NHS is designed to connect the capabilities of modern IT to the delivery of the NHS plan. The core of the strategy is to take greater control of the specification, procurement, resource management, performance management and delivery of the information and IT agenda. From a procurement perspective, there are four key elements the Programme intends to manage:

- infrastructure: provision of secure broadband connectivity over an NHSnet backbone and the completion of e-mail and directory services;
- integrated care record services (ICRS) – a broad portfolio of services covering the generation, movement and access to health records;
- electronic appointment booking – an existing project around providing for locally based solutions on booking secondary care appointments and implemented within a national framework;
- electronic transfer of prescriptions – providing a service for the rapid and safe generation and transfer of prescriptions from primary care to the pharmacy of the patient's choice. As far as the procurement strategy is concerned, it must take into account the individual needs and current progress of the four main elements and then develop a strategy for bringing their procurement together into a cohesive whole that the NHS and industry can understand and manage.

131

At the core of the procurement strategy is 'strategic outsourcing', that is, selectively outsourcing major components of the Programme with delivery of some components at a national level via the NHS Information Authority and maximum use of national framework contracts for other services which will comply with national standards. The various elements of the Programme will be outsourced to Prime Service Providers (PSPs) who will manage approved sub-contractors.

This case example illustrates the intention of the NHS to have a procurement process in place which will support its general objectives of improved care and services. These objectives as such have nothing to do with IT, but IT is considered to be an important enabler of the transformations needed to achieve these objectives. Because the information systems which will be deployed will have to support the transformations, it is important to have alignment between the information systems strategy and transformations strategy. It is notable that the Department of Health (DOH) has chosen not just to be explicit about the function of the information systems required (National Programme for IT) but also on the way in which they will have to be procured. This may indicate that the DOH considers the procurement process to be a considerable risk to the success of the National Programme for IT and through that to the success of the general health care programme objectives.

The Procurement strategy may be seen as one layer in the IT-hierarchy of the strategy portfolio of the NHS. The National Programme for IT is meant to be subordinate to the National Plan to improve care and services in the NHS, the Procurement strategy subordinate to the National Programme for IT. The same 'layering' of strategies occurs in other functions of the health care system, such as human resources, buildings and technical services, medical equipment, etc. Maintaining a logical and efficient fit between the overall strategy, the strategy layers of one function and the strategy layers of the other functions is called alignment. In the case of the NHS, alignment is felt to be needed for the entire health care system on a national scale. In many other countries, where the main decision making authority has been vested with regions or individual institutions, the scope of the alignment issue may be smaller.

SHOULD STRATEGY IN HEALTH CARE BE DIFFERENT?

If we focus our attention on the health care industry, the question arises why this sector would merit a different approach than other types of industry. 'Health care is different' is a statement heard quite often from those who are working in the health care industry, mostly to explain to 'outsiders' why concepts used in industry couldn't be applied to health care. Discussing the possibilities for the standardization in health care work, for example, Strauss *et al.* conclude that coordination of care, for which personnel are constantly striving but know they are not often attaining, is something of a mirage, except for the most standardised of trajectories. Its attainment is something of a miracle when it actually occurs.

(Strauss *et al.* 1985, p. 155)

Apart from reasons cited in Part I of this book complexity is identified quite often as an explanation for being different. The word has been and will be used a lot in this book. What do we mean by the word and are we using it correctly, in the sense of not exaggerating?

Many of the present day strategy[2] development situations can be characterized as complex (Mason and Mitroff 1981), because

- Any strategy development situation comprises many problems and issues.
- These problems and issues tend to be highly interrelated. Consequently, the solution to one problem requires a solution to (all) the other problem(s). At the same time, each solution creates additional dimensions to be incorporated in the solutions to other problems.
- Few, if any, problems can be isolated effectively for separate treatment.

Connecting all of these problems are active networks of stakeholders, which are not neutral, in the sense that they will change when one or more problems change. This is called organized complexity. In such an environment, changes in one problem may be transmitted to other problems, changes can be magnified, modified or reverberated, so that the system takes on a life of its own. Problems of organized complexity are also called 'wicked' problems (Rittel 1972). They are characterized as follows:

- *Interconnectedness*. Strong connections link each problem to other problems. As a result, these connections sometimes circle back to form feedback loops. 'Solutions' aimed at the problem inevitably seem to have important opportunity costs and side effects. How they work out depends on events beyond the scope of any one problem.
- *Complicatedness*. Wicked problems have numerous important elements with relationships among them, including important feedback loops, through which a change tends to multiply itself or perhaps even cancel itself out. Generally, there are various leverage points where analysis and ideas for intervention might focus, as well as many possible approaches and plausible programmes of action. There is also the likelihood that different programmes should be combined to deal with a given problem.
- *Uncertainty*. Wicked problems exist in a dynamic and largely uncertain environment, which creates a need to accept risk, perhaps incalculable risk.

Contingency planning and also the flexibility to respond to unimagined and perhaps unimaginable contingencies are both necessary.

- *Ambiguity*. The problem can be seen in quite different ways, depending on the viewer's personal characteristics, loyalties, past experiences, and even accidental circumstances of involvement. There is no single 'correct view' of the problem.

- *Conflict*. Because of competing claims, there is often a need to trade off 'goods' against 'bads' within the same value system. Conflicts of interest among persons or organizations with different and even antagonistic value systems are to be expected. How things will work out may depend on interaction between powerful interests that are unlikely to enter into fully cooperative arrangements.

- *Societal constraints*. Social, organizational and political constraints and capabilities, as well as technological ones, are central to both the feasibility and the desirability of solutions.

For those practising in health care, many of the characteristics of complexity will be very recognizable. Why is this important? Not because it is useful to classify health care as 'more complex' than other types of industry. There is no benefit in a competition in complexity. It is useful however to recognize many problems in health care as wicked problems, because this will help the health care practitioner in developing approaches to his (strategic) problems and it will provide directions (see the next section, p. 136).

Looking at Porter's answer to the 'What is strategy?' question, there may be another reason why the hospital industry may actually differ from other industries. For managers of hospitals, the liberty to choose a *different* position is in many countries severely limited because of budgetary and other restraints. Quite the opposite, governments and the public opinion in many countries strive for the same quality of care for everybody, regardless of income, age or place of residence. The context, in other words, does not allow health care managers much freedom to design their own goals. On the contrary, there are many incentives to be *the same*. If we follow Porter's reasoning, this inevitably leads to a focus on operational effectiveness and a best practice culture concentrating on standard *individual activities and not on aligning some of these activities into a unique service or product not available elsewhere*. If the unravelling and redistribution of (information handling) tasks (see Chapter 5), requires such an integration of individual activities, i.e. change *beyond* operational effectiveness, strategy development in health care organizations may be seriously hampered. Maybe this explains why there is so little literature on strategy for hospitals, at least in the European context, as opposed to literature on hospital management (focus on operational effectiveness). Certainly, literature comparing strategy approaches on the hospital level in Europe is rare (McKee and Healy 2002).

A final issue differentiates health care from many other industries and heavily influences the abilities of health care providing organizations to develop and implement strategies. In Chapters 2 and 3, we described the tensions between traditional characteristics of medical work and the (potential) impact of technology. As most highly trained professionals, medical professionals and IT have a problematic relationship. IT enables codification of medical knowledge, transparency in medical treatments, standardization of work processes and new ways of collaboration with less qualified professionals (task redistribution), all of which have a direct impact on the professional autonomy and identity of medical professionals. IT, in other words, has the real potential to affect the professional and economic position of medical professionals: the development of the patient–doctor (1:1) relationship into a patient–health care team (1:many) relationship requires a sometimes dramatic redefinition of roles, responsibilities and positions.

If health care organizations were hierarchically structured like 'ordinary' companies, the professionals' worries may be overcome through enforcing the required organizational change (although in such 'ordinary' environments this is by no means easy either). In professional bureaucracies like hospitals, there is no simple hierarchical line of command between the hospital directors and the medical staff. 'Resistances' of the staff (one of the most frequent reasons for PCIS implementation failure) have to be overcome through argument, through emphasizing benefits and a host of other such instruments.

In this environment, the development of a framework to build strategies certainly is no easy task. Implementing the strategy and achieving alignment (fit) may be even more difficult. Therefore, we will now turn to the question of IT strategy in hospitals and health care.

CASE STUDY

Case II: on strategy implementation: the UK – NHS experience

The NHS has a long history of ambitious IT strategies. Equally, however, it has a long history of disappointments in meeting the targets set out in the strategies. Even if alignment is produced on paper (see the previous Case Study Box), *in practice* the NHS IT strategy has generally favoured a technology-driven approach over an organization-driven approach. In doing so, it has similarly massively underestimated the complexities of providing IT that provide 'solutions' for problems that practitioners actually have (see also Chapter 2). One can plead for an 'integrated record' including NHS organizations and private nursing homes, for example, but this is hardly a technical problem: this is first and foremost about ensuring *cooperation* between NHS sites and private nursing homes. Thinking about how that cooperation should look, who should initiate it, who should bear what costs cannot be second thoughts to a technology-driven 'solution'. All this, two observers argued in 2001, is 'a massive organizational development project involving the whole NHS. That beige box on your desk is the agent of fundamental changes in clinical work, whose implications have not yet been established' (Wyatt and Keen 2001).

IT STRATEGY IN HEALTH CARE ORGANIZATIONS

General criteria for strategy formation

In Part I of this book, the practice of IT development in health care has been discussed. For the purpose of this chapter, searching for strategy tools to support better system development and implementation practices, it will suffice to repeat the conclusion that the implementation of IT as a process-supporting tool has been very problematic. Many aspects of IT strategy and IT management (the terms sometimes overlap) in health care have been intensively researched, but, as with general strategy, there is insufficient basis to select just one proven approach.

In health care as well as in other industries, there is a distinction between strategy formation and strategy implementation. IT strategy and organizational strategy should be linked, and the internal IT capabilities and characteristics should be well developed. The importance of strategy formation should not be underestimated: after all, a well executed flawed strategy heads down the wrong path. Crucial are in particular the 'concepts, ideas and definitions, that govern how an organization views a particular IT challenge or opportunity. The importance of foundational concepts and view . . . is significant' (Glaser and Hsu 1999, p. 126). Finally, the IT strategy should be an integral, ongoing component of the overall organizational strategy development process (see also Chapter 8). The characteristics of strategy implementation in general and health care in particular (complexity, alignment of heterogeneous actors, the need for a strong vision) require specific ways of approaching strategy development. First of all, wicked problems of organized complexity (Mason and Mitroff, 1981) have two major implications for the design of strategy-making processes:

- There must be a broader participation of affected parties, directly and indirectly, in the decision making process.
- Strategy making must be based on a wider spectrum of information gathering from a larger number of sources.

For *strategy formation* in complex organizations new general criteria are needed for the design of real world problem-solving methods (ibid.). We focus on these methods because the content of the strategy can be very different from case to case. These criteria are:

- Methods need to be *participative*: since the relevant knowledge necessary to solve a complex problem and also the relevant resources necessary to implement the solution are distributed among many professional and independent individuals, the methods must incorporate the active involvement of (groups of) people with an interest or stake. This implies first building an organization and network that is able to deal with sometimes dramatic changes in both the external (new government regulations or de-regulations) and the internal context (re-distribution of tasks, re-organizations). Second, the personal development of the stakeholders involved should be promoted in order to provide them with the insights, maturity and flexibility needed to support such an organization. Third, use flexible information systems to facilitate the necessary transformation and development process (sometimes supporting it, sometimes provoking it, sometimes enabling it). Fourth, unleash the creativity of the professionals by providing them with the (IT) tools that allow them to contribute to desired strategic outcomes, without squeezing them in a top-down approach.
- Methods need to be *adversarial*: in complex problems, the best judgement on the assumptions embedded in certain opinions or choices is rendered in the context of opposition. Doubt is the guarantor of mature decisions. To enable this, fostering a culture of openness and critical discussion throughout the organization, including top management is necessary. Individual and/or group coaching can support this. Permanent evaluation of strategies and projects will also improve transparency and provide opportunities to deal with new developments.
- Methods need to be *integrative*: a unified set of assumptions and a coherent plan of action are needed to guide effective strategy formation. Participation and the adversarial process tend to differentiate and expand the knowledge base. Something else is needed to bring this diverse but relevant knowledge together in the form of a total picture, which can be the basis for day-to-day decision making. This implies permanently building and maintaining coalitions in order to create the basis for coordinated action by the organization. In the professional context of hospitals, *maintaining support* for strategy implementation is at least as important as the strategy formation itself. Also, focusing on long-term outcomes of the combinations of organizational development and information technology is necessary. This is a management responsibility (top-down). However, getting results requires constant tinkering on the implementation level, which may create bewilderment and distrust in the organization. Management should realize that integrative also means that the strategy should be *borne* by the organization instead of *accepted*, thus creating the basis for dealing with the confusion of the actual implementation.
- Last but not least, methods must be *managerial mind supporting*: most problem-solving methods and computer aids focus on 'decision support systems', that

is, on systems that provide guidance for choosing a particular course of action to solve a particular problem. Problems of organized complexity however, are ongoing, ill structured and generally 'wicked'. The choice of the individual courses of action is only part of the manager's need. More important is the insight into the nature of complexity and to formulate concepts and world-views for coping with it. It is the manager's thinking process and his mind that needs to be supported. This implies that leadership and leadership develop-ment, not just for and by top management, are essential to allow health care providing organizations to address the challenges of this decade. Deliberate management development programmes combined with intensive (external) training programmes will prepare managers to develop personalities which are able to deal with the sometimes bewildering complexity of the sector (education through – international – comparative health care (IT) manage-ment studies, knowledge transfer, experience sharing, project coaching, inter-vision, etc.).

All in all, a core insight is that it is the pre-existing capabilities of an organization to procure the tools it needs, which determines its ability to deliver new compe-tences. These pre-existing capabilities are rooted in the institutional arrangements and the culture of the organization, which govern not just the execution of current routines, but also the enactment of new socio-technical innovations (Ciborra 2001).

CASE STUDY

Case III: On organizational learning: the Danish National Health Informatics Strategy 2003–2007

The central vision for the future information systems in the Danish health care sector is one of a generally accepted, common information model enabling comprehensive digital reuse of shared clinical data. A generic 'Basic EHR struc-ture' has been developed for this purpose by the National Board of Health. The strategy contributes to the national political goals for health: high quality, shorter waiting lists, satisfaction with care delivery, reliable information on service and quality, efficiency and effectiveness and freedom of choice. The health informatics strategy is intended to support these goals through the full interoperability and digital reuse of clinical information.

The objectives for the planning period are:

■ empowering consumers for active participation: citizens are able to interact on a basis of access and control over their health information;
■ the patient in a central position: shared information relevant to the health care process between different parties;

- IT to become an integrated part of the clinical process: integrated into daily work in the form of EHR, health information systems and seamless communication;
- IT to support health care: all hospitals should have an EHR by the end of 2005, sharing a common information model and standards for data, classifications and coding systems;
- to gain the potential medical and organizational benefits of IT in health care (Lippert and Kverneland 2003).

In this case, the objectives of the Danish government are not primarily related to IT but to improved outcomes of the health care system. On the individual hospital level this implies a process of socio-technical change. If a hospital's capacity to deliver new competences is indeed based on its pre-existing capabilities to procure itself the tools it needs, the focus of the Danish project should be on growing mature and professional attitudes towards change and acquiring or organizing the supporting resources. It will be a major effort to develop such attitudes, particularly because they will have to be grown over time instead of just being communicated. Communication between different parties and seamless communication, as the strategy intends to deliver, make this challenge all the more daunting. The nature of medical work and the position of health care professionals make the objective to have all hospitals use an EHR by the end of 2005, sharing a common information model and standards for data, classifications and coding systems a really ambitious one indeed.

Handling the 'installed base'

The challenge thus is to design infrastructures, which can support new ways of operating, but also, in parallel and particularly during implementation, to stretch the capabilities of the organization beyond what it can achieve today. This implies complex exercises of organizational learning.

Because of their fragmentation, hospital information architectures consist of many 'local orders', which interact *and* interfere with each other. The more connections there are, the more unintended side effects – and the more disorder is created when pursuing local order. A twofold strategy might deal with this. On the one hand, architectures should be built that avoid being trapped into the installed base (the fight against the installed base). Thus, the architecture should be as flexible as possible through modularization and simplicity (see also Chapter 5). This implies independent systems for smaller units, simple interfaces and the use of gateways. On the other hand, the installed base may be made an ally, by designing new infrastructures that build upon it, rather than establishing a new one (Hanseth *et al.* 1996; Ciborra 2001; Timmermans and Berg 2003).

Case IV: On obtaining a functional and flexible IT portfolio: single-source strategies – one-stop shopping for health care software

As opposed to 'best-of-breed' strategies, the single-source strategy relies on just one IT vendor for the majority of information systems. Because health care IT becomes more complex, having a strategic relationship with one major vendor is more important than buying a product. Obviously, the vendor should be a stable partner in the long term. In the unstable health care IT market this may pose a challenge.

Benefits reportedly include:

- more attention and support from vendor;
- cost reduction on maintenance;
- cost reduction on integration, better integration;
- improved integrated technology management;
- less management effort to achieve integrated network and systems.

Potential disadvantages are:

- missing out on more sophisticated applications offered by other vendors;
- dependency in case vendor is purchased or goes out of business;
- vendors may charge integration fees anyway.

Some hospitals even outsource their IT departments to the single source supplier. Some organizations hold shared strategy sessions with their supplier. Most single source suppliers will integrate systems from other vendors if clients decide to choose for such a solution or they may have an alliance with vendors of systems which they cannot provide themselves and act as main contractors. An intermediate approach is the so-called 'best-of-cluster' strategy (Kelly 2002).

From the hospital strategy point of view, IT capabilities should be aligned with process improvement or other developments in the organization. In practice, obtaining the proper systems can be the subject of a complicated internal nego-tiation process, which will also involve external stakeholders, such as (potential) vendors and consultants, amongst others. Given the great number of systems hospitals tend to use on the one hand and the need for integration of information on the other, alignment of the IT portfolio as a whole is imperative. Long term contracts may facilitate or hamper an organization's ability to adapt to evolving strategies. Careful consideration of which systems may qualify for a single source strategy is necessary.

IT infrastructures that are intended to standardize work processes on the level of the organizations as a whole are adopted locally in many different ways. The *deployed* infrastructure (i.e. as it is being used) thus has to be considered as the outcome of interactions between 'top-down' design and 'bottom-up' adoption. Insights from the local level frequently are adopted at the top level. Combining 'top-down' and 'bottom-up' approaches creatively will allow organizations to harness the power of the periphery, as opposed to seeing it as a source of resistance (ibid.).

SUMMARY

In this chapter, we have discussed strategy issues, related to integrating IT in health care work. Building on the first part of this book, we have taken the position that the formation and implementation of health care IT strategy has proven to be problematic. We have set out to find out why this may be the case and to discover approaches that may be more successful.

Based on the work of Porter, we have described strategy and distinguished it from operational effectiveness. We have then demonstrated that there is no agreement among practitioners, scientists and theorists as to what strategy actually is. We have asked the question whether the health care sector deserves special attention regarding strategy formation and implementation and have identified several characteristics that indeed set it apart from most other types of industry. The most important characteristics can be described by the terms 'organized complexity' and 'wicked problems'. Combined with the fluidity of the strategy concept, these characteristics confront health care managers with a considerable challenge.

We have concluded that it is wise to be wary of simple, straightforward recipes for the integration of health care work and IT. The strategic application of IT in health care is primarily an effort of process improvement, organizational development, developing a vision and culture, and a network of aligned interests, which is able to initiate and complete the changes related to this type of development.

DISCUSSION QUESTIONS

1   In some countries, like the UK and Denmark, the national government has developed a strategy dedicated to the use of information systems in hospitals. These strategies presuppose relatively standardized approaches to the implementation and use of these systems. What would be the preconditions for such a strategy to be successful? Which alignment issues would be likely to occur? What could be done to deal with these issues?

2   In countries like Sweden the health care system is run by county councils, politically elected leaders. Would their political background lead to different

information strategies than in countries in which individual hospitals are independent in designing their (information) strategy? And what if these hospitals would be for-profit instead of not for profit? Explain and argue.

3   When dealing with wicked problems, changes in one aspect influence (many of the) other aspects and possibly are influenced themselves again by the waves this process creates in the organization. What influence do developments in the information systems industry, such as the Open Source movement or digital imaging, have on strategy development in health care organizations? Do these influences generate new alignment issues and if so, consider which ones.

4   Standardization within the field of health care informatics is by many considered to be a precondition for a properly functioning health care system, allowing professionals to communicate about their patients in a seamless way. Implementation of standards is however lagging. Design a strategy to increase acceptance of standards in health care and to speed up building these standards into systems.

NOTES

1   For the sake of simplicity, we will not go into a discussion of managers versus executives and will use the term manager in a broad sense of someone having responsibility for parts of or the whole organization.

2   In their original work, Mason and Mitroff use the term 'policy'. For the purposes of this chapter, this term can be used interchangeably with 'strategy'.

REFERENCES

Ciborra, C. U. and associates (2000) *From Control to Drift, the Dynamics of Corporate Information Infrastructures*. Oxford: Oxford University Press.

De Wit, B. and R. Meyer (1998) *Strategy: Process, Content, Context*. London: International Thomson Business Press.

Glaser, J. P. and L. Hsu (1999) *The Strategic Application of Information Technology in Health Care Organizations*. Boston: Jossey-Bass.

Hanseth, O., E. Monteiro and M. Hatling (1996) Developing information infrastructure: the tension between standardization and flexibility, *Science, Technology and Human Values* 21: 407–26.

Kelly, B. (ed.) (2002) Single-source strategies: one-stop shopping for health care software, *Health Data Management* August.

Lippert, S. and A. Kverneland (2003) *The Danish National Health Informatics Strategy 2003–2007*. Denmark: The National Board of Health.

Mason, R. and I. Mitroff (1981) *Challenging Planning Assumptions*. Chichester: Wiley.

McKee, M. and J. Healy (eds) (2002) *Hospitals in a Changing Europe*. Buckingham: Open University Press.

Porter, M. E. (1996) What is strategy?, *Harvard Business Review*, November–December.

Rittel, H. (1972) On the planning crisis, systems analysis of the 'First and Second Generations', *Bedriftsokonomen* 8: 390–6.

Strauss, A., S. Fagerhaugh, B. Suczek and C. Wiener (1985) *Social Organization of Medical Work*. Chicago: University of Chicago Press.

Timmermans, S. and M. Berg (2003) *The Gold Standard: An Exploration of Evidence-Based Medicine and Standardization in Health Care*. Philadelphia: Temple University Press.

Wyatt, J. and J. Keen (2001) The new NHS Information Technology strategy, *British Medical Journal* 322: 1378–9.

FURTHER READING

On strategy

Andrews, K. (1980) *The Concept of Corporate Strategy, 2nd edn*. Homewood, IL: Dow-Jones Irwin.

Johnson, G. and K. Scholes (2000) *Exploring Corporate Strategy*. Englewood Cliffs: Prentice Hall.

Liddell Hart, B. H. (1967) *Strategy*. New York: Basic Books.

Mintzberg, H. (1994) *The Rise and Fall of Strategic Planning*. New York: Prentice Hall.

Sanchez, R. and A. Heene (eds) (1997) *Strategic Learning and Knowledge Management*. Chichester: John Wiley and Sons.

Steiner, G. (1979) *Strategic Planning*. New York: Free Press.

Treacy, M. and F. Wiersema (1994) *The Discipline of Market Leaders*. Reading, MA: Addison-Wesley.

Tregoe, B. and J. Zimmerman (1980) *Top Management Strategy*. New York: Simon and Schuster.

Chapter 8

Developing the information strategy

Cé Bergen and Marc Berg

KEY POINTS OF THIS CHAPTER

- Given the importance of information technology for health care institutions, the choices embodied in the information strategy directly affect organization strategy. They should thus be a responsibility of the Board of Directors.
- The information strategy document should state clearly which IT projects will be undertaken and how these relate to the organizational ambitions.
- Formulating the information strategy consists first of listing the organization's ambitions and priorities. Second, corresponding ambitions for information management should be formulated. Finally, projects should be outlined to realize the information system functions that, in their turn, will materialize the stated ambitions.
- The Board of Directors and line management are responsible for the proper use of IT as a tool to reach business objectives. The information management department advises them, and is responsible for the technical functioning of the software and hardware.
- Information management expertise is necessarily decentralized across the organization.
- Guidelines for technical infrastructure and technical standards are mandatory to afford decentralized information management.
- The projects and activities that stem from the information management ambitions can often not be carried out concurrently. A ranking principle needs to be agreed to determine the sequence.

KEY TERMS

- Information strategy development
- IT alignment
- Integrated patient logistics planning
- Standardized care path

INTRODUCTION

In the previous chapter, we discussed the importance of developing an information strategy, and we outlined some of the difficulties that await strategy development in complex environments such as health care institutions. In this chapter, focusing on the individual health care organization, we will provide the reader with steps and guidelines for developing the information strategy.

Information technology is recognized by most health care organizations as a critical success factor in achieving the levels of ambition the organization sets itself. Given the importance of information technology to the organization, the choices embodied in the information strategy are strategic choices and thus a responsibility of the Board of Directors (BoD). The Board should issue the order for the drawing up or updating of the information strategy, and should chair the taskforce that takes up this task.

The information strategy lays down which IT developments the health care organization will occupy itself with in the coming years, which priorities it implements in this respect, and in what period the developments will lead to tangible results. In particular, an information strategy is about *choices:* which of the many possible and desirable IT developments and applications to pursue, which to postpone, which to let lie. It should state clearly which IT projects will be undertaken and how these relate to the organizational ambitions.

This chapter on information strategy development in health care organizations is intended as a practical manual for the information manager allowing him or her to develop a health care organization information strategy. The chapter first considers the aims of the information strategy document and the process of evolving the information strategy. Thereafter it deals with the most important themes to be considered in an information strategy. We will pay particular attention to the first step of setting up the information strategy: how to set the IT ambition level in proper relation to the organizational ambition level. This is part and parcel, of course, of ensuring the 'alignment' discussed in the previous chapter.

PURPOSE OF THE INFORMATION STRATEGY DOCUMENT

The purpose of the information strategy document is to enable a coordinated vision on the information management of the health care organization. The time frame for this vision should be something between three and five years: after all, IT possibilities can change dramatically in such a period.

As argued in the previous chapter, the information strategy must be a derivation of the organizational strategy, or, better still, an integral part of it. That is to say, the information strategy should include a coordinated vision on the care the health care organization provides, and on the supporting processes that make this care possible. This vision should subsequently inform the framework for positioning and testing individual IT activities. The need for such a coordinated vision is particularly evident given a rough average of some 130 projects requested in a mid-sized health care organization, in the context of the annual planning and control cycle.

Furthermore, the information strategy must provide a clear framework that will support and structure the discussions within the organization on IT expectations. Finally, the information strategy needs to be inspirational, and should lead to support within the organization for its content. Figure 8.1 illustrates this.

DRAWING UP AND UPDATING THE INFORMATION STRATEGY

Given the importance to the organization of information management, the information strategy is drawn up at the request of the Board of Directors. Often a special task force will be created to develop the information strategy document. This task force should be chaired by the Board member responsible for the information management portfolio, or, alternatively, by the institution's information manager. Given the importance of the information strategy document, it is crucial that the task force has a chair positioned at a high level in the institution's management hierarchy. The task force should further comprise line managers who are mandated by their peers to make strategic decisions on topics that address departmental interests.

The initial writing of the information strategy document can easily take between three and six months. Most of this time is spent on discussions with a broad group of strategic and tactical managers in the organization. These discussions are crucial to reach a mutual understanding and to align the information strategy with the departmental and organizational strategy. (In practice, this often implies a *mutual* adjustment of the organizational to the information strategy and vice versa.) This time investment, however, will be repaid through broad support for information management within the organization.

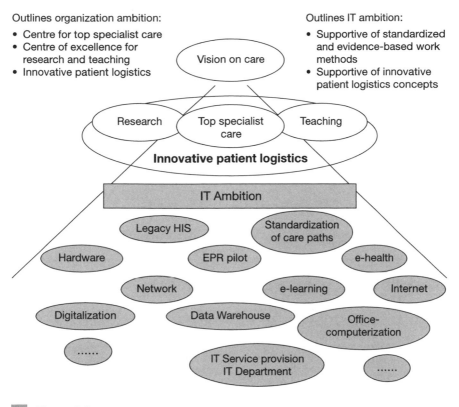

Outlines organization ambition:
- Centre for top specialist care
- Centre of excellence for research and teaching
- Innovative patient logistics

Outlines IT ambition:
- Supportive of standardized and evidence-based work methods
- Supportive of innovative patient logistics concepts

Figure 8.1 *IT ambition offers a vision on the positioning of individual IT activities.*

A good working model for drawing up the information strategy is a small core team within the task force that conducts interviews within the organization and prepares the task force meetings. The task force meetings are held in the form of workshops. One or more workshops are conducted per information strategy theme.

Three rules are important when drawing up the information strategy:

1   Drawing up the information strategy is a top-down process. In making the core choices and laying out the overall framework, the Board of Directors have to take the lead to make choices in the frequent conflicts of interest between organization sections, strengthened by the zero sum game of the budgeting process.
2   Drawing up the information strategy starts with listing the organization's ambitions and priorities. A clear and concise list of ambitions allows grounding the choices that will have to be made later. This rule is also vital to avoid

starting with a summary of all the shortcomings of the *current* information management and IT situation. The danger is that a plan is drawn up to address today's problems, without considering the necessary longer-term developments.

3   The discussion on whether funds are or are not available has to be postponed to the last phase of the information strategy development. This is necessary to allow the required future visions to clearly emerge. Only when the outlines of the information strategy have become clear should discussion focus on the resources needed.

Once drawn up, the information strategy needs to be kept updated in tandem with the planning and control cycle. This will often mean that the information strategy is updated in the spring of each year. Excluding exceptional circumstances, the information strategy is commonly rewritten every two to three years.

THEMES OF AN INFORMATION STRATEGY

An information strategy should generally deal with the following themes:

- a generic conceptual model that categorizes the institution's work process areas and corresponding IT support, into relevant building blocks;
- the ambitions for information management, in relation to the organization ambitions;
- responsibilities and organization of information management;
- guidelines on the development or selection of information systems and information system implementations;
- guidelines on the technical infrastructure and standards;
- priorities for information management and the financial framework.

Of course, depending on the institution's specific situation, other themes can be relevant as well.

Generic conceptual model of building blocks

As we saw in the first part of this book, health care organizations are organized around a complex production process: the process of care delivery. There is an enormous diversity of specialized care delivery processes, for example outpatient planning, laboratory sample processing, etc. And the health care organization, just like any other organization, also has its normal organization-supporting work processes: financial work processes, material logistics work processes, etc. In drawing up the information strategy, a broad area of work processes is covered.

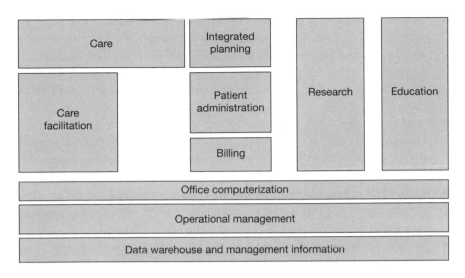

Figure 8.2 *A generic conceptual model of work process areas structures the discussion.*

The conceptual model shown in Figure 8.2 helps to structure the discussion. It offers a starting point for the information strategy that is centred on work processes rather than on organizational departments or traditional information system module divisions. Simultaneously, it offers a starting point for augmenting these work process areas with 'best of breed' information system modules.

This categorization, for example, would lead one to consider a clinical trajectory planning system, instead of separate waiting-list registration and operation room planning systems. Similarly, rather than considering purchasing, warehousing and financial handling systems separately, one would here consider material logistics as an integrated purchase-order-to-delivery work process requiring integrated information systems support.

A short explanation of the segments:

- *Care*: This segment consists of the work tasks of the primary care providers and the information system functions aimed at supporting this work: electronic order entry and result systems, electronic order status management, electronically supported care pathways and so forth.
- *Care facilitation*: This segment consists of the work processes of those diagnostic and therapeutic activities that are carried out by separate units to facilitate the primary care work: radiology, laboratories, pharmacy, pathology, functional departments and so forth. It includes the information system functions intended to support these departments (laboratory information systems, radiology information systems, PACS).

149

- *Integrated planning*: This consists of the organization-wide integrated planning work processes, sometimes performed by a separate care activities planner, and the information system functions aimed at supporting this. To make the step towards integrated patient logistics, this segment needs to result in a fully integrated agenda of the patient, making visible all activities provided for the patient.
- *Patient administration*: This consists of the patient-administrative work processes, such as patient registration, contact registration and activities registration for financial ends, and the information system functions supporting these tasks.
- *Billing*: This segment consists of the invoicing process, and the information systems supporting this. As the patient administration segment, this segment is primarily concerned with the role of administrative worker.
- *Research*: This consists of information system functions aimed at supporting the work processes associated with the role of scientific researcher;
- *Education*: This consists of information system functions aimed at supporting the work processes associated with delivering health care education;
- *Office automation*: This segment consists of information system functions aimed at supporting the role of office worker, in broad terms;
- *Operational management*: This consists of information system functions aimed at supporting work processes aimed at financial administration, purchasing, building maintenance, human resource management and so forth.
- *Data warehouse and management information*: This consists of information system functions aimed at supporting the work processes associated with generating, refining and distributing management information, in broad terms.

The perceptive reader will realize that this categorization of work processes already assumes a certain orientation of the organization and the information strategy. This patient-centred and work-process oriented model, after all, separates 'integrated planning' as a distinct and core health organization work process, for example. It is therefore less useful for organizations that do not *want* to plan in an integrated fashion, or attempt to position the planning of the patient's trajectory as leading to the planning of the individual capacities. This model, in other terms, already assumes a set of ambitions resembling those explicated in Chapter 5. This is not to say that this model is *only* useful when one *fully* embraces these aims: the point to note, here, is that models such as these are not neutral to one's aims. In the remainder of the chapter, we will therefore assume that the health institution's organization strategy resembles (some of the core parts of) the ambitions outlined in Chapter 5.

Aligning ambitions

The first step in formulating the information strategy is listing the organization's ambitions and priorities. Then follows the process of formulating a corresponding ambition for information management, and the listing of an outline of projects that follows from the stated information management ambition: the project's Master Plan.

CASE STUDY

Southern Medical

In this paragraph, we will use the example of Southern Medical, a large general hospital.[1] This hospital's ambitions are:

- to achieve a high standard of health care delivery as a general hospital for the region;
- to provide highly specialized care for a selected number of medical domains;
- to further strengthen its position as a teaching hospital;
- to fundamentally improve patient logistics, while
  - starting from the perspective of the patient;
  - increasing the number of patient cases handled each year; and
  - keeping total costs at the current level.

In order to meet these primary targets, the hospital has embraced the principles outlined in Chapter 5 as the core means through which to meet these goals.

Care, care facilitation and integrated planning: the 'primary proccsses'

The segments care, care facilitation and integrated planning, as described in the previous paragraph, together make up the health care organization's primary process. Since from the perspective of the care provider, these segments are closely related, they are here listed together. (This paragraph will not address specific IT ambitions of individual functions of the organization, such as medical specialties or diagnostic departments. See further on the rules for dealing with such ambitions.)

The starting point of formulating the information strategy management ambitions is the listing of the organization's ambitions.

CASE STUDY

Southern Medical's visions on care, care facilitation and integrated planning

Core concepts for the work processes of care, care facilitation and integrated planning:

- Our hospital is a general hospital for the region, providing the full range of medical facilities that may be expected from a general hospital.
- Our hospital aims to be an innovative teaching hospital for the population in the region, with selected highly specialized functions.
- In order to strengthen our capacity to become an innovative teaching hospital with top specialist functions, our focus is on optimal evidence-based care provision and the generation of medical evidence.
- To us, the quality of, and care for, employees is crucial.
- In addition, our hospital strives towards streamlining work processes of care delivery in a patient-centred way. This should lead to a higher standard of quality of care, and a reduction in pre- and in-hospital waiting times. This streamlining should also lead to improved possibilities for offering high quality coordinated patient care for patient groups at a favourable cost.
- Finally, our hospital aims to promote cross-functional integrated care delivery in the region; to improve patient logistics region wide. This refers primarily to collaboration with family doctors, nursing- and elderly-homes and home care organizations in the region.

The next step in formulating the information management ambition is to match these organizational ambitions with statements on how IT will contribute to realizing these ambitions. At the most generic level, the use of IT is aimed at striving towards an optimal availability of information and an optimal support of the work processes with information systems. More concretely, following the ambitions laid out in Chapter 5, core considerations are to realize that professionals have:

- a complete overview of all available patient information, from multiple dimensions (see Figures 8.3 and 8.4);
- the ability to request and monitor standard care paths electronically;
- one organization-wide patient agenda (see Figure 8.5);
- the ability to initiate and monitor care activities. In order to allow task re-distribution, who may do which activities should not be too restricted (for example, a registered nurse must be able to order and plan an outpatient visit preceded by a radiology examination).

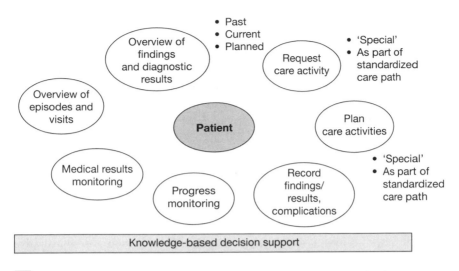

- Past
- Current
- Planned

Overview of findings and diagnostic results

Request care activity

- 'Special'
- As part of standardized care path

Overview of episodes and visits

Patient

Plan care activities

Medical results monitoring

Progress monitoring

Record findings/ results, complications

- 'Special'
- As part of standardized care path

Knowledge-based decision support

Figure 8.3 *Overview of elements of IT support in care and care facilitation.*

The overview of elements of the patient care information system in Figure 8.3 is primarily concerned with the type of functions necessary in the primary process in order to be able to work using standardized care paths. Knowledge-based decision support is a crucial feature in the initiation and monitoring of care activities – but as is indicated in Figure 8.4, it should not be the first step in realizing a PCIS. Figure 8.4 shows the development in the availability of functions of patient care information systems, starting with a 'bare' electronic patient record, that are necessary to develop this mode of working.

Phase 5: ?

Medical data

Phase 4: knowledge-based Organize using advanced algorithms

Phase 4: initiating and monitoring of standardized care paths

Care process

Phase 3: presenting in context Adding intelligent filters and search systems

Phase 3: initiating standardized care paths Request of treatment trajectories

Phase 2: organizing Organize using 'tab pages'

Phase 2: initiating Ordering activities

Phase 1: completing Striving towards more complete information

Phase 1: registering Retrospective registration of activities

Figure 8.4 *Advancement towards a fully developed PCIS, with ever more powerful accumulating and coordinating functions. The increasing phases match an increasing standardization of work processes, data and decision criteria (see Chapters 3–5).*

153

Having one organization-wide patient agenda is crucial in achieving patient-centred logistics, or care pathways. In initiating care activity for a patient, one then has insight into all other care activities for that patient. Likewise, in initiating a treatment plan for a patient, one is then able to book care activities from all departments for all departments. In addition, striving towards an organization-wide patient agenda is part and parcel of striving towards *integrated planning*. This begins with making all planning information visible. For example, at any time one should be able to provide an insight into planned and actual capacities (facilities, nursing capacity and expertise, and medical capacity and expertise), and in relation to this into the actual flow of patient groups per care trajectory (care demand). Or in retrospect, one should have insight into the actual and prognosticated patient flow per patient group and into the actual and prognosticated capacity supply, in any given time period.

In all this, of course, it is imperative to aim at the reduction of administrative handling and at the overall increase of efficiency in the care process. Therefore, the use of IT should also be aimed at supporting delegation of routine activities, as part of standardized care pathways.

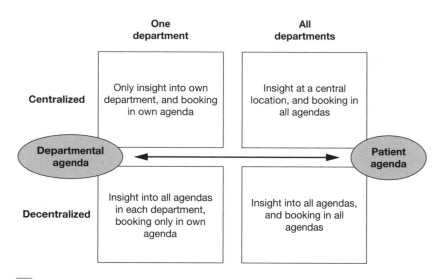

Figure 8.5 *One integrated patient agenda.*

In considering how to support its organizational ambitions with IT, Southern Medical is also considering heavily investing in patient-oriented IT. So, as part of the strategy development process, Southern Medical is investigating introducing the Internet to provide the individual patient with tailored information about individual diagnostic and treatment plans. Or to expand the types of contact with the patient, through for example e-mail and tele-consulting.

Three to five year Master Plan for care, care facilitation and integrated planning

The final step in formulating the ambitions for information management for the segments care, care facilitation and integrated planning, consists of identifying the main projects needed to put in place the information system functions that will materialize the stated ambitions. In this step, a shift is made from being descriptive and generic, to becoming very practical. Projects are identified aimed at implementing specific functionalities. These functionalities are part of modules of information systems that the health care organization already has in place, or will have to acquire.

A three to five year Master Plan, therefore, is very organization specific. It depends on the actual situation of the organization's information systems infrastructure, and the specific priorities for that health care organization.

A danger to be prevented here is that in starting to realize parts of these system functionalities, the overall ambition is lost from view because of practical hurdles. No currently existing PCIS has all the functionalities available to fully support all the ambitions laid out above. At least several different information system modules will have to be linked to cover the full breadth of work processes involved. The resulting incomplete support of what should have been a seamlessly integrated work process makes it easy to fall into the trap of perfecting individual functions instead of improving the total work process. A good example is the ambition to implement integrated patient planning. As no off-the-shelf solution for integrated patient planning exists, it is easier to implement and perfect separate planning systems, for example, outpatient planning and radiology department planning. The common result is that the patient needs to make two visits to the hospital, where one could have been sufficient.

CASE STUDY

Southern Medical's Master Plan Outline for care, care facilitation and integrated planning
This outline will serve as a guide for adding the desired functionalities and ultimately arriving at the stated ambitions:

Care process
This aims at the role of the care provider. The systems involved are PCIS modules, various specialist workstations, regional EPR. Core functions include: orders, results, findings, standardized care paths.

155

Over the next five years, we will take the following steps:

- introducing and utilizing PCIS modules:

    - complete availability of all relevant findings;
    - complete availability of orders, results and medication history;
    - computerized physician order entry;

- carrying out pilots: protocol based work processes and care pathways;
- introducing medical outcomes registration;
- introducing specific medical specialist workstations;
- carrying out pilots: access to PCIS for regional partners, regional integrated patient planning.

Care facilitation
Should aim at the role of provider of care support activities. This role has as its most important aspects:

- the acceptance (or initiation) of examination requests, the subsequent planning and monitoring of the progress, and finally making the results available. Also dealing with the care-supporting activities administratively;
- the support of the specific work process of the execution of the examination requests, or alternatively the comprehensive computerization of the execution.

The information systems involved are: Radiology, Laboratory, Pathology, PACS, Medication, etc. Functions include: orders, planning, results reporting, work flow management, management information reporting, etc.

A particular aspect for this segment is the digitized availability of images and analogue signals (a Picture Archiving and Communication System (PACS)). This accords with our efforts to make all patient information available. Supplementary to the argument for improved availability, we will aim to introduce a PACS on the basis of reducing the operational costs of image-producing departments.

Over the next five years, we will take the following steps:

- implementing hospital-wide PACS;
- implementing electronic order and results communications in all care-supporting departments;
- achieving one patient agenda by integrating all departmental agendas in one master patient agenda.

Integrated planning
Should aim at the role of planner of care activities. This could be individual care activities, or care activities in the context of hospital-wide integrated planning. We will have to investigate whether we will aim at introducing treatment

trajectory planners, or whether we will work with departmental planners (capacity planners), or with a mixture of both. This role has as its most important aspects:

- planning and monitoring care activities from the viewpoint of one patient agenda, individually or in the context of a care pathway;
- the earliest and furthest possible planning of care activities in the context of a protocol or care pathway, within a department, hospital-wide and ultimately in a regional context;
- the earliest and furthest possible planning of care activities in the context of a single capacity or multiple capacities (mostly a traditional departmental focus). For this, insight into all resources (people, space and equipment) constituting a capacity is necessary.

The information systems involved are: integrated planning system, planning modules order management systems or departmental systems, specialist workstations, etc. Functions include: care activities planning, capacities planning, treatment trajectory planning, care pathway management, etc.

Over the next five years, we will take the following steps:

- introducing and utilizing an integrated planning module;
- achieving one integrated patient agenda;
- defining care pathways and treatment protocols;
- piloting treatment trajectory planning;
- providing access to planning functionality in a regional context.

Patient administrative processes, billing and the other segments of the conceptual model

In this chapter, we will not discuss all segments of the conceptual model: their elaboration follows a similar path to the principles outlined in the previous subparagraphs. The segments of patient administrative processes and billing are dealt with together given their close relationship: correctly carrying out administrative recording activities, for one, prevents many corrective operations surrounding the invoicing. The organization ambition level, and thereby the IT ambition level for these segments, will generally be lower than the ambition level for the segments of care, care facilitation and integrated planning. This implies, then, opting for information systems with a more limited and modest functionality set, which adequately covers the most prevalent patient administrative and billing activities.

CASE STUDY

Table 8.1 *Southern Medical's strategy starting points for the segments patient administrative processes and billing*

Ambition level	Derived IT ambition level
The ambition for the patient administrative processes and billing is to have adequate administrative and financial information for care and operational managers. We will pursue the lean collection, and first time right processing of administrative data, with a minimal workload for care professionals. The support of the patient administrative and billing processes should adhere to the following requirements: ■ broadly available; ■ timely; ■ reliable; ■ 'first time right'.	The derived IT ambition level for the patient administrative processes is as follows: ■ a reliable patient administrative information system, which fits seamlessly in the primary work processes of care and care facilitation; ■ recording close to the source, as efficiently as possible, with effective administrative support; ■ emphasis on the existing administrative organization; ■ emphasis on checking during entry; ■ one-time entry; ■ 'end to end' handling of financial/administrative data (linked systems).

Based on the ambition level described in Table 8.1, our five year Master Plan for patient administration and billing will concentrate on improvement initiatives for the administrative organization. Replacing information system components will be limited to necessary replacements.

With regard to office computerization, it is important to note that the contribution of a state-of-the-art office computerization environment to the improvement of a health care organization's efficiency is all too often underestimated. After all, a health care organization is a large-scale, complex and information-intensive office environment, with intensive interaction with the outside world. E-mail, fast internet-access, high-level text processing software and so forth are no luxury in such environments. Not investing in high-end office computerization, then, is often a poor strategic decision, especially because the necessary technologies and services are commodities with relatively good price/quality performance.

With regard to the operational management processes, it is similarly important to realize how much efficiency can often be gained. Health care organizations are complex organizations, requiring, for example, information systems which offer high-quality support for financial management in a complex company (providing support for prospective, current, retrospective and multidimensional analyses). An important strategic consideration, here, is whether (on replacement) a tightly integrated information system is chosen for the operational management functions, or whether a choice is made for linked component systems. Tightly integrated means an integration of work processes, root files and databases (the integrated principle of Enterprise Resource Planning (ERP) systems). The advantage of such a choice is that it enables a work process based organizational structure, instead of a function based organization by department. The disadvantage is a relatively heavy implementation and familiarization phase because a redesign of existing company processes is necessary.

CASE STUDY

Southern Medical's strategy five year Master Plan for the segment Operational Management, having opted for a component-based approach, is aimed at:

■ redesigning the work process for the most common operational processes (20–80 rule: 20 per cent of the workprocesses take up 80 per cent of the work and are amenable to redesign and standardization), aimed at increasing the efficiency of the working methods and eliminating non-added-value activities (NAVAs);

■ providing decentralized access to the functions of the Operational Management systems using Intranet;

■ focusing on executing projects aimed at generating control information from the Operational Management systems;

■ introducing and utilizing career management functionality in the Human Resource system.

Finally, management information and the associated supporting data warehouse is a crucial part of the information provision for the operational processes of administration and general management. The ambition level of a health care organization for this segment is heavily dependent on the ambitions for research and education, and, similarly, dependent on the management philosophy of the organization (centralized/decentralized, use of Balanced Score Card-like steering models and so forth). As always, embarking on a data warehouse project *without* having these organizational visions clearly stated is a certain dead-end route.

As was argued in Chapter 3, generating management information, of course, is only partly a question of technical infrastructure. Standardizing data and registration procedures is equally important – while keeping the additional work-load for the primary care process in check.

Responsibilities and organization of information management

This paragraph discusses the organization-wide division of responsibilities for information management. In particular it considers the role distribution between the organization's departments, clusters and so forth, and the organizational unit responsible for information management.

Often the organizational unit responsible for information management is set up as a staff department, or a facilitative department, or a combination of both. In essence we are concerned with two forms of information management service provision to the organization:

1   the technology-related, generic IT service provision (network, hardware, operating systems and database management systems);
2   application related support (process management, knowledge of the adminis-trative organization, software package knowledge, database queries).

This classic division into technology-related, generic IT service provision (Hardware) and application support (Software) still provides a practical basis to organize the responsibilities and activities for organization-wide information management. The elaboration in this paragraph assumes a centralized organiza-tional unit, the Information Management department (IM department), with responsibility for the organization-wide information management. Following the two forms of information service provision, the IM department's responsibility for information management is twofold:

1   the facilitation, coordination and stimulation of organization-wide application support;
2   the supply of technology-related, generic IT service provision in line with agreed Service Level Agreements.[2]

The responsibilities surrounding information management are elaborated in two sets of guidelines:

1   general, outlining the responsibilities at the strategic/tactical and the tactical/operational level;
2   information system development, selection and implementation.

General guidelines for responsibilities in information management

In outline the responsibilities for information management are as follows:

- the BoD sets the rules for information management;
- the organization units determine the 'what' (the business objectives), followed by the IM department which adds the 'how' (the guidelines for facilitating the business objectives using IT);
- the IM department, at the request of the BoD:

  - formulates the framework for information management;
  - monitors the coherence, across the organization, of the organization's information management;
  - warns when the parts threaten to become less than the whole (for example, when systems are considered that do not interconnect, or when a department's IT strategy is at odds with the overall organizational/information strategy). The IM department is answerable to the BoD, after which the BoD decides;

- the responsibility for the use of IT to reach business objectives lies with the organization units;
- the responsibility for the quality of data in the information systems lies with the organization units;
- the responsibility for the technically correct functioning of information systems and infrastructure lies with the IM department.

It follows from this division of responsibilities that information management expertise is necessary both at a central level (BoD and the IM department) and decentralized across the organization units. In the discussion on information management expertise that is needed at the centre and within the organization units, it is important to draw a distinction between strategic/tactical and tactical/operational information management.

Strategic/tactical information management

Strategic/tactical information management deals primarily with the development and the practical application of the information strategy. Practical application in daily business means making the translation to tactical measures to resolve recurring operational problems. Or, in other words: having developed a strategy, one wants to implement it. Strategic/tactical information management is primarily the responsibility of the line of business managers and the BoD. The IM department has a pro-active, but facilitating role.

161

The organization units are responsible for the 'what' for their own work areas. That is to say, they are responsible for the proper use of IT as a tool to reach their business objectives. In translating the business objectives into information management requirements, and vice versa evaluating IT as an enabler to their business, the organization units must be supported with information management expertise. Information management expertise can be decentralized, in the form of an information management function located within the organization unit, or centralized in the form of a centrally-located information management function.

Independent of their central or decentralized location, all information management personnel report functionally to a centrally-located Information Manager. For the purpose of this chapter, this role is located in the IM department (alternatively, the role could also be positioned as that of CIO on a Board of Directors level). A centrally-located Information Manager is important, since many information management issues surpass individual organizational units. Different requests and developments from *within* units, therefore, may often require channelling with concurrent developments in other units or at the more central level. The IM department has an advisory role regarding the 'what' and is responsible for the 'how'. The 'how' denotes the introduction and proper functioning of the software and hardware. A part of the 'how' is the elaboration of the IT architecture, the coherence of the information system components and the performance of the IT infrastructure.

Decision-making about strategic/tactical information management takes place in the management hierarchy. However, it will often not be practical to reach a

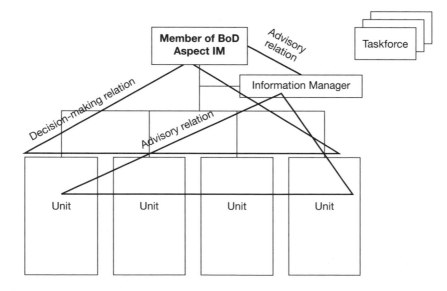

Figure 8.6 *Information management decisions are taken in the management hierarchy.*

decision with all responsible managers on issues that transcend the organization unit. In this case, task forces can be used. These are commissioned to produce an advisory report, which is then used as input for decision-making in the management hierarchy.

Depending on the size of the organization and the capacity made available for the introduction of information management expertise, this expertise will be more centralized (smaller organizations), or more decentralized (large organizations).

Tactical/operational information management

Tactical/operational information management is largely concerned with effectuating tactical measures, identifying recurring operational problems, and the practical resolution of disruptions. Tactical/operational information management should take place as closely as possible to the shop floor, while at the same time ensuring central coordination and harmonization. A well thought out centralized and decentralized distribution of capacities and responsibility is therefore crucial. This is illustrated in Figure 8.7.

Key-users are employees who are decentralized broadly in the organization, with a tactical/operational information management task. It is typical that information

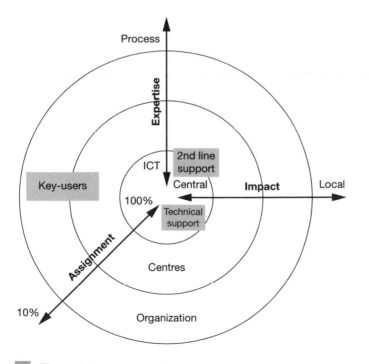

Figure 8.7 *Positioning key-users, second-line support and technical support.*

management is a part-time *assignment* for them, utilizing at maximum 50 per cent of their time, and that they report to their superior in the management hierarchy. For their information management task they report functionally to the Information Manager. Their *expertise* lies primarily in the field of their own work processes, alongside which they are trained in relevant information systems and information management skills, such as process analysis and documentation of the administrative organization. The *impact* of their information management activities is primarily local, within their own type of work processes. With the increase in importance of information systems for the progress of all business processes, the number of key-users will rise correspondingly. Every work unit, for example an outpatient clinic, must have one or more key-users.

Second line support are employees centrally placed in the IM department, with a tactical/operational information management task. The characteristics for a second line support employee are the following. Information management is a full-time *assignment* for them, requiring 100 per cent of their time, and they report both functionally and hierarchically to the Information Manager. Their *expertise* lies primarily in the field of IT, the knowledge of relevant information systems and information management skills. The *impact* of their information management activities is central. They administer the root files which determine the arrangement/operations of the information systems, they coordinate the work processes which transcend the organization unit, and they provide second line advice on the information systems.

Where tactical/operational information management is primarily carried out locally for a specific work process, often in centres (for example the patient administration office, the medical coding department), or in specialized departments (for example laboratories, or billing department), the *assignment* is often full-time, and the *expertise* in IT is larger. However the *impact* of information management activity in these centres is local, remaining within the boundaries of the centre's work processes. This type of tactical/operational information employee is often known as an application administrator (of the laboratory system, or the pathology system, etc.).

Technical support are centrally placed employees within the IM department. They carry out the technical management of the hardware components as part of the information management. This refers to the network, the central servers, the clients, the operating systems and the database management system.

Key-users and second line support together perform the tactical/operational information management, under the leadership of the information manager. They carry active responsibility for the continuous harmonization between the work processes and the information systems, in a tactical/operational sense. Issues which transcend the organization unit, or which require the adaptation of the work processes or the information systems, are presented to the strategic/tactical information management.

Guidelines for information system development, selections and implementation

This paragraph consists of three sections:

- guidelines for the development or selection of information systems;
- the 'make or buy' issue;
- guidelines for implementation.

Guidelines for development or selection of information systems

For the development, selection or upgrade of information systems, the same responsibility division applies as described above for strategic/tactical information management. The organization units determine the 'what'. They set the business goals, desired outcomes of the support of business processes with IT, and the functional programme of requirements. Furthermore the organization units supply the chairman of the information system selection team and/or development team.

The IM department determines the 'how'. They set the technical programme of requirements, specifically the criteria in relation to the overall IT architecture. They also set the programme of requirements for systems management, both technical and functional.

The BoD, finally, endorses the approach and the proposed selection. If the desired information system transcends the organization unit, the BoD decides on the source of the budget to be made available (central or non-central) and where in the management hierarchy the decision-making will take place (central, non-central or task force).

'Make or buy' issue

The complaint is often heard in health care organizations that there is no information system on the market that fits their specific situation well. This is said particularly about patient care information systems. This complaint certainly has a degree of truth, because the development of care-supporting information systems is still in its infancy.

Therefore, many health care institutions still consider the possibility of making their ideal system themselves. The most important consideration for health care organizations confronted with the 'make or buy' issue, however, is not whether the health care organization *can* produce the desired functionality itself, but whether it can sustain the long-term determination needed to maintain a home-grown product. As an application increases in scope, maintenance becomes steadily more complex. The complexity of maintenance increases still further as a broader group of users comes into being, working with various releases and versions. In choosing for in house development, the health care organization must consider

165

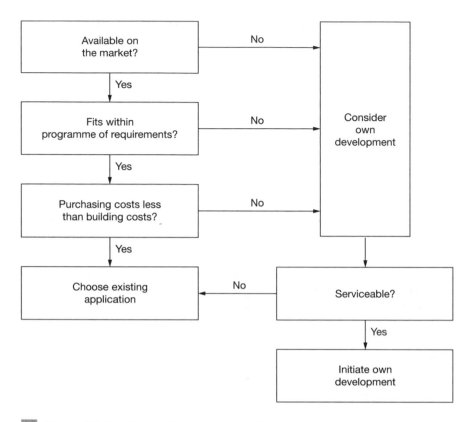

Figure 8.8 *Decision outline 'make or buy' issue.*

whether they will be able to guarantee the quality of maintenance over the longer term. Figure 8.8 shows a decision outline for the 'make or buy' issue.

Guidelines for implementation

The two most important guidelines for information systems implementation are:

1   Every project must have a sponsor in the management hierarchy. This puts the organization in the lead in the implementation of new IT applications, and anchors responsibility within the management hierarchy.
2   Before it can start, every project must have the guaranteed participation of work process experts. Work process experts are actually released in advance for participation in the project. This applies particularly to projects in the care process in which the participation of doctors, nurses and line management is essential.

The effects of work process experts not participating in an implementation are sufficiently well known. The result is that the relevant work processes immediately hit problems as soon as they are introduced, because of a discrepancy in the working methods of the professionals and the process design in the information system. This is known as the post-implementation dip. It is a fact that the post-implementation dip can be avoided by intensively preparing and supervising the transition to new working methods in advance. (See further Chapter 10.)

Guidelines for technical infrastructure and standards

Guidelines for the technical (IT) infrastructure and standards follow from the balance between, on the one hand:

- the general endeavour towards 'optimal availability of information, any time and any place in a work-related and personally relevant context';[3]
- the requests and requirements of the organization units for information management, as expressed in the IT ambition level;

and on the other hand:

- manageability in accordance with the agreed level of functioning and the associated costs;
- general organizational considerations, such as financial and legal rules.

If an imbalance exists between desires and manageability, it will manifest itself through high costs for low infrastructural quality (downtime and incorrect functioning). Commonly seen problems when an imbalance exists are for instance incompletely implemented systems that never reach their full potential, infrastructural instability because of conflicting systems, infrastructural rigidity because of a multitude of special solutions, and an unmanageable back log of system maintenance activities.

To preserve the balance between requests and manageability, it is mandatory that all organization units comply with guidelines for technical infrastructure and standards.

The first guideline is compliance to an organization-wide standard infrastructure:

- The 'standard IT infrastructure' is supported unconditionally on the basis of a Service Level Agreement (SLA).
- 'Special solutions' for unavoidable deviations from the standard are determined case by case. They are supported with customized SLAs per case.
- IT solutions outside these two categories are not supported. When such solutions may produce conflicts or overall information system rigidity (because of added complexity), these systems are not allowed.

167

The utilization of a standardized IT infrastructure leads to a reduction in systems management effort and thus to lower costs, and/or higher quality. Purchasing savings can also be realized by adhering to a standard.

This standardized infrastructure concept applies to all IT infrastructure components. It is often beneficial to reduce network components to one type of model, for example, one type of switches from one supplier. Similarly, allow servers to be only from one brand, and within that, one scalable server-type. Scale back to one operating system for the entire server park. Scale back to one brand and type for the clients, with one identical image for all clients. Finally, maintain one database management system and one developmental environment.

Of course, obtaining one standardized IT infrastructure is a gradual process – and may never be completely achieved. The essence is that the standard is associated with an SLA, and that 'special solutions' are simultaneously recognized as such.

The second guideline is compliance with a version and release policy for the standard infrastructure. The IT infrastructure is kept up to date:

- A hardware life cycle is adhered to, in step with the functional lifespan of the hardware. For example, clients and servers have a functional lifespan of between 2 and 4 years.
- A software version and release policy is adhered to, upgrading operating system software and database management systems at a pace which is at a maximum one year behind software industry developments.

Not having a version and release policy will result in infrastructural rigidity and instability. Ever increasing hardware or software malfunction incidents, caused by a growing diversity of models and software versions, will lead to increasing costs of systems management.

Besides improving manageability of the infrastructure, the two guidelines will also form the basis for a multi-year planning of ICT infrastructure maintenance and development.

Standardization of the IT infrastructure and working with service level agreements also lays the groundwork for a well-funded reflection on the merits of in-, co- or out-sourcing of the IT infrastructure. It may be expected from co- or out-sourcing that a supplier of IT infrastructure and associated services has lower costs because of economies of scale, and that it also has more specialized in-house knowledge. Co- or out-sourcing is a consideration if the health care organization thus enjoys lower costs and/or higher quality of its IT infrastructure.

PRIORITIES FOR THE INFORMATION MANAGEMENT AND FINANCIAL PRECONDITIONS

The previous paragraph listed what should happen as far as ambition and necessity are concerned. This deliberately did not consider the financial aspects. Neither was a ranking of importance made for the desired projects and activities.

In all probability, however, an initial tally of the necessary manpower and finances for executing the projects and activities will produce figures above those reserved by the health care organization for information management. Two questions then arise: how large should the health care organization's expenditure be on information management, and what ranking principle can be applied to the sequence of projects and activities?

Financing, not budgeting

How large the expenditure on information management should be, should ideally be determined by the expected returns. The tally of business cases (determined per project/activity) determines the IT expenditure in a multi-year estimate.

Unfortunately, the returns of PCISs can only partly be expressed in economic terms. Benefits include the increase in effectiveness of care, and the satisfaction of patients and care professionals (see also Chapter 11). The quality, speed and scope of information provision should improve, after all. Also, there are intangible benefits, such as being a front-line organization, and/or being an attractive organization for care professionals and researchers to work. In addition, the organizational impact and process changes associated with IT implementation make it difficult to calculate a simple economic yield (see Chapter 11).

Listing the tangible and intangible information management benefits must be undertaken, however. No matter how imperfect, it provides a footing for the discussion on the funds to be channelled to information management.

Simultaneously, comparative data from other information-intensive industries are helpful in the strategic discussion on the percentage of the budget that should be devoted to information management. Information-intensive, for-profit companies currently spend approximately 12 per cent of their annual costs on IT. The expenditure by hospitals, for example, is far below this; between 2 per cent and 4 per cent. For other health care organizations, these numbers are generally even lower. These figures make clear that health care organizations – a highly information-intensive industry, after all! – can benefit from pro-actively drawing up a multi-year budget that takes account of rising expenditures for information management. (The expectation of a rise in expenditures can also be built bottom-up, by making a forward projection based on the expansion of the number of users, expansion of functionality, and replacement of existing systems.)

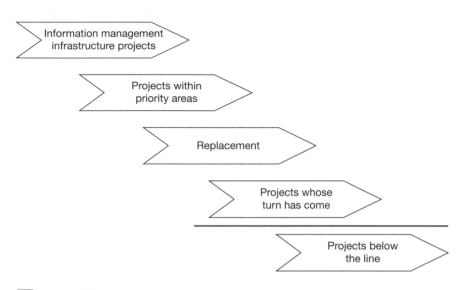

Figure 8.9 *Ranking principle for projects.*

Ultimately it is up to the health care organization's BoD to agree on expenditure on information management in a multi-year framework, in line with the ambition, the strategy and the expected yields.

Prioritizing projects and activities to be carried out

The projects and activities that stem from the IT ambition level, in conjunction with the guidelines, can usually not all be carried out concurrently. A ranking principle needs to be agreed to determine the sequence. Figure 8.9 shows the outline for such a ranking principle.

The starting point is that available resources (both manpower and financial resources) are introduced from top to bottom. Each project is added to the project list (projects are proposed by line managers). Projects which do not fall within the previous categories are placed 'below the line'. The priority 1 projects are first subtracted from the total available budget. A percentile division for priorities 2, 3 and 4 is then made from the remainder. For priority 5 'projects below the line' no budget will be available in the relevant time frame.

Priority 1 are the *information management infrastructure projects and activities*. This refers to the 'fundamental' infrastructural projects, both organizational as well as hardware and software, which are preconditions for the other projects, ambitions and guidelines. For example the elaboration of the guidelines for standardization, or the addition of key-users, etc.

Priority 2 are the *projects and activities within the priority areas*. These are the projects and activities required for fulfilling the ambition. The health care organization needs to make a ranking of the ambition per sector from the conceptual model. Derived from this is a ranking of the projects within the sector areas. The ranking determines the sequence of diminishing importance and cuts right across the sector areas. An estimate of costs and required manpower is made for each project, from which a tally offers an insight into what the budget depletion will be. When reaching the previously determined percentage of the budget (after subtracting the costs for infrastructure), the remaining projects are placed below the line.

Priority 3 are the *projects and activities surrounding replacements*. This refers to the necessary or planned replacement of existing information systems. Replacement is placed lower in the priorities to let growth and strategy-driven renewal prevail above retaining current functionalities. Here too, costs are estimated, and projects that no longer fit go below the line.

Priority 4 are *projects and activities whose turn has come*. This refers to projects which do not fall within the previous categories, but for which funds should be released for other reasons considered desirable or necessary. For example for legal obligations, or to prevent the neglect of a particular organization unit. The amount of resources released for this category is determined in advance in relation to the rest.

Priority 5 are the *projects and activities below the line*. These are projects for which there is a need but which were not sufficiently highly ranked. These will not be carried out in the relevant time frame.

The result of this priority setting exercise is an outline of the development and project plan expressed in time, along with an estimate of costs.

CONCLUSION

Building on the visions for the future directions of health care work processes presented in the previous chapters, this chapter gave guidelines on how to draft an information strategy, and on what it should contain. Examples were given of how ambitions for improved health care work processes can be translated into corresponding ambitions for the use of IT.

DISCUSSION QUESTIONS

1   PCIS vendors are currently introducing Tablet PC based applications. The Board
    of Directors asks you, as the information manager, to give an advice on
    introducing the Tablet PC into the health care organization. Which topics would
    you address in your advice to the BoD?

2   Your Board of Directors asks you, as the new information manager, to update
    your department's five year old IT strategy document. As the BoD is a strong
    practitioner of integral management by the business unit managers, you are asked
    to work directly with each of the 12 business unit managers. How would you
    structure the process of formulating the strategy? Make a project outline,
    addressing intermediate deliverables in a time-line.

3   European health care organization are mostly not-for-profit organizations that
    rely strongly on financial management of their organization units by budgeting.
    In this situation IT expenditures for each unit and for the organization as a whole
    are known in advance for at least the upcoming two to three years. Given these
    considerations, does it still make sense to you to start an information strategy
    formulating process by putting budgetary constraints at the very end of this
    process?

NOTES

1   This example is a fictitious case history, built up from several real life experiences.

2   A Service Level Agreement: pre-agreed contract for content, amount, quality of
    services and response times.

3   Please note that 'any time and any place', does not indicate 'any context'. As has
    been elaborated on in Chapter 4, information is highly context sensitive.

FURTHER READING

See Chapter 7. For the US situation, two books are worth exploring for additional
practical insights into information strategy development:

Glaser, J. P. and L. Hsu (1999) *The Strategic Application of Information Technology
in Healthcare Organizations.* Boston: McGraw-Hill.

Johns, M. (2002) *Information Management for Health Professions.* Alabama: Delmar
Publishers.

Implementing information systems in health care organizations

Myths and challenges

KEY POINTS OF THIS CHAPTER

- Whether information systems are 'successful' or 'fail' is not easy to establish. 'Success' is a multi-dimensional concept, which can be defined rather differently by the different involved parties. These definitions evolve over time.

- There is no list of critical success or failure factors that will guarantee success. There are, however, several prevalent myths that need to be avoided, and some core challenges to be tackled (see also Chapter 9).

  - Myth 1: PCIS implementation is the technical realization of a planned system in an organization.
    - ▶ Challenge 1: see and manage a PCIS implementation project as an organizational change process, or as organizational development.

  - Myth 2: You can leave PCIS implementation to the IT department
    - ▶ Challenge 2: the organizational development process requires a project group that finds the balance between top-down and user-led direction.

  - Myth 3: PCIS implementation can be planned, including the required organizational redesign.
    - ▶ Challenge 3: The unpredictability of PCIS implementation requires that its management resembles a careful balancing between initiating organizational change, and drawing upon IT as a change agent; between steering towards implementation targets and stimulating the learning processes that will inevitably transform these.

  - The challenge of health information management is to find ever more synergy between PCIS, primary work processes and secondary work processes.

KEY TERMS

- Implementation
- Success and failure factors
- Organizational development
- Business process redesign
- Synergy
- Iterative and incremental

INTRODUCTION

As we already mentioned in Chapter 2, the implementation of PCISs in health care practices has proven to be a path ridden with risks and dangers. It has become evident that there are many more failure stories to tell than there are success stories – and the more comprehensive the technology, or the wider the span of the implementation, the more difficult it appears to achieve success. In addition, the preceding chapters have made it clear that organizational issues are just as important in successful PCIS development and use as technical issues. Of course, inadequate design of an information system (e.g. an inadequate user-interface) or its poor performance (e.g. slow response times) will reduce its chances of being successfully implemented. Yet even in cases of clear-cut technical difficulties, the question whether the implementation is seen as a success or a failure is ultimately not a mere technical matter. In the end, this final decision is about the attachment of the label 'success' or 'failure' (or anything in-between) to a particular situation. Some health care organizations might decide to muddle through with a given system, or to invest more resources so as to improve the problems perceived to be most problematic; other organizations might, in similar situations, decide to abort the project, and accept their losses. In the end, then, the question whether an implementation has been successful or not is *socially negotiated* (Woolgar 1988; Kaplan 2001).

In addition, organizational issues are key because technical difficulties can be the *result* of poorly managed development processes. When users are not sufficiently involved in the design process, the user-interface may become illogical from the users' point of view, for example, or the sequence of actions prescribed by the system may run against the users' working routines (see also Chapters 3 and 4). Or, likewise, some groups of users might have a political agenda embedded in the new system: insight in the working patterns of other groups, for example, or access to another group's information resources. Such agendas might lead to open conflict with other groups, thus leading to non-use of the system (Schneider and Wagner 1993).

These small examples illustrate the deep interrelation of technical and social aspects in systems development. Technical problems may have organizational roots, and result in organizational conflicts; a well-functioning system exemplifies a match between the functionalities of the system and the needs and working patterns of the organization.

In this chapter, the issue of successful implementation will be addressed from this perspective. Three myths will be introduced that often underlie implementation failure, but that still seem to be surprisingly alive. Concurrently, alternative and more fruitful viewpoints will be introduced, drawn from the scientific literature on organizational change and technology development, our experience, and illustrated with concrete examples.

TOWARDS 'SUCCESSFUL' IMPLEMENTATION: TWO CAVEATS

What is a 'successful' implementation?

When is a PCIS implementation successful? As stated, in real-life projects, whether an information system is 'successful' or not is decided on the workfloor, by the middle management, by top managers – and it is the outcome of all these interactions that in the end settles the system's fate. It is of course also possible to be less relativistic, and to set a success measure outside of an organization's own deliberations (for example, 'the percentage of professionals using the system for the majority of their patient contacts'). Only in this way, after all, can one compare different implementation processes. Also, only in this way can one build an argument whether a given organization has perhaps set its own standards too high – or too low. Yet the ongoing negotiations about the degree of 'success' of any given system should at the very least open our eyes for the fundamentally multidimensional and contested nature of the concepts of 'success' and 'failure'. A system can be a success economically: the implementation project may not have exceeded its budget, for example, or management may have succeeded in reducing the administrative workforce by the target set in the implementation plan. 'Success' could also mean that the system is up and running on time, for example, or it could mean that it is widely used. Alternatively, it could mean not so much the factual *use* of the system but the *appreciation* of this use by the users, or (and this need not coincide) the appreciation of this use by those users' managers. More specifically, for an order-entry system, a specific success measure could be a reduction in errors in medication deliveries; for a reminder system attached to an electronic patient record of hypertensive patients, the measure could be a reduction in the average blood pressure of these patients (McDonald *et al.* 1984; van der Lei *et al.* 1993).

175

Success, in short, has many dimensions: effectiveness, efficiency, organizational attitudes and commitment, worker satisfaction, patient satisfaction – and not all parties in and outside of the implementing organization may agree about which dimension should be the most relevant. What is more, not all parties may agree just what the proper effectiveness measure is, for example, or what costs and benefits should be incorporated in an evaluation of the system's efficiency. Should an implementation of a Picture Archive Communication System (PACS) be judged by the reduction of administrative worktasks (by both supporting staff and nursing and medical professionals)? Or should one also include the more tacit benefit of facilitating research, and the improved availability of diagnostic information with the concurrent – but generally very hard to quantify – improved quality of the primary care process? If views on these issues differ, whose view should prevail? The question about the success of a system, then, becomes the question of success *for whom*?

In addition, due to the complexity of the implementation process (see further) and to the multi-dimensional nature of the concept of 'success', what counts as 'success' at any given time may fluctuate. 'Success', in other words, is a *dynamic* concept, not a static one. After sometimes many months or even years of hard work, management and health care professionals alike might have changed their view about what a 'successful' implementation of an information system might consist of.

CASE VIGNETTE

During the introduction of a physician order-entry system in a US Academic Medical Center, management slowly realized that direct, substantial savings on personnel costs were not to be expected. Rather, the very restructuring of the professionals' work tasks that the system implied (creating order entry at the 'point of care') should in itself be seen as an important success. 'Quality of care' and 'being a state-of-the-art Academic Medical Center' became more important criteria for success than the originally projected cost-savings that were a major factor in the decision to acquire the system (Massaro 1993a).

'Success', then, is a multi-dimensional concept, which can be defined rather differently by the different involved parties, and which evolves over time. From these queries it should not be deduced that speaking about or striving for a 'successful' implementation is meaningless. Rather, it implies that managing towards a 'successful' implementation implies careful attention to what success parameters are used, whether the different parties involved in the implementation process share these goals, and how the inevitable evolution of the criteria of 'success' will be handled.

How successful are success factors?

Another caveat that should be addressed is that it is not possible to list a definite set of 'success' and/or 'failure factors' that will provide a certain recipe towards implementation success (or failure). Even in those (rare) cases in which there is total agreement on the goals of an implementation, there exists no simple formula for success. This is due, in one sentence, to the *complexity* of the enterprise at stake. A core feature of IS development processes within complex organizations – and we will return to this point later – is their fundamental *unpredictability*. The technology itself is already very complex. Consisting of a host of interrelated hardware components and thousands or millions of lines of code, its behaviour never becomes fully transparent, even to those intimately involved in its construction. In addition, the number of parties who have a stake in and an influence on the IS implementation and use is large, and their reactions to the (in itself never fully predictable) behaviours of the technology cannot be fully foreseen.

Given this unpredictability, it is not at all evident that an implementation strategy that was successful in one organization will be similarly successful in another. Even if what will count as 'success' is fixed, determining a definite list of success or failure factors is impossible because what has worked in one case might not be relevant at all in another. Even within a tightly delineated domain such as health care, and even if we limit our analysis within this domain to, say, management information systems, this still would hold. Different organizations, with different sizes, different leadership styles, different cultures, different financial situations and different environments, may and will react very differently to a similar technological innovation, or to a similar implementation strategy.

This is not to say that we cannot outline certain insights that seem to be a *sine qua non* to the realization of successful systems – however defined. Indeed, in the following paragraph, some of these insights will be discussed in the form of prevalent 'myths' that stand in the way of fruitful implementation projects. Yet any such discussion runs the risk of reducing what can only be fine-grained discussion of individual cases to bland, almost empty slogans such as 'the importance of leadership' or 'the involvement of users'. It is not that leadership is not important, but just how a specific leadership style in any given situation works out cannot be predefined. Likewise, involving users is essential, but there is no recipe for this that will work in any given case. More often than not, the proper leadership style for a specific implementation process, or the optimal way to involve users, can only be *discovered during* the process itself. In other words, the complexity of the account can only be reduced at the expense of losing its validity. This is why speaking of 'factors' is so problematic, since that projects the notion that there is a fixed list of pregiven capacities, resources, characteristics and so forth that will do the trick. This chapter therefore rather speaks of 'insights': issues, complexities, pitfalls to be *aware* of. In this and the following chapter, in other words, we are more concerned with understanding, acting upon and structuring the implementation process than with the futile attempt to isolate individual contributors to either 'success' or 'failure'.

THREE MYTHS ABOUT IS IMPLEMENTATION

Myth 1: PCIS implementation is the technical realization of a planned system in an organization

Overlooking the fact that PCIS implementation will fundamentally affect the health care organization's structures and processes is one core reason for implementation failure. All too often, still, we hear project leaders or IS professionals speaking about 'rolling out' a system, or planning its 'diffusion'. Such terminology underestimates that whether it is anticipated as such or not, the implementation of an information system in an organization involves the mutual transformation of the organization by the technology, and of the system by the organization. As emphasized in Chapter 2, this is a two-way process. On the one hand, the technology will affect the distribution and content of work tasks, change information flows, and affect the visibility of these work tasks and information flows. Because of this, it will also change relationships between (groups of) health care professionals and/or other staff. Electronic patient records, for example, inevitably change one's recording practices, and raise questions about who will get access to whose data, under which conditions. This may seem self-evident and innocuous, but such changes inevitably trigger subtle (and sometimes not so subtle) social and political processes about who gets to fill in what parts of the record, who 'owns' what information, and who gets to check on whose work. In the case study of the implementation of a physician order-entry system mentioned above, Massaro describes how physicians reacted forcefully against the need to be more structured and precise in their writing of their orders. The fact that Massaro chose to describe the physicians' slow adjustment to the system in terms of Kübler-Ross's phases of mourning (denial, anger, acceptance and so forth) is an indication of the depth at which these change processes can affect existing organizational realities (Massaro 1993b).

Such organizational processes in their turn inevitably affect the system. Pressures on the implementation staff may lead them to change authorization procedures, for example, or to throw out elaborately coded entry-screens that (in the eyes of the users) take up too much time.

> **CASE VIGNETTE**
>
> In a PCIS developed for a mental health care organization in the Netherlands, we found that discussions about access rights to patient information had resulted in an unwieldy explosion of over 25 different authorization levels. In this case, the specification of every new level resulted in renewed discussions about the exact mutual relationships between all the involved professionals – leading to more dissent, and more requests for diversification.

Because of the impact of the PCIS on the organization, then, and because of the consequent repercussions of these impacts back on the shape, use and functioning of the PCIS, it is imperative to see and manage a PCIS implementation project as an organizational change process. Even better still, PCIS implementation should be conceived as organizational *development*, since that term implies that the information system is strategically *intended* to affect the organization.

> **CASE VIGNETTE**
>
> The mental health care organization mentioned above had aimed at co-developing the organization and the information system. Their aim had been to transform previously independent care delivery units into one integrated care delivery system, encompassing both ambulatory and clinical care for an entire region. Through the use of IT, they could introduce case managers that would coordinate and oversee the handling of a client throughout different phases of his/her treatment, irrespective of traditional organizational boundaries. The PCIS system afforded the case manager to consult patient records and care professionals' agendas irrespective of their actual physical location, and in this way underwrote the process of organizational change.

As argued in Chapter 5, this possibility to draw upon IT to generate new organizational forms of delivering care – that would not be able to exist without IT – is one of the core challenges for the field of medical informatics and for the strategies of health care organizations.

Myth 2: You can leave PCIS implementation to the IT department

PCIS implementation, then, should not be run as a 'mere' technical project. It should be managed as a process of organizational development, in which IT is drawn upon as a strategic asset to transform organizational structures and routines, and further the organization's goals. When seen as such, it becomes obvious that the implementation of any medium to large scale PCIS has to be managed by a project-group that includes the IT department, but that is not limited to it. Crucially, it should include both representatives from future users, and representatives from the institution's top-level management.

Adequate user-involvement, first of all, is of paramount importance to foster ownership of the system by the future users, and to allow the implementation of systems that will actually match work processes – current or future. 'User-involvement' is an easy slogan, yet its importance cannot be overstated. It is not enough to 'include' a few potential users in the project group, to have them negotiate system specifications, and to discuss implementation plans and the achievement of socio-technical 'fit' in meetings once every so often. User involvement should be taken much more extensively and literally. Users are generally very bad in speaking the language of 'specifications', and in imagining what specific configuration of the technology they 'need' or what would work 'best' in actual work situations. Such judgement skills can only develop over time when users are taken on board in the development process early and systematically, and when careful attention is paid by those responsible for the implementation to the actual work processes that these users take as their starting point. Ethnographic methods, studying the detailed social organization of actual working practices through participant observation methods and in-depth interviews, can be highly useful here. Such methods can illuminate interdependencies between worktasks, and demonstrate, e.g. how tasks that seem to be executed in a highly variable way are actually fine-tuned to match a context that is highly variable (see also Chapters 3 and 4). Such issues, highly relevant for choosing system configurations and planning implementation trajectories, easily disappear from view when the 'work' to be 'supported' by the PCIS remains too abstract a category. In addition, to draw upon the skills users *do* have, they should for example be allowed to try out proposed system configurations in their actual work settings. Here again, ethnographic methods can help to elucidate more practical human–computer interface designs, or more efficient ways to interrelate the demands of the actual work tasks with the demands of the chosen PCIS (see also Chapter 6).

Yet in and by itself, proper and thorough user-involvement is only half of the picture. Many PCIS projects run to the ground, even when users have been thoroughly involved from the outset.

180

CASE VIGNETTE

In a regional Dutch hospital where a system rather similar to the order-entry system mentioned on p. 176 was introduced, the concept of 'user-involvement' was taken at heart. Health care professionals were heavily involved first in the acquisition of the system, and later in the implementation process and the tailoring of the system to the specific needs of this hospital. This implementation group, that did much of the tailoring work, consisted mainly of nurses and physicians who had worked in the same wards and offices that they were now fine-tuning the system's functionalities for. This work consisted mainly of designing 'screens': electronic forms, with structured queries and preformatted fields to fill in. At the time we conducted our investigation, the system was implemented only partially in only a few wards. Yet at that time already, the number of individual screens was getting out of control. On the neurological ward alone, for example, nurses had access to up to 10,000 screens. The screens were linked to each other in various ways and formed several paths (to order medication, to order an investigation, to seek information, to report patient data and so forth), each consisting of up to 30 individual screens. All in all, the system consisted at that time of 27,000 different screens (Goorman and Berg 2000).

A core problem of the system encountered in this case study, not unlike the labyrinth of authorization levels mentioned above, was that the number of screens was exploding beyond manageability. Dedicated to their previous work environments and colleagues, the implementation team dutifully translated each request and 'need' from the hospital's shop floor into a new screen. This is only one example of a common problem in projects that have users 'in the lead': the trajectory of user-led design processes tends to lose direction and momentum due to the multitude of different voices pushing the process into different directions – or to nowhere at all. In health care settings, usually characterized by a host of different professional, paraprofessional, technical, administrative groups and so forth, this problem is even more pronounced.

The balancing act between user-directedness and manageability, then, between the need to be 'flashy' and to be 'robust', or between the needs and desires of different usergroups can only be made when the users' presence in the project group is *itself* balanced by a proper and strong presence of upper management. Overall, the project group should lie out a vision that creates and restricts the space *within which* user-involvement can emerge and can express itself. This requires the existence of that vision at the level of the upper management, and the adequate operationalization of that vision into adequate means, mandates

181

and manoeuvring space for the project group. This vision, which should be first and foremost about the future of the *organization* (maybe inspired by IT possibilities, but not primarily centred around IT) should be both robust enough to frame and direct the PCIS implementation process, yet it should be open-ended enough to be adaptable to newly upcoming challenges, in part deriving from the PCIS implementation process itself. In the next subsection, we will take a deeper look at the need for this flexibility, and at the core insight that organizational development – including PCIS implementation – is more about improvization and organizational learning than about top-down planning and 'process redesign'.

Myth 3: PCIS implementation can be planned, including the required organizational redesign

Although one can and should *intend* to have a PCIS development trajectory affect one's organizational structure and processes, this 'intention' should not turn into an attempt to fully plan and control this process. In much literature on IS-related organizational change, *business process redesign* or *re-engineering* (BPR) is embraced as the sure route to competitive advantages and organizational survival. Originated in the private sector, BPR, in short, propagates a *process* view of organizations, in which the whole organization is organized around the customer and the product he desires, rather than the traditional *functional* view, in which the organization is organized around its core, internal functions. BPR states that managers should be willing to radically redesign business processes so as to optimize the processes' effectiveness and efficiency. Translated into health care idiom, an organization's 'core business' is the primary care process (the work of health care professionals to manage patients' trajectories). The necessary redesign is usually taken to be the creation of PCIS-dependent integral care delivery systems, radically restructuring the traditional, 'functionally organized' health care organizations.

These ultimate aims are crucial, and the ambitions explicated in Chapter 5 are deeply influenced by these views. Also, it is an important insight that it is not possible to maximize IT's contribution to organizations without affecting the very nature of these organizations. Yet the idea that current business processes (including current information systems) should be radically redesigned from scratch, and that this should be done top-down, is simply wrong. In strictly hierarchically oriented companies, where the processes to be redesigned are relatively predictable and standardized, such an approach might be feasible. In such instances, senior management can simply impose wholly new working routines and cooperation patterns on its employees. In health care, however, the 'core business process' consists of highly knowledge-intensive, professional work, typified by a complexity that defies the predictability and standardization required for simple reengineering. Moreover, the professionals ultimately responsible for this process are powerful actors in the organization, and cannot be simply told to change their work patterns by senior management.

It all adds up: the complexity of the primary care process, the complexity and unpredictability of the IS itself and the sheer number of parties involved in PCIS implementation (see Myth 2, p. 180) results in a process which is *fundamentally* unfit for a strict planning and controlling approach. The uncertainty and unpredictability of PCIS implementation processes is an *inherent* characteristic of such processes, which should be accepted and even nurtured rather than 'overcome'. Attempting to impose more controls to weed out surprises is a sure route to disaster: unexpected problems should be taken as instances to *learn from* and *adapt to* rather than as obstacles to overcome. Similarly, unforeseen spontaneous alternative uses of the system should be carefully investigated as possible unexpected ways to draw out unforeseen benefits from the system (Ciborra 1997).

CASE VIGNETTE

In a study of an electronic patient record developed for use in the care for hypertensive patients, for example, we found that the designers, in close cooperation with one or two leading hypertensive specialists, had opted for a very structured interface. The record consisted of several screens in which doctors could enter (coded) complaints, diagnosis, blood pressures, examination results, medication and so forth. The IS professionals and specialists had designed this record to facilitate their research: in this way, the structured information they required for their clinical investigations could be drawn directly from the databases of the patient record. For this purpose, the system functioned well: in this sense, the system was successful. In the everyday processes of outpatient care, however, the system appeared to be less functional. Many physicians complained that the system was too 'rigid' to capture the essence of a patient's visit. The list of coded complaints, pressures, examination results and so forth was very useful to track some overall parameters — yet it could not capture that the core reason of the patient's visit was his increased anxiety about his hypertension, for example, triggered by the recent death of his father. To overcome this limitation, many physicians started to use the one small free text section that the system had ('conclusion') as a field to enter such information. This resulted in a somewhat awkward use of the system, with physicians maximally using the limited amount of text they could put in this small field, and having this lower right corner of one of the screens function as the central focus during patient visits.

From the perspective of the original aims of the system described in this case vignette, generating 'good research data', the developments described could be seen as a problem. The one field that generated unstructured data that were almost impossible to aggregate was heavily used – often at the expense of the more structured fields. When framed as such, an appropriate response might be to try to eliminate this unstructured usage, and to attempt to structure this field as well, or restrict its utilization. A more creative response to this unplanned use, one that would be sensitive to the multiple and changing viewpoints that characterize any implementation, would be to make this field more readily accessible and enlarge it. The structured items could be regrouped around this field so that the required back-and-forthing between the fields would be designed to facilitate the evolved usage as much as possible. In this way, a compromise between different demands would be optimized, and a *synergy* between the computer's aggregating and ordering powers and the physician's recording routines would be carefully crafted.

The transformation of success criteria, the resetting of what it is the system aims to do during the very process of implementing the system, characterizes larger scale examples just as much – or even more – than this small scale example. This is what happened in the order-entry system implementation project described by Massaro: once it was realized that cost-savings were not going to be immediate, the overall goals of the project slowly changed. One can introduce a PCIS to reduce administrative costs, and find that the increase in administrative efficiency is paralleled by an increase in the amount of information required by external parties. System requirements *evolve* in and through the process of learning from unexpected workarounds and unforeseen usage of the IS (Hartswood *et al.* 2000). The following two case vignettes illustrate this phenomenon.

CASE VIGNETTE

A PCIS is a double edged sword for health care professionals: it may facilitate and support their work, but it often does so through importing novel constraints to their work, and facilitating the scrutiny of their work for outsiders. In the case of four US order-entry using hospitals, the use of carepaths gave nurses both more autonomy and less. They received less orders that were difficult to decipher or interpret, and could create their own order sets, yet they regretted the loss of subtle influence that they used to have in helping doctors formulate orders. In such situations, one often does not know how care professionals will react: for young interns, the possession of 'individual' order sets gave an unexpected sense of 'control and even pride'. Such reactions cannot be predicted, yet are key: when carefully nurtured and acted upon, they can help further the creation of truly powerful PCIS (Ash *et al.* 2003).

CASE VIGNETTE

In an increasing number of hospitals in the Netherlands, clinical workstations are being placed where the physician can gain access to all the patient information present in the Hospital Information System. The systems do not support data entry, but the data retrieval is well designed, using a Windows-based graphical user-interface, with many visual clues indicating what information is present and all this information just a few mouse-clicks away. One may criticize this system for its lack of data entry capacities, but that would overlook the phenomenon that it is in fact the very *presence* of this read-only system that *generates* a new 'need'. Whereas in most of these hospitals, 'computers' were low on these physicians' priority list, the coming of these workstations has sparked their interest. It is the very confrontation with its potential capacities that have *turned* the physicians into fervent supporters of a more aggressive PCIS strategy.

Radical redesign is doomed to fail, to destroy much tacit knowledge, and to produce massive organizational upheaval and chaos. A much wiser approach is to learn from the embedded wisdom and already present synergies between work and (often paper-based) tools in existing working practices, and to work from there. This does not mean that one can or should not envision radical changes in work practices – this is not a plea against ambition! It does mean, however, that starting from scratch may be a useful thought experiment, but it is not a wise implementation strategy. It means, also, that we should carefully reconsider what paper-based information technologies *do* do well – their simplicity and robustness, for example, or their unsurpassed efficacy in small-group communication (see Chapters 3 and 4). See the last case vignette: it is likely that a more radical implementation of a fully operational, electronic patient record in most Dutch hospitals' outpatient offices would have failed. Data entry by professionals is a well-known bottleneck, and the current implementation, one could argue, combines ease of (electronic) retrieval with ease of (paper-based) data-entry. At the very least, the current implementation has made physician resistance much less likely. As Glaser and Hsu put it, 'the use of information technology to improve care is a form of guerilla war' (1999): an ongoing set of initiatives, constantly changing tactics, constantly changing targets. 'Guerilla war' might be a rather aggressive metaphor, but it does capture the fundamental limitations to blueprints, precise planning, predictions of future needs and desires, and top-down implementation strategies. Rather, it emphasizes the need to seize opportunities when they emerge, and creatively turn disadvantages into advantages – which often includes a radical reconstruction of what exactly the 'advantage' *is*.[1] In such instances, one does not

185

know at the outset where one ends: one does not 'redesign' according to some plan; one rather 'drifts' with the currents, attempting to steer one's project through the ever changing environment (Ciborra *et al.* 2000).

STRIVING FOR SYNERGY: SUCCESSFUL IMPLEMENTATION REVISITED

A proper implementation process, then, attempts to reach a situation as described in Figure 9.1. The primary work processes denote all the work directly linked to patient care (the central work tasks of doctors, nurses and other health care professionals). The secondary work tasks consist of the work processes that support, complement and steer the primary care process. This includes the whole gamut ranging from resource management, management of medical equipment, food services, billing, to overall organization management. The arrows indicate a relationship of *mutual* transformation. The IS should help transform the primary work processes (affording, e.g., integral care processes, or new ways of quality control), and, likewise, should help transform the secondary work tasks (affording, e.g., new, efficient resource management, or more strategic use of primary care process information). Part and parcel of this is, of course, that the primary and secondary work processes become more aligned – a development that is already taking place throughout Western medicine, but that is requiring a re-ordering of some of the fundamental ordering principles of the classic model of the professional bureaucracy.

The figure depicts both some *ideal*, future state of an organization *and* the continuous process of striving towards that ideal – which itself will inevitably change over time. It indicates that every step taken in the gradual 'growth' of a PCIS should one way or another be a step *within* this process: towards a transformation of primary work processes, secondary work processes and/or the interrelation of the two. How exactly the 'ideal' looks, of course, is a highly political issue if only because of the organizational turmoil involved in any realignment between primary and secondary work processes. Information systems can never be a neutral player in this ongoing battle, typical for any professional bureaucracy. In addition, the complexity of the issues at stake here makes prediction impossible: every novel development (whether in- or external to the PCIS implementation process) will result in new challenges to meet, and new, often unexpected opportunities for new information systems functionalities.

The task of achieving this synergy, then, is the task of creating the circumstances so that PCIS functionalities can bring primary and secondary work tasks to new levels of quality, efficiency and/or work satisfaction – whether that means an enlarged span of control for administrative personnel, an improved grip on the patient's trajectory for the health care professional, or a novel sense of autonomy

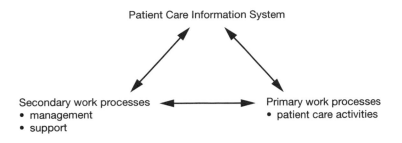

Patient Care Information System

Secondary work processes
- management
- support

Primary work processes
- patient care activities

Figure 9.1 *Striving for synergy.*

for the patient. Most of all, it is the task to create a situation in which eagerness to mutually *learn*, a desire to constantly further develop both the PCIS and the work process, has become default. As has become clear, where and how exactly this synergy will be found, and to where it can then further develop, or where it will be thwarted by organizational politics, cannot be planned or predicted. (As we will discuss in Chapter 10, a *sine qua non* for this mutual learning to develop is ongoing, in depth, multi-level *evaluation* of the implementation process.)

This is the PCIS implementation challenge: managing the implementation so that these synergies can be found, nurtured and developed. It is an *iterative, incremental* process: going step by step, recreating new synergies while dissolving older ones, and – hopefully – coming closer to bridging the quality gap described in Chapter 5. This implies taking the uncertainty of every single step as the rule rather than as a problem, to fully realize the political nature of the processes set in motion, and to carefully monitor and learn from spontaneous experimentation on the workfloor.

CONCLUSION: THE CHALLENGE

In this chapter, we described how the implementation of a PCIS in health care organizations is a process of mutual transformation. The organization is affected by the coming of this new technology, and the technology is in its turn inevitably affected by the specific organizational dynamics of which it becomes a part. This empirical fact can become highly problematic when IS implementation is seen as a mere matter of 'diffusing' a technology, or of merely 'rolling out' a technical fix. In such instances, 'barriers' and 'obstacles' appear from the blue in the guise of 'user resistance' or suboptimal 'returns' of the PCIS. When anticipated, however, when *seen* as a process of organizational development, PCIS implementations can be strategically intended to transform the organization, and the technology can be allowed to grow along, gradually becoming part and parcel of the basic organizational work routines.

We described, likewise, how such a process can only get off the ground when properly supported by both central management and future users. A top-down vision and framework for the implementation is crucial: only *with* such a framework can 'user needs' be articulated that transcend individual wish lists. In setting the stage this way, user-input can become a coherent, steering force that in its turn transforms and specifies the overall vision – and that creates a solid basis for the organizational transformations that will then certainly ensue.

Finally, we emphasized how the management of PCIS implementation processes resembles a careful balancing between initiating organizational change, and drawing upon IS as a change agent, without attempting to pre-specify and control this process. It is a balancing act between setting goals and targets for the implementation – yet stimulating the mutual learning processes that will inevitably transform these goals and targets. Accepting, and even drawing upon, this inevitable uncertainty might be the hardest lesson to learn – yet time and time again, the most 'successful' implementation processes appear to be those in which an obsession for control and planning is replaced by an obsession for experimentation and mutual learning. It implies finding the difficult balance between setting the direction for change, and to let oneself drift with the current thus formed. Time and time again, the exact role of the PCIS in the organization is only discovered *during* the implementation process.

In the next chapter, we will attempt to translate some of these insights into practical guidelines for project management, the distribution of responsibilities, and the modes in which we can organizationally realize this 'management of uncertainty'.

DISCUSSION QUESTIONS

1   Figure 9.1 describes the interrelation between PCIS, primary and secondary work processes. Select a PCIS you are familiar with, and describe this interrelation. Can you discern synergies? Are there also negative interactions in which the PCIS is involved?

2   Does the critique on lists of 'success' and 'failure' factors imply that such lists are useless?

3   Explain the following seeming paradox: 'not changing the success criteria for one's technology is a certain sign of failure' (after Latour 1996).

NOTE

1   Atkinson and Peel use a much more 'peaceful' metaphor when they speak of 'growing' rather than 'building' information systems (Atkinson and Peel 1998).

REFERENCES

Ash, J. S., P. N. Gorman, M. Lavell, T. H. Payne, T. A. Massaro, G. L. Frantz and J. A. Lyman (2003) Physician order entry: a cross-site qualitative study, *Journal of the American Medical Informatics Association* 10: 188–200.

Atkinson, C. and V. J. Peel (1998) Growing, not building, the electronic patient record system, *Methods of Information in Medicine* 37: 285–93.

Ciborra, C. U. (1997) Improvising in the shapeless organization of the future. In C. Sauer and P. W. Yetton (eds), *Steps to the Future: Fresh Thinking on the Management of IT-Based Organizational Transformation*. San Francisco: Jossey-Bass, pp. 257–78.

Ciborra, C. U., K. Braa, A. Cordella, B. Dahlbom, A. Failla, O. Hanseth, V. Hepso, J. Ljungberg, E. Montiero and K. A. Simon (eds) (2000) *From Control to Drift. The Dynamics of Corporate Information Infrastructures*. Oxford: Oxford University Press.

Glaser, J. P. and L. Hsu (1999) *The Strategic Application of Information Technology in Healthcare Organizations*. Boston: McGraw-Hill.

Goorman, E. and M. Berg (2000) Modelling nursing activities: electronic patient records and their discontents, *Nursing Inquiry* 7: 3–9.

Hartswood, M., R. Procter, M. Rouncefield and M. Sharpe (2000) Being there and doing IT in the workplace: a case study of a co-development approach in healthcare, *Proceedings of the CPSR/IFIP WG 9.1 Participatory Design Conference, New York, 28 November – 1 December*: 96–105.

Kaplan, B. (2001) Evaluating informatics applications: some alternative approaches: theory, social interactionism and call for methodological pluralism, *International Journal of Medical Informatics* 64: 39–56.

Latour, B. (1996) *Aramis, or the Love of Technology*. Cambridge: Harvard University Press.

Massaro, T. A. (1993a) Introducing physician order entry at a major academic medical center: I. Impact on organizational culture and behavior, *Academic Medicine* 68: 20–5.

Massaro, T. A. (1993b) Introducing physician order entry at a major academic medical center: II. Impact on medical education, *Academic Medicine* 68: 25–30.

McDonald, C. J., S. L. Hui, W. M. Tierney, S. J. Cohen, M. Weinberger and G. P. McCabe (1984) Reminders to physicians from an introspective computer medical record. A two-year randomized trial, *Annals of Internal Medicine* 100: 130–8.

Schneider, K. and I. Wagner (1993) Constructing the 'Dossier Représentatif': Computer-based information-sharing in French hospitals, *Computer Supported Cooperative Work* 1: 229–53.

van der Lei, J., E. van der Does, A. J. Man in 't Veld, M. A. Musen and J. H. van Bemmel (1993) Response of general practitioners to computer-generated critiques of hypertension therapy, *Methods of Information in Medicine* 32: 146–53.

Woolgar, S. (1988) *Science: The Very Idea*. Chichester: Ellis Horwood.

FURTHER READING

On the contested and multi-dimensional nature of 'success'

Markus, M. L. and C. Tanis (2000) The Enterprise Systems experience – from adoption to success. In R. W. Zmud (ed.), *Framing the Domains of IT Research: Glimpsing the Future Through the Past*. Cincinnati, OH: Pinnaflex.

Star, S. L. (ed.) (1995) *Ecologies of Knowledge: Work and Politics in Science and Technology*. New York: State University of New York Press.

Woolgar, S. (1988) *Science: The Very Idea*. Chichester: Ellis Horwood.

On why systems fail

Checkland, P. and S. Holwell (1998) *Information, Systems and Information Systems: Making Sense of the Field*. Chichester: Wiley.

Kling, R. and W. Scacchi (1982) The web of computing: computer technology as social organization, *Advances in Computers* 21: 1–90.

Latour, B. (1996) *Aramis, or the Love of Technology*. Cambridge: Harvard University Press.

Sauer, C. (1993) *Why Information Systems Fail: A Case Study Approach*. Henley-on-Thames: Alfred Waller.

On the challenge of implementation in complex organizations

Atkinson, C. and V. J. Peel (1998) Growing, not building, the electronic patient record system, *Methods of Information in Medicine* 37: 206–310.

Checkland, P. and S. Holwell (1998) *Information, Systems and Information Systems: Making Sense of the Field*. Chichester: Wiley.

Ciborra, C. U., K. Braa, A. Cordella, B. Dahlbom, A. Failla, O. Hanseth, V. Hepso, J. Ljungberg, E. Montiero and K. A. Simon (eds) (2000) *From Control to Drift. The Dynamics of Corporate Information Infrastructures*. Oxford: Oxford University Press.

Sauer, C. and P. W. Yetton (eds) (1997) *Steps to the Future: Fresh Thinking on the Management of IT-Based Organizational Transformation*. San Francisco: Jossey-Bass.

On user-involvement and ethnography in design

Goguen, J. A. and C. Linde (1993) Techniques for requirements elicitation, *Proceedings of the International Symposium of Requirements Engineering* 1993: 152–64.

Greenbaum, J. and M. Kyng (eds) (1991) *Design at Work: Cooperative Design for Computer Systems*. Hillsdale, N.J.: Lawrence Erlbaum Associates.

Hartswood, M., R. Procter, M. Rouncefield and M. Sharpe (2000) Being there and doing IT in the workplace: a case study of a co-development approach in healthcare. *Proceedings of the CPSR/IFIP WG 9.1 Participatory Design Conference, New York, 28 November – 1 December.*

Kaplan, B. (1997) Addressing organizational issues into the evaluation of medical systems. *Journal of the American Medical Informatics Association* 4: 94–101.

Zuiderent, T. (2003) Blurring the center: On the politics of ethnography. *Scandinavian Journal of Information Systems* 12: 59–78.

Business process redesign and its critique

Davenport, T. H. (1993) *Process Innovation: Reengineering Work through Information Technology.* Boston, MA: Harvard Business School Press.

Sauer, C. and P. W. Yetton (eds) (1997) *Steps to the Future: Fresh Thinking on the Management of IT-Based Organizational Transformation.* San Francisco: Jossey-Bass.

Chapter 10

Project management of innovative PCIS implementations in health care

Cé Bergen

KEY POINTS OF THIS CHAPTER

- Project management is key, especially when projects are inherently unpredictable.
- The project definition should reflect the dual aim of reaching specific targets and learning from the process of attempting to do so.
- The project organization should be designed to optimize possibilities for the steering of PCIS implementation processes.
- Project organization is essentially about structuring project decision making, and being clear about the allocation of responsibilities.
- An important consideration in designing the project organization is the amount of 'managerial weight' needed to keep the project moving.
- The project manager should get a clear ranking from the steering committee with regard to the order of importance of the basic project variables time, money and scope.
- Key to staffing a project is to get significant and dedicated time from project team members.
- Keeping the project on course – while allowing the course to evolve – should in a large part be an inherent functioning of the project organization.

KEY TERMS

- ■ Project management
- ■ Incremental change
- ■ Project organization
- ■ Steering group
- ■ Project group
- ■ Work group
- ■ Risk management table

INTRODUCTION

This chapter focuses on themes that are of special interest to those involved in the management of innovative PCIS implementations in health care. Project management, of course, is a field in itself, the basics of which we can hardly hope to cover in one chapter. Here, we will zoom in on a few core issues that are crucial for IT project management in health care settings: incorporating the unpredictability of implementation projects, for example, and staffing projects in professional bureaucracies. Project definition and project team design, then, will be at the centre of this chapter. This reflects the conceptualization of a PCIS implementation project as a learning and evolving experience, as described in the previous chapter.

THE CASE FOR STRONG PROJECT MANAGEMENT OF PCIS IN HEALTH CARE

As argued in the previous chapter, PCIS implementation in health care does not show a good track record. From a project management point of view this is not surprising, since PCIS implementation is a fundamentally unpredictable process. Project management is often defined as attaining predefined goals, at a predefined time, and within a predefined budget. Yet is this attainable in health care, given the previous statement? According to the previous chapter, goals should evolve during the project and the learning process should remain relatively unstructured (it can hardly be pressured by setting a time for it). Given uncertain times and goals, moreover, a fixed budget would be an illusion.

We will argue here that project management can and should be done – *especially* for the most unpredictable of projects. The key lies in the 'management' part of project management. The art of this management is that – in the midst of all uncertainties – the project has to be steered in the desired direction. To do this,

CASE VIGNETTE

Some years ago, a medium sized hospital had the opportunity to select a new Hospital Information System (HIS) vendor, because the contract with their previous supplier had come to an end. Grasping the opportunity, they set high ambitions for their new HIS and dedicated a significant amount of money for the purchase and subsequent implementation of their new HIS. Their ambition stated that the new HIS must be a real Patient Care Information System. True to their ambition, they selected an innovative and capable HIS/PCIS vendor that had all the functionality on offer to support the work of doctors and nurses. The system included, amongst others, fully fledged order communication with advanced order-set functions, integrated patient planning based on a central patient agenda, a highly flexible forms generator to support customized electronic record building, and so forth. Before moving on to the advanced PCIS functions, of course, the project started with ensuring that the traditional functions supported by the old HIS would be properly replaced.

After two years, having lost the Board of Directors, the project manager, and surviving a near bankruptcy, the old HIS's functions had been replaced with the new HIS/PCIS. This implementation had taken three times the money and twice the time as had been planned. In hindsight, the main reason was that the new HIS/PCIS required that a patient episode had to be selected or registered and an order had to be entered before any other action could be initiated for a patient. Only after having done this, for example, could an admission be performed, or an outpatient visit be planned. Administrative personnel, nurses and doctors alike revolted at this seemingly unworkable process.

Now, seven years later, the nuisance of obligatory order entry and episode registration have been removed from the system by reprogramming parts of it. The basic HIS functions perform adequately. Recently, the medical staff has requested permission from the BoD to start a scan of the marketplace to find an innovative PCIS.

some beacons have to be decided upon to *always* keep in view. Amongst such beacons, an initial set of parameters for the desired goals, time and budget ranks high. In addition, the project organization can be *designed* to optimize possibilities for the steering of such enterprises as embarked upon here. First of all, it should be a project organization that is capable of recognizing the need to redefine goals, time and budget, and has the structure to do so. Second, it should be a project organization that is capable of measuring progress and making decisions that ensure continuing progress.

PCIS implementation in health care will likely fail unless focused effort is taken to structure the detailed decision making process by a broad group of professionals. This decision making process is fundamental to designing redesigned or new work processes – the basis of a successful PCIS implementation.

DEFINE THE PROJECT

Project management starts with the process of defining the project at hand. Given the insights from the previous chapter about the 'learn as you go' nature of PCIS projects (or any innovative project), the project definition should reflect the dual aim of reaching specific targets and learning from the process of doing so. This goes as far as to make redefining the targets based on what is learned, *part* of the project. This is as good a recursive definition as you will find!

In practice, a trade off is made between *having* targets and being able to learn as you go (and thus changing them), through phasing the project. First an overall definition is made by stating what business objectives the project should serve (see also Chapter 8). For example: the project implementation of a Medication System aims to reduce medication errors. Or: the project implementation of a Physician Order Entry System aims to fundamentally improve patient logistics.

Then the project is phased in time by defining intermediate goals. The end of each phase is a natural moment for a thorough evaluation and a rethinking of the targets for the next phase, based on what was learned (see also the next chapter). For example: 'the project Electronic Prescription System phase 1 is the proof-of-concept pilot at cardiology. Phase 2 is implementing the system in the whole of internal medicine. Further implementation is to be defined after completion of phase 2.'

Phase the project smartly

Phasing PCIS projects is crucial. Phasing is basically about reducing complexity. This is much needed, because with the often large scope and high ambition of PCIS projects, uncertainty and unpredictability are high as well. One is looking for ways to divide the project into building blocks (phases) around intermediate goals that can be delivered with less uncertainty and unpredictability.

Delivering a pilot implementation, as 'proof of concept', is in almost all innovative PCIS implementations a good first phase. Delivering the pilot means that the application and its technical infrastructure are working technically correctly, freeing up time and energy to focus on getting the work processes right before attempting a next step.

Other lines along which to phase a PCIS implementation are for example first delivering parts of the project that can be termed as purely technical (e.g. technical infrastructure), or parts of the project that bring the user added value without requiring a change in his work process (e.g. showing examination results). Another example is phasing by sequentially delivering discrete steps of the total work process, e.g. first improving patient intake, then improving patient discharge, and only then starting on patient throughput and integrated patient planning.

Many projects go wrong when after the termination of a pilot phase, 'roll out' is defined as the next phase. A sudden increase in scope of the project increases its uncertainty and unpredictability. Proper time should be allotted for the organization and technology to learn from each other. That is to say: incremental change, introducing smartly dosed next steps one by one, is an ideal way to allow optimal learning from unexpected problems and synergies.

CASE VIGNETTE

When setting high ambitions in care process redesign and IT process support, as in the case of Southern Medical (see Chapter 8), it is important to start work around substantial patient flows. Importantly, care areas should be targeted where 'quick wins' can be achieved, and where professionals frequently encounter bottlenecks. In some cases, it may be appropriate to *not* start with the introduction of IT so as to not overload the targets for the first step. The complexity of the organizational change, in other words, can lead one to wait with IT (to delay introducing further complexity) until the outlines of the new working methods are realized.

Be clear on scope, deliverables, milestones, initial timetable and budget

For each phase of the project, the scope, deliverables, milestones, timetable and budget should be defined. The scope should clearly state which work processes will be included (and which will be excluded). Milestones and deliverables should be placed on a timeline, resulting in the initial timetable for that phase of the project.

Special attention should be given to milestones and deliverables to make sure that these are phrased in such a way that they can be easily reported on. A common mistake is to phrase a milestone as an activity. For example saying 'training cardiologists to use electronic ordering in the month September', instead of saying 'all cardiologists trained to use electronic ordering by end September'. It is crucial that the project team and the steering committee unambiguously understand when the project is in danger of getting bogged down. A clear phrasing of milestones and deliverables is fundamental to creating an understanding of the dynamics of the project.

Next, based on the initial timetable for milestones and deliverables, a resources requirement estimate is made. This results in an initial project budget stating personnel and materials requirements. Guidelines for determining the personnel requirements will be discussed on page 198–202.

Be absolutely clear on the choice of the basic project variables

Project management is based on three generic parameters: time, money and scope. The parameter time is obvious: when should the project be delivered? The parameter money is meant in a broad sense, covering internal and external personnel costs, and all required materials. The parameter scope is meant to cover all activity areas following from the stated objectives and ambitions for the project.

The project goals must be absolutely clear on the order of importance of these three parameters. Having delivered the initial project plan, the next task of the project manager is to get a clear ranking from the steering committee with regard to the order of importance of time, money and scope. This is not an easy task for the project manager. Most steering committees will at first choose for the obvious. Time, money and scope are equally important, and the project manager is reminded he was hired to deliver on preset targets for each of these parameters. In the discussion that should follow, the project manager and steering committee should unearth what the project will entail in this organization, with these set ambitions. If the project is found to be highly predictable in its outcomes, then fixed targets can be set for all three project control parameters. But most likely, since we are dealing here with PCIS implementations, the discussion will clarify the inherent 'learn as you go' nature of this type of project at this point in time. Then the steering committee must again be asked to rank the order of importance of time, money and scope.

CASE VIGNETTE

A famous example of the outcome of the ranking of time, money and scope, is the project aimed at putting the first man on the moon. Scope and time were fixed parameters: the competition with the USSR was a leading driver of the project. Money, then, was the variable, of which as much was used as needed to deliver the project. Had this variable been fixed as well, the project would have most likely never succeeded.

In a hospital setting, money will not likely be the last in the ranking of importance of project control variables. Often, time is last in the ranking, giving the possibility to delay project delivery in order to reach the desired scope. When scope is the last in the ranking, ambitions are trimmed in order to meet the project delivery deadline within budget.

DESIGN THE PROJECT ORGANIZATION AND STAFF THE PROJECT

Determine the amount of 'management leverage' needed

An important factor when designing the project organization is the amount of 'managerial weight' needed to keep the project moving. This is not meant ironically: it is imperative to be able to recognize and resolve issues as they occur during the project. This ability is directly related to line management representation within the project team, or the mandate that the project team has been given to resolve issues. The more innovative, the larger, the more ambitious the project, the more impact the project will have on the organization, and the more top management should thus be involved in the project (see Figure 10.1).

If a hospital-wide project is innovative, involves a large number of people, aims to standardize work processes, and involves behavioural change, then it must be clear that this project should be led on a Board of Directors level. The introduction of a Physician Order Entry System would be an example of such a project.

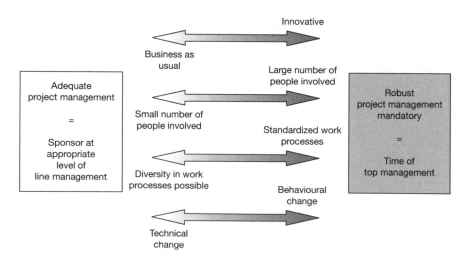

Figure 10.1 *Positioning the project on the basis of project characteristics.*

Structure the decision making on content

Having decided on the level of management representation in the project team, the next question is how to structure the ability of the project team to resolve issues related to the content of the work processes at hand. During the implementation of a Medication System, for example, issues will inevitably arise that are specific for the treatment of a patient group. Similarly, as we discussed in the previous chapter, the introduction of a Physician Order Entry System affects the way doctors and nurses cooperate.

There are three basic structures in the design of the project organization: the steering committee, the project group and work groups. The steering committee controls time, money and scope. The project group coordinates the work of the work groups, resolves issues that span more than one work group, and serves as the project office for the project. The work groups, of which there can be several, work on specific tasks in the course of the project. In small projects, depending on the number of people involved, these basic structures could be compressed into two or even one group. In a large project all three basic structures will be needed.

In addition to these basic structures, a complex project might also make use of a matrix structure for 'horizontal themes' that cut through the domains of several work groups, and sounding board groups. The former includes themes such as end user training, master indexes, data conversion, methodology for describing the administrative organization and so forth. See Figure 10.2 for an example.

199

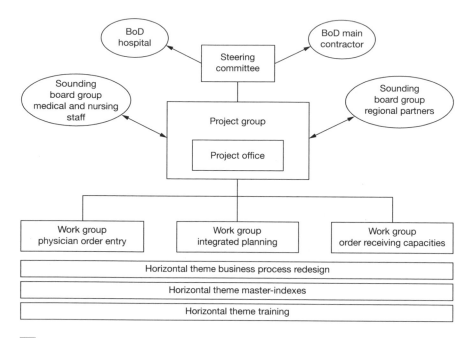

Figure 10.2 *Example of project organization.*

The steering committee controls time, money and scope

One main task of the steering committee is to manage the project parameters time, money and scope. The members of the steering committee should be line managers of a level corresponding with the need for management input of the project (see above). Another main task of the steering committee is to authorize new and redesigned work processes that are put forward by the project group. In the consensus driven world of hospitals, this is a crucial task if any deadline at all is to be made: bottom-up consensus does not combine well with deadlines.

One could consider including a high level manager of the project's main contractor (consultancy company, and/or IT vendor) in the steering committee. In this way the main contractor is made into a collaborating partner, instead of a remote provider of products and services.

The project group coordinates and facilitates decision making

The project group is the coordination point for the project. Chairman of the project group is the project manager. The other members of the project group are predominantly the chairmen of the work groups. In the project group, issues that span more than one work group are resolved, the project planning is done, and the change management activities are coordinated.

The ability of the project group to effectively execute decision making on the content of the work processes, where needed backed by authorization from the steering committee, depends largely on selecting the right chairmen for the work groups. The project group designs the interaction between the various high-level work processes. To put it bluntly, this is where the general rules are made on how the various work processes will work together. To put it a bit more mildly, this is where agreement is reached on what will be proposed to the Board of Directors on the rules of working together in the redesigned work processes. For example, the project group decides just how specialized nurses supported by computerized care protocols will be positioned in the care pathway of geriatric care. Or, another example, whether primary care physicians will have access into all planning systems of the hospital, supported by a computerized referral index, is a decision that will be made (or at the very least 'pre-cooked') by the project group.

The project office is a staff function to the project group. The main task of the project office is to provide a standardized set of methodologies and templates for the participants in the project. All work groups need BPR methodologies, process mapping methodology, change management methodology, project management methodology and so forth. The project office is the main driver for the efficiency of the work processes of the project itself.

The work groups get the work done

The task of the work groups is to get the work done. (Re)designing work processes, customizing the information system, debugging the work processes and information systems in simulation runs, end user training, producing documentation on work processes and the information system, and finally giving support during and after 'going live'.

Work groups are formed around a high-level description of work processes. The choices made at the formation of the work groups are dependent on the goals of the project. If a fundamental redesign is considered, then the work groups might change with the phases of the project. First a small core group, aided by ad-hoc work groups, may make the high-level work process design, for example. Then work groups may be formed around the different high-level descriptions to make the detailed design. And finally, the project team members may be rearranged in work groups formed on the basis of the implementation strategy. During a PCIS implementation, one may have one work group on clinical work processes and another on outpatient work processes; alternatively, a process redesign of the care process in the detailing phase might have a work group patient intake, a work group integrated planning, and a work group patient discharge.

The responsibility area and staffing of a work group should be such that most questions on content can be handled within the work group itself. The chairman must be the process owner for the work process under its responsibility. This is a challenge in most hospitals for most work processes. For instance, consider the work process integrated patient planning. In cases such as this, a process owner should be found whose authority will have to cut through the existing organization, and who reports to a process sponsor on Board of Directors level. If work groups are ordered by patient groups, natural process owners for most work processes can be found more readily. The natural process owner of a care pathway is the head of the medical specialty or multi-disciplinary treatment group.

In addition to the chairman, further roles in the work group are: a member responsible for planning and methodology, one or more information system experts, and subject matter experts.

Sounding board groups anchor the project in the real world

Sounding board groups are important. By installing them and presenting to them the project's progress, content under development, and issues, a reality check is introduced for the project team. A good name for the sounding board group meetings is challenge sessions. Sounding board group members are invited to speak their mind about the content under development and the project itself.

To be effective, the steering committee chairman should chair sounding board group meetings, and the invitees should be stakeholders. This ensures proper stature for the meetings, so that they can simultaneously occasion as commitment building meetings for stakeholders that are not members of the project team.

Core rule for staffing: committing dedicated time

A certain recipe for project failure is to have many people cooperating, with each person donating a little bit of their time. Staffing must start with freeing up people from other duties to serve on the project. This is a tough task in most health care institutions. Health care institutions operate in a paradigm of scarcity, causing projects to be routinely understaffed. A good way to start is to put in place a small dedicated core team as soon as the decision for the project is made. The core team does the initial project planning, identifies the roles needed, names people for these roles, and makes an estimate of how much time of each individual is needed. Then the project manager starts the negotiations to free up the required persons to meet the project ambitions.

The amount of time that is needed for each role is, of course, very much dependent on the project at hand, especially on the ambitions for that project. For any ambitious, innovative ICT implementation, there are some rough measures one should heed to be effective in each role. A Board of Directors member must at a minimum reserve half a day per week for the project. A line manager – chair person of a work group – at least one day per week. Subject matter experts – members of work groups – three days per week to full time. The project manager must be at this job full time. A team member responsible for planning and method-ology, and an information system expert: both also full time.

The equilibrium between internal and external staff

Finally it is a consideration for the health care organization to involve external experts in the implementation trajectories. Particularly with large-scale imple-mentation trajectories, the health care organization can reap benefits through hiring parties who have built up routines relevant to large-scale trajectories, or who have a specialized contribution to make.

Adding senior consultants from the application's vendor (and/or process redesign experts) to each work group is an effective way to quickly build up appli-cation expertise (and/or process redesign expertise). To be effective these consul-tants should be planned to be part of the team at least three days a week and must really be experts in their area. A word of caution is in place here: the health care organization should not fall into a trap of their own making to bring in external consultants because it is so hard to free their own personnel from their existing duties. This will result in a lack of organizational learning during the project and the dire consequence of ending up with somebody else's information system.

KEEPING THE COURSE

Keeping an eye on the beacons set should for a large part be ensured in the inherent functioning of the project organization. Most work is done in the work groups, and these check their own progress against the milestone plan. Only when they run into issues that are outside their ability to solve do they alert the project group.

The project group, mainly through the project manager, has the job of keeping an eye on the overall progress and the speed with which upcoming problems are solved. The milestone plan is the basis for measuring progress. The list of prob-lems to be resolved, and especially the speed with which they are resolved, gives an indication of future progress.

In addition, the project manager maintains a *risk management table*. This table contains a list of potential risks to the project, and a corresponding list of measures to prevent these risks from materializing. If prevention is not a realistic option, then the measure should consist of early recognition of the problem and scenarios to deal with its occurrence.

A very important aspect of keeping the project on course – while allowing this course to evolve – is the role of project management in actively enabling the steering committee to actually steer. Steering committee meetings should be on a predefined schedule, for example each month or six weeks, and should not be cancelled. Especially when there is no progress to report, steering committee meetings *should* be held. If there is no progress, after all, something is definitely going wrong.

During a steering committee meeting the project manager should report progress against the milestone plan, an assessment of workload and morale in the project team, change management issues, and budget overview. Then the project manager should clearly state which decisions are to be made by the steering committee in order to maintain progress of the project, including authorizing project group proposals and potential changes to targets, milestones or the overall course of the project. Finally the steering committee should discuss the Risk Management table.

DISCUSSION QUESTIONS

1   One of the fundamental definitions of a project is that it must have a clear start and end. With all that has been said about PCIS implementation, it must be clear that it is more or less impossible to define a clear end. *How is this solved?*

2   A new health care organization, the result of a merger of two home care organizations and a large nursing home, gives you, as the project manager, the task to integrate their three as yet separate Information Systems into one system for the whole new organization. Integration should be achieved in a newly acquired Care Information System with advanced PCIS functionalities. The project must become a flagship case! The BoD asks you to present a first outline of a milestone plan, the project organization and the required staffing. *Build this outline.*

3   Under great pressure by the professional staff, your mental health care organization has contracted a software company to integrate all electronically available patient data in a so-called professional workstation. The software company will use Internet technologies to unlock the different organizations' information systems that contain patient data. The chairmen of the psychiatric and psychological staff send you an enthusiastic e-mail saying that they will nominate you as chair of the Steering Committee overseeing the building and implementation of the professional workstation.
Reflect on your own position in relation to this honourable nomination. Then propose a project organization for this project and a proposal for phasing the project.

FURTHER READING

General project management literature

Bowen, H. K. (1996) *Project Management Manual.* Boston: HBS Press.

Davenport, T. H. (2000) *Mission Critical: Realizing the Promise of Enterprise Systems.* Boston: HBS Press.

Senge, P., A. Kleiner, C. Roberts, R. Ross, G. Roth and B. Smith (1999) *The Dance of Change – The Challenges of Sustaining Momentum in Learning Organizations – A Vth Discipline Resource.* London: Nicholas Brealey Publishing.

Project management of PCIS implementation

To our knowledge, there is no additional literature on this specific subject.

Chapter 11

Evaluation of patient care information systems

Theory and practice

Arjen Stoop, Heather Heathfield, Marleen de Mul and Marc Berg

---

KEY POINTS OF THIS CHAPTER

- Evaluation of PCISs is a balancing act between limited resources and the need to focus on a wide spectrum of possible effects of the use of the system.

- Formative evaluation offers better opportunities to improve PCIS development and use than summative evaluation.

- The use of randomized clinical trials in PCIS evaluation does not lead to suitable management information for organizational decision-making about a PCIS.

- Integrating qualitative and quantitative methods leads to a better understanding of the effects of the implementation of PCISs than the concentration on one of the two.

- Textbook descriptions of 'how one should perform an evaluation' are useful, but are of limited value because of the complexity of evaluation in real-life settings.

KEY TERMS

- Randomized controlled trials
- Formative and summative evaluation
- Objectivist and subjectivist evaluation methods

INTRODUCTION

Evaluation of patient care information systems (PCISs) has become increasingly important. Handling the increased complexity of health care processes, many argue, is impossible without the use of PCISs such as electronic patient records, patient data management systems, physician order entry systems and decision support systems. Many benefits are claimed: such systems will 'enhance the quality and efficiency of care', 'empower the patient', 'provide an answer to labour shortages', 'help reduce medical errors' and so forth. Yet such claims can only be validated through evaluation of the performances and the effects of (using) these systems. In addition, the introduction and maintenance of PCISs consumes large amounts of resources and implementation failure is a very traumatic event for an organization. Decision-makers and those who are responsible for the procurement or development of IT are expected to demonstrate that resources spent on IT provide benefits in clinical outcomes, cost savings, and/or to the health care process. Furthermore, evaluation is increasingly important since there is a need to understand the effects of PCIS on the social, professional and organizational context in which they are used.

Those responsible for the design and implementation of evaluation studies, in the meantime, are faced with a bewildering and often conflicting array of choices and dilemmas concerning evaluation criteria, study designs, data collection methods and analysis techniques. In this chapter, we discuss some of the choices and dilemmas in PCIS evaluation, and provide the reader with practical guidance. While evaluation can be aimed at many audiences, we here focus primarily on PCIS evaluation aimed at informing professionals and organization management in their decision-making about the development, implementation and use of the PCIS.

This chapter covers the following topics:

- the randomized controlled trial debate;
- evaluation from a sociotechnical point of view;
- steps to designing an evaluation: theory and practice.

THE RANDOMIZED CONTROLLED TRIAL DEBATE

In the field of evaluation of PCIS, two kinds of evaluation are distinguished: formative and summative. Formative evaluations focus on the continuous improvement of the system. Research is done throughout the lifecycle of a system, aimed at facilitating the organizational learning that is imperative for successful system design and implementation. Summative evaluations, on the other hand, are done to account *post hoc* for the promised or expected benefits, such as financial savings or the effectiveness of information systems in terms of clinical outcomes. Where formative evaluations are internally oriented, providing insights for the work groups, the project and steering group alike, summative evaluations are externally oriented, towards those paying or politically responsible for the PCIS.

From the literature on evaluation of PCIS in health care it is clear that (literature on) summative evaluations are predominant in the field of PCIS evaluation. More specifically, since the field of PCIS evaluation is strongly influenced by the health care context in which it finds itself, the golden standard for evaluating new technologies – as in medicine – is the Randomized Controlled Trial (RCT). An RCT used for testing a new drug, for example, means that two randomly selected groups of patient are created: one group that is given the intervention (the drug) and a control group that is not exposed to the intervention (by being given a placebo). The doctor and the patients are both 'blinded': they do not know whether the treatment consists of the drug or the placebo. As a consequence, neither doctors nor patients know whether the drug causes the effect of the treatment or not. Randomization and blinding are means to eradicate confounding variables and biased interpretation. RCTs are regarded as optimally suited to prove whether a new medical technology is effective or not – or whether the effectiveness lies in the eye of the beholder, in the placebo effect and so forth. However, given the need for a control group, to control for unwanted variables, and the need for a strict definition of and protocol for the measurements targeted for improvement, RCTs take up much work and are expensive.

Given the fact that IT is also a technology, it is not so strange that health care professionals, medical journals and, in their wake, many health care managers are primarily focused on the RCT as the model for evaluation. Hence, the history of PCIS evaluation is replete with RCT-like studies proving the effectiveness in terms of clinical decisions of, for example, alert and reminder systems (see Kaplan 2001).

Yet over the past two decades, more and more authors have voiced their concern about this dominance of the RCT model for PCIS evaluation. RCTs are criticized because of different reasons. First of all, the fact that conceptualizing (parts of) PCIS systems as 'the intervention' that a RCT focuses on, supposes that it makes sense and is possible to isolate the functioning of this 'hardware' from the social processes that surround it and are integrated with its current functioning. Yet as we have seen time and time again in this book, this assumption is dubious

– to say the least. In practice, it is often impossible to disentangle the 'effect' caused by the PCIS itself from the 'effect' caused by the changes in the work practices induced by the PCIS implementation. (In fact, as we argued in the last few chapters, PCIS systems *should* be introduced as part and parcel of an organizational development process, which renders a search for the 'unique effects' of the information technology wholly elusive).

Second, a properly executed RCT is labour intensive and expensive. Conducting an RCT means that randomization has to be accomplished: by patient, or groups of professionals. In the former, the same doctor may use a decision support system on randomly allocated patients, for example. In the latter (also known as clustered randomized trials), individual professionals, departments or whole hospitals are randomized to use the Decision Support System or not to use it. However, generating these kind of 'objective' circumstances is often impossible. For example, patient-randomized trials have a strong risk of the 'carry-over' effect, i.e. doctors learn from the system and apply this new knowledge to the treatment of control patients as well as intervention ones. Clustered RCTs may not provide comparable control and intervention groups, given that no two professionals, departments or hospitals are likely to be the same. In both types of trial it is not possible to 'blind' the participants from the presence of the health care PCIS.

In addition, generating these kind of 'objective' circumstances is often also undesirable. The specific routines, work processes, leadership patterns, cultures of professionals and departments within and between hospitals differ – and such issues are often key in understanding why systems may fail in one situation and succeed in another. While RCTs will give 'hard data' (in the form of establishing relations between) on a very limited set of pre-set parameters, it cannot answer the *why* or *how* questions that are often the most relevant when one wants to understand PCIS implementation. Nor can it grasp all the unanticipated consequences, like sabotage of a system because of user resistance, that are often crucial to the fate of PCISs. RCT researchers themselves often stress that their designs are of limited 'real-world' use due to the artificial, laboratory circumstances (e.g. simulation patients, inexperienced subjects) in which the data are produced. Knowing more about these issues requires methods that are able to understand the way information systems work in daily practices and the interaction between the system and the user. In much recent literature on ICT evaluation, qualitative methods like interviews, participant observations and focus group meetings are seen as much more suitable for this goal (see also further).

Finally, social scientists have argued that 'scientificness' comes in many guises, of which hypothesis testing is only one. Building a theory explaining a specific social phenomenon, for example, is an equally scientific endeavour, which may or may not be amenable to quantification, or to 'testing' through an RCT.

FORMATIVE EVALUATION OF PATIENT CARE INFORMATION SYSTEMS

Partly due to this historical entwinement with the RCT as 'gold standard', the PCIS evaluation literature still sharply divides 'objectivist' and 'subjectivist' approaches to PCIS evaluation. The objectivist position starts with the assumption that the merits and worth of an information system can and should be quantifiable. 'To measure is to know', it is often stated, and observations should be as objective as possible. In this way, it is argued, two observations of the same phenomenon will yield the same results, without being affected by how the resource under study functions or is used. Much attention, therefore, is given to the avoidance of measurement error, and the prevention of biased observation. Such issues, indeed, are crucial for any definite summative evaluation. For formative evaluations, we will argue however, an overly stringent focus on objective measurement is beside the point.

On the other side of the spectrum we find the subjectivist position, which argues that the impacts of health care ICT are often social and organizational in nature. In addition, even when one focuses on primarily medical or financial targets, social and organizational issues are co-responsible for the results. Therefore, some authors argue that proper health care ICT evaluation (summative and formative) requires the use of qualitative methods instead of quantitative methods. From this position, the results obtained from observation and interviews are context-dependent, and since the researcher is part of this context, 'objective data' are an illusion *in principle*. What is important is to understand and document the different opinions that individuals and groups hold on issues, and the social and organizational processes that lead to a certain effect – such as the 'success' or 'failure' of a PCIS (see e.g. case study step 5 below).

Contrary to the assumptions underlying the use of RCTs, a formative PCIS evaluation should consider factors like limited time and resources, logistics, contradicting cultural, social and political forces between different stakeholders and so forth as research data. For this, qualitative methods are key. However, this does not mean that the value of quantitative research methods is denied. In fact, in formative evaluations, qualitative and quantitative research methods should be seen as complementary. Qualitative research methods such as interviews, observations and document analysis are optimally suited to understand a phenomenon from the points of view of the participants, and in its particular social and institutional context. They are capable of getting to the *what*, *why* and *how* of a social phenomenon: how users perceive and experience a system, for example, what the influence is of the social and organizational context on system use, or why an implementation strategy that worked in organization A does not work in organization B.

Quantitative research methods are most suitable for establishing the *size, extent* or *duration* of certain phenomena (*how much*), or to establish *that* a specific cause or intervention results in a pre-specified effect. The 'how much' can be answered using different measurement techniques such as questionnaires, time studies or tracking of clinical outcomes. To establish a causal relationship, a broad range of more or less 'rigorous' designs is available, such as before–after designs, meta-analysis, cohort studies, case-control studies and observational studies.

For summative, scientific purposes, of course, purely qualitative or quantitative studies (including RCTs) may be very useful. In the case of user resistance, for example, it is important to know what the exact nature of the resistance is and what the impact is on the way professionals work in an organization. It is, on the other hand, also important to know how many users experience resistance and what the consequences of not using a system are for clinical outcomes. Yet when evaluations at the organizational level are concerned, aimed at informing decision-making about the PCIS, a comprehensive evaluation requires the use of quantita-tive *and* qualitative methods. Only in that way is it possible to look at all the different relevant domains (technical, organizational, professional, economic, ethical/legal issues) that come to play in such decisions and generate a balanced judgement.

Combinations of qualitative and quantitative methods in information systems evaluation have been made – albeit infrequently – since the end of the 1980s. In such studies, qualitative results were usually seen as the exploratory 'first steps' that could at best inform the 'real' research of generating hypotheses to be tested using experimental or statistical techniques. During the last decade, more sym-metrical integrations have been proposed under the label of the 'multimethod' approach, where the different methods each produce their own data, without an implicit proposed hierarchy between them. One of the reasons for the importance of 'multimethod' research is that the use of different methods is needed to capture the diverse and diffuse nature of information systems' effects. Another reason is to strengthen the robustness of research results by looking at the way in which research results coming from different methods support each other (or not), which is called triangulation.

Though we agree with these insights, we would like to argue that this is still a very loose 'integration' of qualitative and quantitative methods. At best, qualita-tive and quantitative researchers cooperate, and jointly decide on issues best amenable for qualitative or quantitative evaluation. Having thus 'divided the turf', studies are usually done rather independently and, more often than not, the results discussed follow these borders drawn. In addition, the results from the different studies are often phrased in such different idioms that 'integration' becomes completely (practically and theoretically) impossible.

True integration requires joint design and execution of the study, where data from one method are used as *input* for the other. Hereby we mean to take results from one method as a starting point for research of the other method. In this way it is possible to capitalize on the strong points of each method in order to gain more understanding in the 'that' *and* the 'how' or 'why'. After all, it is obvious that having established *that* something is the case is a rather useful input to investigating *why* that is so. And, vice versa, the insight *'how'* a specific effect is achieved can be greatly strengthened by the knowledge *how often* this is so. Explained like this, the interrelation of the two methods becomes almost all too obvious. Yet truly integrated designs are still rare.

Using results from one method as input for the other makes it possible to capitalize on the strong points of each method and increases the understanding and strength of the overall results. Applying methods in this way supposes a careful sequencing of the design. Qualitative research often is a prerequisite for quantitative research, because qualitative methods are best in identifying and selecting research topics for investigation. Quantitative research can, after that, be used to quantify these topics. Interpreting the results from quantitative research, subsequently, requires qualitative methods. For example, to conclude whether the results can be regarded as 'bad' or 'good', or to understand fluctuations or apparent contradiction in measured scores, qualitative interpretation is required to make sense of the numbers obtained. For formative evaluations, integrating quantitative and qualitative research methods in this way requires that these quantitative designs should be quite 'modest' in nature: before–after designs are useful, but more strictly experimental designs (like RCTs) exceed their aim. Their design is too rigorous to be of help, often directly hinders the organizational change process that is occurring, and they yield very few results in the light of their costs.

In the next paragraph we will elaborate on the different steps that come to play when designing and conducting an evaluation.

STEPS IN DESIGNING AN EVALUATION

In this paragraph we will describe the design of an evaluation as following several, successive steps (as shown in Figure 11.1) (Heathfield *et al.* 2001). We will focus primarily, but not exclusively, on formative evaluation. In reality, the individual steps are often difficult to separate, and usually impossible to manage as a simple and steady sequence. The process of designing an evaluation is one of adjustment and compromise, where choices concerning study design, evaluation criteria and data collection methods must be offset against the constraints of conflicting stakeholders' aims, deadlines, resources available, the intrusiveness of the evaluation and ethical considerations. The design of an evaluation is as much a social and political process as that of IT procurement and implementation itself. By using case material (from the UK and the Netherlands), we will show that taking these steps can be quite complicated. Every next step is determined by the situation at hand. Though the cases differ in technology, set up and success, both can be seen as a realistic example of the implementation of a PCIS in health care. The more general

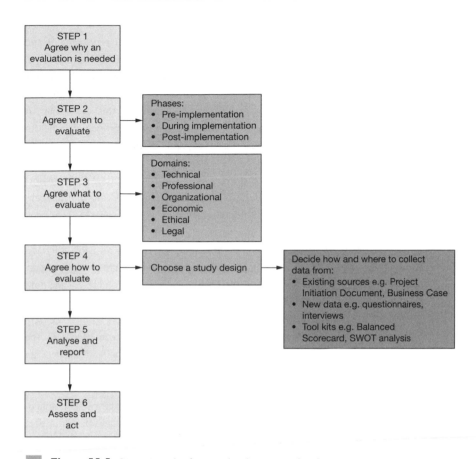

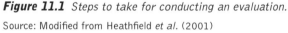
Figure 11.1 *Steps to take for conducting an evaluation.*
Source: Modified from Heathfield *et al.* (2001)

'Issues' and 'Lessons learned' at the end of each step are based on material from these two sites as well as other case material.

CASE STUDY

The first case is based upon a study in which the UK NHS Executive, through its Information Management Group, initiated two programmes of work which sought to improve patient records using information technology: the Electronic Patient Record (EPR) project and The Clinical Workstation (ICWS) project. The EPR project was a three-year research and development programme to assist clinicians in acute hospitals to provide better care to patients through the use of electronic patient record systems. The ICWS project was a two year project concerned with providing interface facilities to an EPR. A number of sites with established Hospital Information Systems and sites in the early stages of procurement and implementation but with an organizational commitment to an EPR were selected. External evaluation was seen as essential to both the EPR and ICWS projects and the evaluation covered all five sites. Several stakeholder groups, at both national and local levels, were interested in the results of this evaluation. A multidisciplinary team was assigned to evaluate the project, including health economists, social scientists, computer scientists and health services management specialists (Heathfield *et al.* 1999).

The second case refers to the late 1990s, when the Intensive Care Departments of a large Medical Centre in The Netherlands agreed to invest in information technology. The purchase of a Patient Data Management System (PDMS) was seen as an important first step towards an electronic patient record for Intensive Care, as it was a system to be used by both doctors and nurses. Like an EPR, a PDMS is an IT application that makes it possible to enter patient data. More importantly, the PDMS is explicitly focused on automatically storing and retrieving data from the heart monitor, the respirator and other electronic devices used in the Intensive Care Units. Moreover, the PDMS can also collect data from other data sources in the hospital, for example the laboratory results from the HIS. The system also makes it easier for the medical staff to order medication, because the system can calculate the right doses based on patient characteristics (age, weight). In addition, the system is able to make all sorts of automatically generated calculations, overviews and reminders, such as the fluid balance and medication overviews, and medication reminders. The system replaced an important part of the Intensive Care paper medical record, the bed chart.

Step 1 Agree why an evaluation is needed

This first step is crucial, because it does not only give direction to the goal of the evaluation and the questions that have to be answered, but, as a consequence, also to the required methods. If one wants to do an evaluation to compare a situation before and after the implementation of a PCIS with the option to return to the old situation when the system does not function well enough, it is important to do a before–after study. This means that one first has to do a measurement of the situation before the implementation (baseline measurement), as to be able to make a good comparison between the situation with and without the system. If the implementation of a system is meant to replace work practices without the option of returning to the old situation without the system, for example, the formative evaluation of the system should focus on improving the way the system functions. In this case, a longitudinal design, throughout the whole implementation process, is appropriate.

CASE STUDY

In the EPR case study there was considerable difficulty in getting the stakeholders and commissioners of the evaluation to agree on the very *reason* for the evaluation. Many did not perceive an evaluation's role in promoting successful system implementation, for example. At last the team agreed on questions such as: What is the impact of the technology on clinical management regarding individual patient care, management of services and resource management? What is the experience of living and working at the implementation sites? During the study, however, it appeared that these questions were still far too general to answer directly, and that views on the concrete purpose of the evaluation were still diverging.

In the PDMS case the complexity of the question 'why evaluate' was caused by the fact that the evaluation had to serve different goals. On the one hand, the evaluation of the pilot had to deliver 'objective results' because the Board of Directors was about to decide about further investments in the rollout of the system to other ICUs. The project team therefore had to show the Board of Directors to what extent the goal of the pilot was met (the technical implementation of a PDMS with specific features and functionality). On the other hand, the members of the project team (especially the doctors and nurses) were interested in the impact of the system on work practices and user satisfaction. As a result, the evaluation of the PDMS pilot consisted of different parts, each addressing different evaluation questions, requiring different methods and time scopes.

In this step, different issues come to the fore and several challenges have to be faced:

Issues

- Stakeholders may disagree on why an evaluation is needed, and it is not uncommon that some question if evaluation is necessary at all (i.e., whether doing an evaluation is not a waste of already scarce resources).
- Different stakeholders wish to evaluate for different reasons.

Challenges

- Ensure that everyone fully understands the role and importance of evaluation.
- The project team responsible for conducting the evaluation needs to have enough knowledge about conducting an evaluation.

- Make clear how the evaluation results will be used, whether this is to inform and change the future direction of the project or to simply report and justify expenditure.
- Be aware of different stakeholders perspectives and agendas and make these explicit in the evaluation.

Step 2 Agree when to evaluate

The question when an evaluation is appropriate depends on different matters. First, it depends on the aim of the evaluation. Formative evaluations are geared towards process indicators and/or preliminary outcome measurements and are performed before and during the implementation of an information system. Summative evaluations are geared towards outcome parameters and are often performed before and after the implementation process to be able to compare both situations. Typical summative evaluations are, for example, cost-effectiveness or cost–benefit analyses.

CASE STUDY

In the UK EPR project, the evaluation was only commissioned after the start of the implementation, despite the fact that the commissioners of the work required the evaluation to demonstrate benefits in the post implementation as compared to the baseline situation. Therefore it was not possible to conduct a before–after study. In addition, due to the problem of defining and agreeing on the scope of the evaluation, and the lack of initial access to the sites, the timescales for starting the evaluation slipped considerably.

The project team of the PDMS started to think about conducting the evaluation during the pilot implementation. Here also, when the decision to evaluate was made it was too late to do a before-evaluation of the 'old situation' (without the system). Consequently, topics like possible reduction of medical errors and completeness of medical records could not be evaluated. The project team decided therefore to evaluate user satisfaction during and after the implementation.

Issues

- Stakeholders often do not consider evaluation until late in a project which prevents a before–after study design.
- Evaluating early in the project life cycle can highlight problems and barriers, enabling them to be solved and the project to progress.

216

Challenges

■ Start evaluation planning as early in the project life cycle as possible, prefer-
ably before project initiation.

■ Getting 'evaluation' on the agenda this early in the project often requires an
awareness of the organizational challenges of PCIS implementation that might
not – yet – be present at the project and steering group level.

Step 3 Agree what to evaluate

Evaluations can be focused on different topics, which we will call domains. By
domain we mean the different viewpoints an evaluation can take: it can focus
on the technical performance of the system, on the impact of the system on professional or organizational matters, or on economic, ethical and legal features.
Looking at an EPR, for example, relevant topics from the technical domain are
whether the system is compatible with other systems (like the hospital information system), whether it is easily upgradeable, whether it is easily maintained
and whether the system has a fast response time. Relevant topics from the professional domain are whether the system meets professionals' needs, whether it
is user-friendly, whether it makes the work of professionals easier. From the
organizational domain it is relevant to know whether the organization is ready
for the implementation of a new system, whether the objective of the implementation is clear and whether it fits with the organizational strategy. From the
economic domain it is interesting to know what the costs are of buying the
system, training of personnel, maintenance and so forth. From an ethical point
of view it is interesting to know what the effects of electronic patient data are on
for example autonomy of the patient or the doctor–patient communication. From
the legal domain, finally, topics like the legal status of electronic patient data
are crucial.

When one simultaneously takes the domain and the phase of implementation
in consideration, a whole range of potentially relevant evaluation questions
emerges (see Table 11.1). The importance of the different questions is dependent
on the type of technology and the focus of the evaluation. Paying attention to all
these questions offers the possibility to do a comprehensive evaluation, which
means one can judge the information system on all relevant aspects.

Since one can ask so many questions, the relevance of the evaluation questions
is dependent on the perspective that one takes. There can be as many perspectives
as there are stakeholders in an evaluation project. For example, evaluation questions regarding the technical aspects of maintenance, compatibility with other
systems and possibilities to upgrade are relevant for the IT department, but generally less of a priority for professionals (doctors, nurses) or the manager that is
accountable for the cost-effectiveness of an information system. Patients, for

Table 11.1 *Different domains and moments of PCIS evaluation, with example questions*

Pre-implementation	Implementation	Post-implementation
Technical domain:		
• compatibility with other systems? • upgradeable? • maintenance? • data consistency? • speed? • adaptability to changing requirements?	• possible to tailor information to specific needs of professionals? • downtime (frequency, duration)? • upgradeable?	• how did the system perform on all selected features? • were there unexpected problems and were they solvable?
Professional domain:		
• what are the professionals' needs? • how much time does it take to learn the system/work with it? • does it make work easier? • what are professionals' interests to work with the system? • user-friendliness? • content of information: understandable and complete?	• is it easy to use? • what are the benefits compared to the old situation? • (how) does it affect the content/effectiveness of work? • does it improve patient outcomes (compliance, morbidity, mortality)?	• 'final' impacts on content/effectiveness of work (changing tasks, responsibilities, routines, less errors, time saving, less 'lost' records)? • improved data quality? • impact on patient outcomes? • overall satisfaction? • overall use?
Organizational domain:		
• is the organization ready? • are the different stakeholders ready? • is the objective of implementation clear? • does the investment 'fit' with other organizational strategies? • what kind of preparations/adjustments have to be made in advance?	• does the organization have to make adjustments (procedures, strategy, decision-making, etc.)? • are there unexpected negative effects?	• impacts on work processes and organization as a whole (communication patterns, responsibilities, decision-making procedures, interactions within/between professional groups)? • impacts on waiting lists, provided services, organizational strategy? • impacts on patient satisfaction?

Table 11.1 *(cont.)*

Pre-implementation	Implementation	Post-implementation
Economic domain:		
• expected costs of buying, training, maintenance, etc.? • expected benefits (return on investment)? • reliable vendor?	• unexpected costs (maintenance, upgrading, training)? • are risks being managed?	• 'final' costs? • 'final' benefits?
Ethical domain:		
• data access, data security? • accountability for use of patient data? • possible effects of use of electronic patient data?	• how are patient data being used (by whom, for what purposes)? • who is responsible for use of patient data? • how are patients involved in the implementation?	• 'overall' effects of use of electronic patient data (e.g. decision-making, autonomy, doctor–patient communication, etc.)?
Legal domain:		
• expected registration (quality, presence) improvements/benefits?	• what role do electronic patient data play in legal matters (e.g. legal status)?	• consequences of use of electronic patient data? • (potential) legal (im)possibilities?

Source: Stoop and Berg (2003)

example, are interested in patient outcomes, but probably less interested in the expected costs of buying or the reliability of the vendor. Independent of the reason for the evaluation, the aim of evaluation is to find answers to relevant evaluation questions. This sounds incredibly obvious, yet *defining* what a relevant research question *is* in a given situation often appears to be far from easy. As we argued in different earlier chapters, since it is often less than clear *why,* from the perspective of the organization, a PCIS project is embarked upon, it is also often difficult to establish what should be evaluated. Once this is clear, it becomes relatively easy: systems that are implemented to enhance the quality of care in terms of, e.g., effectiveness, efficiency or satisfaction, should be evaluated by questions that are also geared towards these parameters. An EPR that is primarily implemented to enhance the ability to retrieve data should be evaluated by, e.g., looking at the speed, reliability, completeness and user friendliness of retrieving data. Conducting an evaluation on all these different domains in the different phases of the implementation is in principle impossible – unless resources are unlimited. In addition, doing a comprehensive evaluation requires much knowledge and skills of the evaluators. As a consequence, designing the evaluation implies selecting only the relevant domains and phases.

CASE STUDY

A problem that we saw above arises here in a different guise. In the EPR case study one of the evaluation questions looked at the impact of the EPR on work practices. However, the question was posed as a general question, and did not specifically address questions of interaction between the user and the EPR, dupli-cation of information recording or clinical uses of the information held in the EPR. Therefore it was unclear what the exact focus of the evaluation was. To gain clear results from an evaluation, the topic one evaluates should be very specific. There was also a push from the clients to look at clinical outcomes, although these were unlikely to show up until much later in the system lifecycle.

In the PDMS case the project team did not do a baseline measurement, which made before–after measurements impossible and, consequently, limited the range of possible evaluation questions. Other questions could not be addressed because there was not sufficient knowledge on how to set up an appropriate evaluation. This was the case for economic questions like 'what is the result of the invest-ment in terms of saved resources (staff, time and money)' which was 'promised' by the vendor of the system. Therefore, they decided to focus only on two aspects of the system during and after the implementation phase: doctors and nurses' satisfaction with the system and their opinions of the system's effects.

In this step, the following issues and challenges come to play:

Issues

- Conducting a comprehensive evaluation is generally impossible because re-sources are always limited (knowledge, money).
- Some areas are more difficult to evaluate than others. In particular, the effects of the introduction of a PCIS on clinical outcomes or costs-benefits are hard to measure because these effects take much time to become apparent.

Challenges

- It should be clear from the beginning what the topic of the evaluation is.
- It is important, given the limited amount of resources, to jump upon opportunities to conduct parts of the evaluation (data already gathered, meetings already planned where focus interviews can be held, and so forth).
- The project team has to agree on (and back up) the relevance and feasibility of evaluation questions.
- Evaluation questions have to be specific enough as to generate meaningful data.

Step 4 Agree how to evaluate

Choose a study approach

We have already claimed how important it is to define evaluation questions that are relevant, specific and feasible. Subsequently, the content of the question determines which methods have to be applied. Crucial, in these choices, is the question how – scientifically speaking – 'hard' the data need to be. Though RCTs are seen as the gold standard generating the 'hardest' data possible, we have argued that this design is unsuitable in the field of evaluating PCIS. In practice there has to be a balance between the wish to generate robust data and the reasonableness of the effort to generate these data. Experimental designs, for example, generate 'hard' data compared to non-experimental designs like case-control or before–after studies, but they also require much more effort (time, money, knowledge).

Choosing the study approach, then, is essentially a balancing act between the resources available and the breadth and depth of evaluation information required. Evaluating whether the use of an electronic prescribing medication system leads to gain or loss of time and reduction of errors, for example, would ideally require a design in which doctors' prescribing behaviour is precisely measured and compared between the old and new situation. However, interviewing doctors and those that are involved in reading and acting upon the prescriptions probably gives data that are hard enough to conclude whether the system meets its objective. In addition, though we claim that an evaluation of a PCIS should focus on several domains (see further), this does not mean that a complicated design is always necessary. When we were asked to evaluate the impact of a patient information system in the waiting room of the general practitioner, for example, we were asked to consider the impact in terms of efficiency (a reduction of consultations) and patient satisfaction. A fully elaborated design would require a comparative, longitudinal study. Because of limited resources, we resorted to doing a quick scan of the practices using the system, through brief participant observations in the waiting room and interviewing GPs, secretaries and patients. This gave us already

221

much information – enough to give the feed back that the system would not meet its objectives.

Heavily leaning on 'less than ideal (in the sense of "optimally objective")' designs is not a weak point of formative evaluations. To the contrary: when the evaluation questions are clear, and the evaluators and the members of the project and steering group have a clear understanding of one another's needs and possibilities, a little information can be very powerful. As we argued in the previous chapters, implementing a PCIS is a highly uncertain and unpredictable process, and being able to obtain rapid information from a broad array of relevant issues can be priceless. More 'objective' data would not be able to be at hand when managers actually need it, nor would it be possible to paint the breadth of the issues at stake in the implementation when only focusing on a few parameters measured.

Determine the right data collection method

After having chosen the right design, the question is which methods are most suitable to answer the evaluation questions. If one, for example, wants to investigate user satisfaction, questionnaires often are suitable. One can also do observations or a combination of these two methods. If the aim of the system is to improve clinical outcomes, one can review clinical records and outcome measurements or ask health-care professionals and patients what their perception is. If the aim is to improve completeness, a comparative study with a sample of paper records and electronic records is appropriate. The choice of methods is also depending on the scope of the evaluation: questionnaires and interviews make it possible to cover many topics, whereas time studies (e.g. on the amount of time it takes to use an electronic prescribing system compared to a paper method of prescribing) generate data on few aspects of the implementation. Here again, of course, the issue of 'balancing the costs versus the outcomes' in the evaluation design is crucial. It is often wise to start out with brief interviews and short participant observations to get a sense of the issues at stake. In our experience, we have been surprised how often we were able to feed back crucial implementation advice by just having interviewed a few core actors and having spent a few days on the implementation site.

Decide how to collect data

Data for evaluation studies may come from many sources, some of which exist already, some of which have to be collected from scratch. Existing sources of data are useful for identifying criteria against which to evaluate. Potentially interesting documents are: local, sub-national and national benchmarks on reference costs or quality and performance indicators, project initiation documents, local or national standards. When there are no (available) data one can decide to collect new data, for example by means of questionnaires, interviews, observations, focus groups, workshops, etc. One can also use self-assessment tools, like balanced scorecards, Strengths Weaknesses Opportunities and Threats (SWOT) analysis and benchmarks, which allows stakeholders to identify the project criteria that are important to them, and encourage them to think about these issues in depth. The right size of the study group, finally, depends upon the scope of the system being developed. If one is evaluating a system that is meant to cover a large number of patients but only regarding minimal data items, the potential sample size is large but the potential impact of the system may be small given the fact that the data may be useful only in a limited number of clinical situations. If the system is meant to cover a small number of patients but containing in-depth data, the potential sample size is small but the potential impact on clinical decision-making is greater.

This step, then, is not primarily a question of scientific rigour, but primarily a matter of balancing between the often limited resources of the site, and the evaluation questions that the steering or project group want answered. The choice for a study design is dependent on the time, knowledge and financial possibilities of the evaluation site. Designs like control and intervention studies regarding the implementation of for example an EPR are not realistic (how to find sites that, except for the application, are really comparable?). Regarding the scope of the study, it is again important to balance between the often limited resources and the multitude of possible effects of a system by focusing on those domains that – looking at the evaluation question – are seen as most relevant. Focusing in-depth on one or two effects is dangerous because many other – more important – aspects of the use of the information system might then be overlooked. In addition, it is important to know the relation between the different aspects of using the system. Some effects of the use of the information technology may be caused by each other, e.g. time gain and satisfaction of the user, but others may not be related, e.g. increased efficiency of work practices and the impact on patient outcomes.

CASE STUDY

In the UK EPR case, a number of different techniques were used to answer the evaluation questions. But because these techniques were not in any way adapted to each other there was no match between the study design and the evaluation questions. Hence, it was not feasible to conduct any kind of comparative study with similar non-EPR sites, as each site is unique and the resources available for the evaluation were insufficient to cover the additional control sites.

The project team responsible for the PDMS implementation made a questionnaire for nurses and doctors. This questionnaire was based on a validated questionnaire that was, however, not aimed at information technology, but at a totally different topic. As a consequence, the questions of the original question-naire had to be rephrased, some questions were left out and some new questions were added. This new questionnaire was seen as suitable for the PDMS context. For the evaluation of the technical success of the implementation, a practical study design was found: the functional demands (which were found in an initia-tion document) were compared to the PDMS-in-use.

Issues

- Stakeholders often assume that a (randomized) controlled trial is the only way of evaluating a system.
- There is a lack of understanding about how to match study designs and evalua-tion questions.
- Stakeholders underestimate the skills and time needed to design question-naires and conduct interviews and focus groups.

Challenges

- Ensure that the evaluation resources are appropriate to the size and type of project.
- Convince the project and steering group that a pragmatic research design is the most optimal research design for formative evaluation projects.

Step 5 Analyse and report

The interpretation of the data can be complicated. Even when one has a very clear and limited research question, the effects of the implementation of applications can be diverse and unexpected. Several elements (such as the culture of a hospital regarding innovation, the computer literacy of professionals, work satisfaction or the way professionals work together) can impact the implementation, and should therefore be included in the evaluation. Yet even when this is done, it often remains a difficult task to ascribe the impact of the different elements to the outcomes measured.

Second, though from the data it may appear that the system has no impact, this does not mean that this is the case. For example, results may be contradictory or unclear which makes it impossible to draw valid conclusions. It may also be that though the parameters used in the evaluation do not show any impact, profes-sionals or patients do perceive a difference (on parameters not measured).

Third, the object of evaluation often steadily changes. Because of staff or work-flow changes, software modification, training sessions, etc., the information system may change and be in the end markedly different from what it was at the beginning of the study. In addition, for many applications it is generally difficult to make statements about the success or failure of a system immediately after the implementation phase, because it often takes years for systems to have its maximum impact. It takes time for work processes to find an optimal equilibrium with the new system, for conceptual, design and implementation errors to be repaired, and so forth. This is called the 'evaluation paradox': although it is desirable to get evaluation results as soon as possible so that one can decide on following steps (e.g. adjustments or aborting the system), it is often impossible to generate 'final' results within short time.

CASE STUDY

The EPR case study illustrated the problem of not presenting results as accessible for the client or the commission. Instead of a clear and practical guidance in the form of recommendations, a large report was delivered with different kinds of results – ranging from mainly descriptive material about the way health care professionals work (many hundreds of pages!) to short technical reviews, e.g. on the robustness of the system. As we already said, the results were impossible to triangulate. Subsequently, it was left to the client to search through and identify the salient points (which of course was unrealistic). Furthermore, the report was delivered after major decisions about future EPR initiatives were made.

The results of the PDMS case illustrated the differences in perception of success of the system between and even within groups of stakeholders, for example regarding time investment in the system. Though the system made several manual activities superfluous (like making and checking the 24 hours-list, or copying the medication list and the nursing orders list to every new bed chart), these activities were normally conducted during the nightshift and the gained time remained therefore unnoticed for the dayshift. Also, because of readability and automatic storage of prescriptions, the use of the PDMS on one location (the ICU ward) saved time on another (the pharmacy connected to the ICU ward). Bringing such issues to light is often crucial to prevent mutual frustrations to fester.

Issues

- The implementation of information technology changes both work practices and the technology itself. The phenomenon to be investigated, then, is not stable in formative PCIS evaluation.
- The way in which evaluation data is presented can skew the interpretation.

Challenges

- Ensure that evaluation results are presented in a clear and concise manner.
- Produce different reports for different stakeholders, reflecting their perspectives and need for detail.
- Show how different results link to each other. For example, a qualitative result may explain a quantitative finding.

Step 6 Assess recommendations and decide on actions

An important part of evaluation is the consideration of the implications of the evaluation. By doing this in the right way, continuous improvement and development of a learning culture is stimulated. If we want to learn from evaluation studies, we not only have to publish negative results, but also act on them. This is not always easy, of course. Evaluation results might lead to the conclusion that, looking at the aims of the PCIS, it is best to abort the system. For example, alerting systems that appear to be unreliable or alert too often too fast will not be accepted by personnel or management of a hospital. What is needed, therefore, is a formal documented action plan that is agreed upon by all stakeholders and allocates responsibilities for improvement and identifies timescales. In addition, it is important that there is proper communication of the actions and that necessary adjustments are made in, for example, policies in order to make the actions possible. Finally, this step should be seen as establishing a – new – baseline that is crucial for the next steps in a possible next evaluation.

For the interest of the health care community, it is important that negative findings are also viewed as a basis for shared learning and action planning. Since many local – more or less identical – initiatives are undertaken, it is especially important that these experiences are documented and people are informed about systems and implementation trajectories that are successful and those that have failed. Doing this requires a thorough analysis of the reasons for success or failure of PCIS.

CASE STUDY

In practice, however, negative results are often not published and positive results are not always acted upon. In the UK EPR study, clients were keen to see positive results and the sites that were studied did not wish their projects to be viewed in anything but the most positive light. This made it difficult to present specific examples, lending less weight to the findings.

In the PDMS case, the results of the survey were positive. The evaluation of changing work practices and user satisfaction resulted in several technical improvements of the system and in better communication to the users. However, despite the positive results of the evaluation, the Board of Directors decided not to prioritize the implementation of the PDMS on three other ICU wards, the operating rooms and the Emergency Departments. Faced with a small budget, the project team could only install the system on two wards.

Issues

- Different stakeholders may selectively focus on specific bits of information out of the overall context of the evaluation report, to illustrate their own points.
- Despite positive evaluation results, further steps might be frustrated.
- Often it is unclear who is responsible for taking action on the evaluation results.

Challenges

- Communicate clearly on the core of the evaluation results and appropriate action.
- Defining who is responsible for receiving and acting upon evaluation results should be done at the evaluation planning stage – not later once results appear.

CONCLUSION

In this chapter, we have provided an introduction to the theory and practice of evaluation. To this end, we have given the reader an appreciation of some of the major debates in this area. In addition, we have showed that conducting an evaluation is not simply about following several steps in a certain sequence. Designing and conducting an evaluation is a balancing act between identifying specific and feasible evaluation questions, utilizing the amount of resources available and specifying the sufficient 'objectivity' of the data. However, as elsewhere in this book, distinguishing the steps is useful since they constitute a framework through which to introduce and discuss the relevant issues. In addition, the steps are equally useful as a framework to guide one's own work. Yet the overriding requirement in the practice of designing and doing an evaluation, as in designing and 'doing' a PCIS, is the concrete balancing act between limited resources, ever changing and multidimensional aims, and the changing environment within which any project takes place.

DISCUSSION QUESTIONS

1   What are the differences between the starting points of evaluation from a RCT perspective compared to the sociotechnical perspective?
2   What are the strengths of qualitative and quantitative methods and what is the additional value of integrating them?
3   When you were to evaluate a PCIS implementation you know of, how would you proceed through steps 1–6?

REFERENCES

Heathfield, H., P. Hudson, S. Kay, L. Mackay, T. Marley, L. Nicholson, V. Peel, R. Roberts and J. Williams (1999) Issues into multi-disciplinary assessment of healthcare information systems, *Information Technology & People* 12(3): 253–75.

Heathfield, H., S. Clamp and D. Felton (2001) *Probe: Project Review and Objective Evaluation for Electronic Patient and Health Record Projects*. UK Institute of Health Informatics for the NHS Information Authority.

Kaplan, B. (2001) Evaluating informatics applications – clinical decision support systems literature review, *International Journal of Medical Informatics* 64: 15–37.

Stoop, A. P. and M. Berg (2003) Integrating quantitative and qualitative methods in patient care information system evaluation: guidance for the organizational decision maker, *Methods of Information in Medicine* 42 (in press).

FURTHER READING

On methods of evaluation in (informatics in) health care

Anderson, J., C. Aydin and S. Jay (eds) (1994) *Evaluating Health Care Information Systems*. California: SAGE Publications.

Friedman C. P. and J. C. Wyatt (1997) *Evaluation Methods in Medical Informatics*. New York: Springer-Verlag.

Kaplan, B. and N. T. Shaw (2002) People, organizational, and social issues: evaluation as an exemplar, *Yearbook of Medical Informatics* 91–102.

Øvretveit, J. (1998) *Evaluating Health Interventions*. Buckingham: Open University Press.

Pope, C. (1995) Qualitative research: reaching the parts other methods cannot reach: an introduction to qualitative methods in health and health services research, *British Medical Journal* 311: 42–5.

On the discussion of the use of RCTs

Berwick, D. M. (1998) Developing and testing changes in delivery of care, *Annals of Internal Medicine* 128: 651–6.

Heathfield, H. A., V. Peel, P. Hudson, S. Kay, L. Mackay, T. Marley, L. Nicholson, R. Roberts and J. Williams (1997) Evaluating large scale health information systems: from practice towards theory, *Proceedings of the American Medical Informatics Association Fall Symposium*: 116–20.

Kaplan, B. (2001) Evaluating informatics applications – some alternative approaches: theory, social interactionism, and call for methodological pluralism, *International Journal of Medical Informatics* 64: 39–56.

Kaplan, B. and D. Duchon (1988) Combining qualitative and quantitative methods in information systems research: a case study, *Medical Information Systems Quarterly* December: 571–86.

On evaluation from a sociotechnical point of view

Berg, M. (1997) *Rationalizing Medical Work. Decision Support Techniques and Medical Practices*. Cambridge: MIT Press.

Berg, M. (1999) Patient care information systems and health care work: a socio-technical approach, *International Journal of Medical Informatics* 55: 87–101.

Index

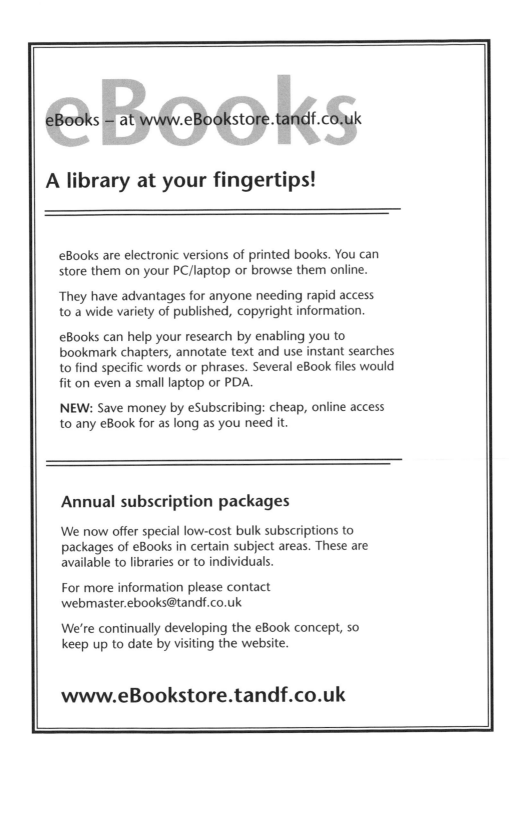